Gettin' Around

Gettin' Around

Jazz, Script, Transnationalism

JÜRGEN E. GRANDT

The University of Georgia Press ☾ ☾ ☾ Athens

Excerpts from "A Drum Is a Woman," "Carribee Joe," and "Pomegranate," words and music by Billy Strayhorn and Duke Ellington, copyright © 1957 (Renewed) by Tempo Music Inc. (ASCAP), Sony/ATV Harmony (ASCAP), and Music Sales Corporation (ASCAP); all rights administered by Music Sales Corporation; international copyright secured, all rights reserved; reprinted by permission. Excerpts from "Rhythm Pum de Drum," "What Else Can You Do with a Drum," and "You Better Know It," by Duke Ellington, are quoted courtesy of Sony/ATV. Excerpts from "If the Drum Is a Woman," by Jayne Cortez, are reprinted from *Jazz Fan Looks Back*, © 2002 by Jayne Cortez, by permission of Hanging Loose Press. Excerpt from "I Wonder as I Wander," by John Jacob Niles, copyright © 1934 (Renewed) by G. Schirmer, Inc. (ASCAP); international copyright secured, all rights reserved; used by permission. Excerpt from "Black, Brown, and White (Get Back)," by Big Bill Broonzy, is courtesy of Screen Gems/Sony/ATV. Excerpt from "Good Morning Heartache," by Ervin M. Drake, Dan Fisher, and Irene Higginbotham, appears courtesy of Sony/ATV, Lindabet, and Microhits. An earlier version of chapter 2 was published as "The Colors of Jazz in the Weimar Republic: Hans Janowitz's *Jazz* Takes the Coltrane," in *Jazz in German-Language Literature*, ed. Kirsten Krick-Aigner and Marc-Oliver Schuster (Würzburg: Königshausen & Neumann, 2013), 73–94.

Paperback edition, 2023
© 2018 by the University of Georgia Press
Athens, Georgia 30602
www.ugapress.org
All rights reserved
Set in Adobe Garamond Pro by Graphic Composition, Inc. Bogart, GA

Most University of Georgia Press titles are
available from popular e-book vendors.

Printed digitally

Library of Congress Cataloging-in-Publication Data
Names: Grandt, Jürgen E., 1968– author.
Title: Gettin' around : jazz, script, transnationalism / Jürgen E. Grandt.
Description: Athens : University of Georgia Press, 2018. | Includes bibliographical references and index.
Identifiers: LCCN 2018019189| ISBN 9780820354354 (hardback : alk. paper) | ISBN 9780820354347 (ebook)
Subjects: LCSH: Jazz—History and criticism. | Music and transnationalism.
Classification: LCC ML3506 .G715 2018 | DDC 781.6509—dc23 LC record available at https://lccn.loc.gov/2018019189

Paperback ISBN 978-0-8203-6485-8

For
Werner Grandt
(1931–2016)

Contents

Acknowledgments ix
Prelude 1

Introduction. Dexter Gordon Gets Around 9

Chapter 1. The Afro-kinetic Passages of Madam Zajj
    Driving Jazz "Home" with Manu Dibango and Duke Ellington 29

Chapter 2. Sheets of Jazz
    Hans Janowitz Takes the Coltrane 58

Chapter 3. High Fidelity on the Black Atlantic
    Rocking Out with Langston Hughes and Nick Hornby 76

Chapter 4. "Good Morning, Heartache"
    Sound, Script, and Improvisation in Paule Marshall's The Fisher King *and Steven Spielberg's* The Terminal 101

Conclusion. Jürg Wickihalder Gets Around 126

Notes 139
Bibliography 161
Index 181

Acknowledgments

"Writing about music is like dancing about architecture" is an aphorism that has been attributed variously to Thelonious Monk, Miles Davis, Frank Zappa, and Elvis (both of them: Presley as well as Costello), among others. In the course of this project, I have felt quite often as if I were indeed dancing about the plans for an imposing, intimidating structure whose contours I could never quite make out let alone chart, whose interior furnishings required lots of plumbing and heavy lifting but which sometimes didn't even include a high-end stereo system. In certain nooks and crannies, *Gettin' Around* still sometimes feels to me like it's not quite finished—but at least my plans and vision for it are now getting around. And while I could not have hoped for a better, smarter, more dedicated construction crew, its members must not be held responsible for inoperable light switches, leaky faucets, or faulty wiring, and least of all for scratches in the grooves of precious vinyls. Many, many hands, minds, ears, and eyes contributed to this project, and I apologize to those whom I may have inadvertently omitted.

But the scholars among them are Tony Bolden, Rashida K. Braggs, Terry Easton, Mary Francis, Julius Greve, Trica Danielle Keaton, John W. Lowe, Barbara McCaskill, Christian Moraru, Aldon Lynn Nielsen, Sascha Pöhlmann, and Arthur J. Sabatini. DoVeanna S. Fulton and R. Baxter Miller keep demonstrating that they can dance to *anything*, even academia: their passion, intellect, and grace epitomize what it means to be "in the humanities." Mark Ekman, Jane Klain, and the fabulous staff at the Paley Center for Media in New York City provided invaluable assistance and insights. Everyone at the University of Georgia Press is a consummate professional who models what scholarly publishing *should* be like, especially Walter Biggins, who answers the phone to share his impressively broad knowledge of all kinds of music even when he, kinetically challenged, is waiting in line at the DMV. The two anonymous outside readers heard what I missed, explained what I needed to reharmonize, and impressed upon me that my manuscript was dancing with the stars.

Among the artists are writers Calaya Michelle Reid aka Grace Octavia, giovanni singleton, and Artress Bethany White; singer Dee Dee Bridgewater; trumpeters Leon "Chocolate Kid" Brown, John Swana, and Robert Wilson; saxophonists Scott Burns, Bob Campbell, Elias Haslanger, Hans-Heinrich Honecker, Nico Kindlimann, Azar Lawrence, John Mills, "The Reverend" Roderick Paulin, Jure Pukl, Mike Smith, Rickey Woodard, and Audrey Betsy Wright; harmonica virtuoso Adam Gussow; pianists Luis Perdomo and Andrew Santander; guitarists Andy Brown, Thomas Erb aka Hank Shizzoe, Robi Lyle, Tim Motzer, and Mike Stern (many thanks also for "Wishing Well"); bassist Tom Kennedy; drummers Joris Dudli and Kenny Washington; world music maverick Fizzé aka Peeni Waali aka Victor Bros de Puechredon; Hackbrett wizard Roland Schiltknecht; the Harmoniemusik Netstal; and the University of North Georgia at Gainesville Jazz Band. Most of all, I am deeply indebted to saxophonist, composer, arranger, and *Hansdampf in allen transnationalen Gassen* Jürg Wickihalder, adopted son of Madam Zajj, whose axe can make any building dance.

My "road crew": the families of Simone and Daniel Althaus, Sandra and Martin Kindlimann, Wanda and Richard B. Lyle III, Sibylle and Thomas Menzi, and Friederike Pohlenz and Stephan C. Brunner.

And finally, all the *right* notes in what follows hark back, in one way or another, to my mom, Yvonne. She and Dexter Gordon never met, so he couldn't have been thinking of her when entitling his 1969 album for the Prestige label *The Tower of Power*. But Madam Zajj must have thought of Yvonne, I am certain, when she gifted Long Tall Dexter with the title.

Oakwood, Georgia, March 2018

Gettin' Around

Prelude

In Zurich, Switzerland, the last day of May is an unseasonably cold one. The thermometer struggles to reach ten degrees Celsius, and the constant precipitation over the last few days has prompted the federal meteorological service to issue a flood warning for all cantons north of the Alps—a rare occurrence in this small mountain republic. Still, steady trickles of people converge on the city's venerable Neumarkt Theater on this rainy evening. The present three-story structure dates to 1742, but its predecessor on this spot was, in the early sixteenth century, home to Konrad Grebel, who with Felix Manz hatched the Swiss Brethren here, a branch of the Anabaptists. In the 1920s the building housed the first headquarters of the Communist Party of Switzerland; a plaque outside commemorates the roughly eight hundred Swiss nationals who volunteered in the Spanish Civil War, and the six hundred survivors who returned dedicated the building to "the culture of international solidarity." Just a stone's throw away, at Spiegelgasse 14, Vladimir Ilyich Lenin had planned a revolution a few years before. At the other end of the narrow alley is the world-famous Cabaret Voltaire, the birthplace of Dada, and a short walk further south, James Joyce used to enjoy a glass of Fendant or two at the Restaurant Kronenhalle. Henry Wirz was born just around the corner from the Neumarkt too, but official tourist brochures don't list Froschaugasse 26 after the plaque commemorating the expat who rose to become commander of the notorious Andersonville POW camp in Georgia—the only high-ranking Confederate officer to be tried, convicted, and executed for war crimes after the American Civil War—was quietly removed some years ago.[1]

On this chilly, drizzly night, though, the Neumarkt Theater doesn't host a poetry reading or experimental play. The poster in the foyer announces a concert billed as "Monk and More . . . ," pairing two of Switzerland's most exceptional improvising musicians. At age seventy-two, pianist Irène Schweizer is widely recognized as a national treasure. Back in the heady 1960s, she was one of the very, very few women among the pioneers of European free jazz, and while she had to work hard and wait long for the well-deserved accolades, the international press has been referring to her as "the First Lady of European Jazz" or "the grande dame of European jazz piano" for a decade or two now.[2] More than a generation younger than Schweizer, saxophonist Jürg Wickihalder is her congenial counterpart. A graduate of the Berklee College of Music in Boston, Massachusetts, Wickihalder returned to Switzerland, although as a first-rate soprano saxophonist and highly regarded composer, he continues to perform all over the world. As Wickihalder explains to the audience that evening by way of introducing his original composition "Last Jump," "*Wir Jazzmusikerinnen sind ja auch Grenzgänger*"—jazz musicians are also commuters across international borders.[3]

Tonight, Wickihalder makes all the announcements from the stage; Schweizer doesn't speak, except during the applause following the Wickihalder-penned numbers when she points, with almost parental pride, to her duo partner, beams a wide smile, and repeats his name. The saxophonist would later concede that it can be difficult to find musical space improvising with Schweizer, whose forceful, percussive style many other high-caliber musicians find challenging.[4] Tonight though, this is truly a dialogue: each listens carefully to the other—Schweizer focuses her gaze intently on Wickihalder, whose posture on his main instrument sometimes recalls Sidney Bechet, the bell of his soprano tracing a high arc, pointing at the ceiling. When he channels Rahsaan Roland Kirk and puts his soprano and tenor saxophones to his mouth simultaneously, it is not a musical gimmick but the compelling response to a call from Schweizer's piano. His eyes are mostly closed, even during the pianist's solo passages when he often retreats to the edge of the stage, crouching, head cocked, hands folded between his knees as if in prayer. This is a conversation, an emotional journey in sound, really; before long, the energy of the performance draws the audience in too, and the listeners no longer simply witness the concert, they become part of it. While his horns can just as easily tell a profound story of loss and longing or hurt and anger, a boyish wit and playfulness are characteristic of Wickihalder's style—one reason the saxophonist gravitated to Thelonious Monk's music early on in his career. At intermission, he jokingly announces that "*Glühwein und Weihnachstchrämli*"—mulled wine and Christmas cookies—would be served in the lobby, and as the concertgoers file out, some can be heard whistling (or trying to) the head of "Little Rootie Tootie," the Monk tune that closed the first set.

What "Monk and More . . ." demonstrated undeniably that May evening is that jazz has been getting around. Or as Langston Hughes had noticed in Paris almost a century earlier,

> Play it, jazz band!
> You've got seven languages to speak in
> And then some,
> Even if you do come from Georgia.[5]

These planetary, polyglot resonances, however, have by and large gone unheard in interdisciplinary cultural studies. Transnationalism so far has not availed itself of the critical potential inherent in what was already the first "world music" long before there was a term for it. The richly symbolic territory alone in which "Monk and More . . ." resounded constitutes a "population of nows, all unsynchronized," but syncopated instead. At the very nascence of the transnational turn, Wai Chee Dimock's search for a "literature for the planet" prompted her to argue that literature "holds out to its readers dimensions of space and time so far-flung and so deeply recessional that they can never be made to coincide with the synchronic plane of the geopolitical map." Literature makes these dimensions legible, but Dimock also stressed the aurality of these dimensions: "Reading allows the ear to come into contact with tongues not spoken in its vicinity, to hear foreign echoes in the midst of native speech. To a practiced reader the hearable world is nothing less than the planet as a whole, thick with sounds human beings have made across the width of the globe and across the length of history."[6] *Gettin' Around* proposes a conceptual turnaround, as it were, of Dimock's epistemology, putting sound before script. After all, transnationalism as an ethically viable critical practice can only work if we not only read but *listen to* each other. As Wickihalder and Schweizer's example demonstrates, improvised music requires such careful, close listening if it wants to make a meaningful statement. Moreover, given the transnational sonorities of jazz, this music is perhaps more conducive than any other to circumvent the pitfalls Robyn Wiegman pointed to more than a decade after Dimock when she asked the question, to her mind a rhetorical one, whether "the transnational analytic" was "functioning as the vehicle through which American Americanists could inoculate themselves against the critique of our global power and authority, such that we could imagine ourselves outside the nationalizing discourses and imperial agency of our object of study regardless of how inside we were to the globalizing U.S. knowledge industry and the authority it conferred on us to define the priorities and scope of the field?"[7]

Wiegman's concern is one that, to varying degrees, underlies the wide variety of critical approaches accompanying transnationalism—from new cosmopolitanism to border studies, from glocalism to diaspora studies, from oceanic studies to planetarism. One who offers his own corrective paradigm is critical theorist Christian Moraru, who posits that since the fall of the Berlin Wall, there emerges from American literatures a "cosmodernist" strain. Cosmodernism endorses "a post-multiculturalist 'politics of recognition'—and with it a less conventional idea of identitarian 'authenticity'—whose motto is no longer the autonomist 'I want to be known for what I am' but the more humbly relational 'I want to be known for what or who I am with.'" Call-and-response is a hallmark of cosmodernist literature as it is "Uncommonly keen on language as vernacularizing practice that flouts the nation-state's repertoire of codifications"; it "transcribes the cornucopia of accents, connotations, styles, and idiomatic vacillations issuing forth in what otherwise we may hear (and utter) as one, as the monoglossic touchstone of identity building and expression." This transcribing process is therefore highly attuned to transnational stories and histories that subvert calcified narratives of homogenized nationhood: "What makes time possible is history—history as a stage on which self and other enact their ethical relatedness. [. . .] With the cosmoderns, we can then safely assume, today more than ever in American and world history, that the only time there is, hence the only time when we can be, where we can figure out who we are and build a culture in the process, is the time of self-other interaction. A temporalization of mutuality, this time *determines culture as a deeply transactional, ethical project.*"[8] If this sounds remarkably like the Ellisonian ideal of a jam session—or like Schweizer and Wickihalder's performance on the stage of the Neumarkt Theater—where the "temporalization of mutuality," of bearing witness in time, is codependent on bearing "with-ness" ethically, not just aesthetically, then jazz music in fact anticipates Moraru's cosmodernist literary paradigm by almost a century. And still, interdisciplinary studies have not yet been getting around to tapping the jazz aesthetic's inherent transnationalism(s), a dearth all the more surprising because both storytelling and music-making are, after all, acts that reimagine the passage of time. Despite Shelley Fisher Fishkin touting jazz music as a synecdoche for the crossroads of American transnationalism in her 2004 presidential address to the American Studies Association, only one article focusing on the subject has been published to date in the *Journal of Transnational American Studies* that Fisher Fishkin herself helped launch in 2009.[9] Conversely, the massive two-volume *Oxford Handbook of Critical Improvisation Studies* totaling over a thousand pages contains the terms *transnational* or *transnationalism* exactly half a dozen times—even though, of course, it is not focused solely on jazz.[10]

To be sure, there have been plenty of *gestures* toward transnationalism in the interdisciplinary field of sound studies. After all, as Johnathan Sterne noted at the onset of the transnational turn, "hearing and listening are foundational to modern modes of knowledge, culture, and social organization."[11] A decade later, Sterne explained that sound studies "is a global phenomenon" that "reaches across registers, moments, and spaces, and [. . .] thinks across disciplines and traditions" precisely because "Hearing requires positionality." But transnationalism as a critical methodology still doesn't make an appearance in *The Sound Studies Reader*.[12] Across the Atlantic from Sterne, Georgina Born argues that sound and music "are particularly fertile conduits for spatial experience in that they have the capacity both to compound and to orchestrate in novel and affective ways the spatial affordances of social life writ large." The nation-state, however, occupies but one sliver of the methodological territory that her collection *Music, Sound, and Space* stakes out, and none of the essays traveling on a transnational route addresses jazz.[13] Of the two that do train their focus on the genre in Born's follow-up, *Improvisation and Social Aesthetics*, not even Eric Lewis's chapter, which carefully listens to the string of albums the Association for the Advancement of Creative Musicians (AACM) recorded in Paris, deploys transnationalism as a critical methodology.[14] Meanwhile, firmly back on U.S. soil, Jennifer Lynn Stoever's "historiographical echolocation" in *The Sonic Color Line* serves an intriguing foretaste of what transnationalism can offer sound studies. In a chapter discussing the twenty-one-month American tour of opera singer Jenny Lind, "the Swedish Nightingale," in the early 1850s, and contrasting the synesthetic spectacle her appearances proffered with the critical reception of Elizabeth Taylor Greenfield, "the Black Swan," Stoever's critical ear and eye limn how transnational resonances became instrumentalized in choreographing American citizenship at a moment of great national crisis.[15] Still, jazz makes no appearance in *The Sonic Color Line* either. Stoever is also the editor in chief of *Sounding Out!*, the widely read sound studies blog that went online in 2009. A search of its archives using the term "jazz" returns almost two dozen pages of results—yet none of the articles deals with jazz extensively.

What accounts at least in part for the dearth of truly interdisciplinary critical investigations is the difficulty, if not the impossibility, of defining *transnationalism* and *jazz* both. In the introduction to the 2017 *Cambridge Companion to Transnational American Literature*, editor Yogita Goyal comments at the outset that "little seems settled about the scope, method, or value of transnationalism."[16] Similarly, the term *jazz* has been highly contested from the beginning. Sidney Bechet, the music's first international ambassador, profoundly disliked the label, preferring "ragtime" instead.[17] For Duke Ellington, "'Jazz' is only a word and really has no meaning. We stopped using it in 1943"—the same year, not coincidentally, the overtly transnational suite *Black, Brown, and Beige* premiered at Carnegie Hall. Continues Ellington, "To keep the whole thing clear, once and for all, I don't believe in categories of any kind."[18] More contemporary exponents of the music also reject the term, proffering a range of alternatives, from "BAM" (Black American Music) to "stretch music" to "autophysiopsychic music."[19] Yet not even the Duke managed to excise the J-word from his autobiography completely.

These tangled morphological skeins still cannot explain why on one hand the transnational turn in the humanities has been so complete that it has become, perhaps, "normative rather than insurgent," as Goyal ventures, but on the other, not very many of Dimock's practiced readers have been lending their ears to the hearable, transnational world of jazz.[20] Among the very few who have is Rashida K. Braggs, whose *Jazz Diasporas: Race, Music, and Migration in Post–World War II Paris* not only reads James Baldwin and Boris Vian but closely listens to Sidney Bechet, Kenny Clarke, and others. What she calls "dislocated listening" offers a valuable critical prism also because it harkens back to the aurality of Dimock's planetary space-time dimensions, even if Braggs limits her critical interventions to the City of Light.[21] Omi Osun Joni L. Jones's *Theatrical Jazz: Performance, Àse, and the Power of the Present Moment* is also "calling on jazz to once again take on the job of standing in for both a politicized Blackness and a counterhegemonic set of aesthetic principles" by combining certain elements of the music with Yoruba cosmology, but it barely listens to the sounds that ostensibly help shape its critical underpinnings: the Yoruba-influenced New Orleans jazz funeral isn't even mentioned, let alone any of the jazz musicians—Steve Coleman instantly comes to mind—whose music draws explicitly and extensively on Yoruba cosmology.[22] Also dealing with artistic and critical optics, the ten essays assembled in *Watching Jazz: Encounters with Jazz Performance on Screen* are generally much more attentive to the music, yet only one focuses on non-U.S. jazzers.[23] The others note, but decline to investigate, the fact that much of the analyzed concert footage of John Coltrane, Oscar Peterson, Miles Davis, and others was shot by European television networks, in front of European audiences. Alfred Appel, though, plays up the European connection in *Jazz Modernism*. Confining himself to the three decades between the Roaring Twenties and midcentury, his critical approach is more often than not playfully allusive rather than analytical: "syncopated dialogue" or "rat-a-tat-tat prose" suffices to classify Hemingway, and even Joyce, as "jazz modernists"—Appel's study, therefore, might more appropriately be titled "Jazz *Age* Modernism."[24] Moreover, the book's unreflexive references to "Negro" culture, paired with recurrent swipes against postmodernism, postcolonialism, and the Black Arts Movement of the 1960s, betray a certain dogmaticism that, in 2002, appears rather reactionary and mars Appel's close readings, listenings, and viewings, also because it runs counter to the very jazz aesthetic Appel purports to champion.

Gettin' Around, on the other hand, deliberately refrains from a narrow, empirical definition of jazz or of transnationalism and, true to the jazz aesthetic itself, opts for a broader, more inclusive scope, even as it listens very carefully and closely to its variegated soundtrack. Such an approach not only seeks to avoid the wistfully museal whiff of a "golden age, time past" but broadens both the appeal and the applicability of the overall critical argument, or such is my hope.[25] For my intents and purposes, the international simply designates currents of people, ideas, and goods between distinct geopolitical entities or nation-states, whereas the transnational refers to liminal dynamics that transcend preordained borderlines, that occur above, below, beside, or along the outer contours of nation-states. What the present study does attempt to offer up is a long-overdue consideration of the ways in which jazz music can inform critical practice in the field of transnational (American) studies. In doing so, *Gettin' Around* employs two specific yet sufficiently pliable concepts, Afro-kinesis and Afropolitanism, which seek to foreground the aurality of transnational space-time dimensions. First and foremost, however, this study is informed by close reading, close viewing, and close *listening*. For without listening attentively to what the other, across the border, has to say, any critical practice, regardless of its terminology or theoretical apparatus, becomes ethically problematic.

At the end of *Invisible Man*, its protagonist wonders, "Who knows but that, on the lower frequencies, I speak for you?"[26] *Gettin' Around* is mindful of these lower frequencies as they travel from the invisible man's coal cellar in Harlem to faraway places, which in turn often transform those frequencies and bounce them back to their place of origin in new, different sounds and scripts. Still, *Gettin' Around* does not purport to be a comprehensive study: for example, the Black Pacifics of, say, a Fred Ho or a Toshiko Akiyoshi remain unrepresented here.[27] It aspires to revisit just a few destinations on jazz music's long, planetary itinerary and in doing so hopes to inspire others to undertake musical journeys of their own. Finally, except where otherwise noted, all translations from the French and German are my own.

INTRODUCTION

Dexter Gordon Gets Around

Of the many African American writers who elected to make a new home in Europe in the years following World War II, James Baldwin kept perhaps the closest ties to the music world. Blues and gospel remained major sources of inspiration for him, and he was a jazz buff too. He had been living in Paris for quite a while already when he authored "Sonny's Blues," the story that would become a "standard" of jazz literature, as well as *Another Country*, a novel featuring a drummer named Rufus Scott. When yet another newspaper article appeared on the phenomenon of black American expatriates abroad, he notified a more recent transplant, tenor saxophonist Dexter Gordon, but the newcomer averred that he was irritated by that term: "I'm not ex-anything." As he later elaborated, "I had not thought of myself as being 'expatriate.' I didn't originally come to stay—as some cats have. When I came, it was just to make a gig."[1]

The conversation—and disagreement—between the novelist Baldwin and the saxophonist Gordon in some ways repudiated Blue Note's marketing plan for the musician: for jazz's most iconic record label, Dexter Gordon was, as one of their album covers touted, *Our Man in Paris* after all, flanked on that particular outing by fellow "expats" Kenny Clarke and Bud Powell as well as Frenchman Pierre Michelot.[2] The music, too, availed itself of the genre's inherent transnationalisms: the album from which this book borrows its title was recorded in 1965, three years after the native Californian had relocated to Europe: *Gettin' Around* incorporates diverse influences, from Brazilian bossa nova (Luiz Bonfá's "Manhã de Carnaval") to French chanson (the original composition "Le Coiffeur"), and therefore also constitutes a reminder that jazz has always already been transnational. Once again, Blue Note clearly sought to capitalize on Gordon's European sojourn with the album's title and with the cover, which shows the lanky Gordon sporting a beret and straddling a bicycle. The European connection was a natural one to make for the label, which after all had been founded back in 1939 by two refugees from Germany, Francis Wolff and Alfred Lion. And even though almost all of the label's output during its heyday, including *Gettin' Around*, was recorded in Rudy Van Gelder's famed Englewood Cliffs studio in New Jersey, a transnational resonance was always present. Musicians fondly remember Wolff casually leaning against the wall in the control room, snapping his fingers, tapping his foot, and, if he gave his clients any musical direction at all, instructing them in his hard, German accent, "We must find the groove! It must shving!"[3]

Blue Note's philosophy also underscores that Gordon's music remained firmly rooted in the African American jazz tradition, and so musically speaking at least, Gordon was correct—he wasn't "ex-anything." Neither was the style of his European colleagues, for that matter. In this respect, his preferred pianist of the period, Spaniard Tete Montoliu, was a congenial partner for the American in Europe. As far as the blind pianist was concerned, Catalan *sardanes* weren't really all that different from hard-charging bebop: "basically we Catalonians are all black," he maintained.[4] But Long Tall Dexter's highly individual style provides an ideal template for this study also because the tenorist always aspired to give expression to a "'story' feeling" in his improvisations.[5] Dex liked to quote, but quotes very often were the launching pad for motivic development within the solo as a whole. Far from musical cutesies, these were often planned ahead of the actual performance, as he also liked to do with cadenzas or solo introductions. One of the staples in Gordon's repertoire of the time was the standard "Three O'Clock in the Morning," and the tenorist frequently liked to interweave a quote from "Take Me out to the Ballgame" into his solos; he was also an avid baseball fan and followed his beloved New York Mets wherever he was. So when he found himself in Stockholm being accompanied by an all-Swedish pickup group, probably no one among the adoring listeners in the audience or the starstruck musicians on the bandstand was familiar with America's national pastime, even if they did recognize the melody. But the musical quote will seem less incongruous or accidental if we recall that 3 a.m. might be last call in the Gamlingen Jazz Club, but at Shea Stadium, it's 9 p.m.

and quite possibly the seventh-inning stretch.⁶ Thus, Gordon's improvisations tell a transnational story of exile, of home, of be/longing—of making connections in music across time zones and national boundaries.

If the tenorist remained committed to a view of jazz as a primarily African American art form, get around he surely did. From 1962 to 1976, he made his home in Europe, eventually settling in Valby, a suburb of Copenhagen, with his new Danish wife, Fenja Halberg, and their son, Benjamin, named after fellow tenor titan Ben Webster. Even after he finally returned Stateside, Gordon still seemed a little overwhelmed by the reception accorded him upon his arrival in the Old World:

> I had no idea of the European love for jazz—and jazz fans. . . . I'd heard that it was beautiful. All the cats that came over spoke about it. But I really had no idea *how* much it was appreciated. It was such a great revelation. And to feel all this respect, as a musician, as an artist. . . . It was quite a new thing for me and, I would say, for most American musicians. Because at that time *jazz* musicians were, in America, just horn-blowers: "Oh, you're one of them *horn-blowers*!" A kind of musical weirdo? Yes. Unless you were Duke Ellington—you had to be on that kind of pedestal to get any respect. But I found it, in England and in Europe. And I found this very heartwarming. As for the knowledge . . . you meet these guys and they know *everything* about you. They've got what you did [. . .] the whole thing . . . at their fingertips. And it wasn't uncommon to run into people like this all over Europe—Sweden, Denmark, Italy, England, Belgium. Everywhere.⁷

The "musical weirdo" felt comfortable, "at home" almost—as much at home as is possible for a touring jazz musician—in the Danish capital. He also picked up the language; he nurtured young, local talent, got involved in the arts community. His base of operations for much of his stay was Copenhagen's fabled Jazzhus Montmartre, whose name itself fittingly signaled a polyglot transnationalism. Long Tall Dexter was a familiar and quite memorable sight in the city, his towering, six-foot-five frame comically dwarfing the bicycle he loved to ride everywhere to the proportions of a mere child's toy. His immersion was such that Webster nicknamed him "Copenhagen Slim" when he decided to pitch his tent in Denmark himself. To the Danes, he became such a beloved figure that when their Home Office rescinded Gordon's reentry visa after the saxophonist was arrested at the Paris airport on drug charges in 1966, there was a spontaneous protest rally outside of the capital's city hall of several hundred people brandishing signs that read, "We want Dexter—we don't want NATO!"⁸

So Gordon's insistence that he was really not "ex-anything" might smack somewhat of disingenuousness. With a much, much smaller pool of top-shelf accompanists—and with the handful of other American jazz "expats" always in high demand—Gordon was forced for the first time in his career to play with musicians who were not American (and white). For a while, he had to make do with rhythm sections comprised of architects and dentists and students. But before long, he spotted local talent that he took under his wing. Still, Gordon felt artistically fulfilled as well. While he regularly played with fellow American musicians making their more or less temporary home in the Old World, the young European musicians he recruited for his working group provided more than just support for the American star: he recognized eager talents such as Danish wunderkind Niels-Henning Ørsted Pedersen on bass, fellow Dane Alex Riel on drums, and pianist Montoliu, comprising Gordon's rhythm section of choice and three youngsters who would go on to become stars in their own right. And the American, in turn, was inspired by them: "I built myself up, I mean it was mutual. That experience became very, very important."[9] His "expatriate period," first in Paris, then in Copenhagen, is recognized by critics and fellow musicians alike as the pinnacle of Gordon's entire career. Scandinavian radio stations broadcast innumerable gigs, most of them from the Jazzhus, and the many surviving air checks from this period present a Dexter Gordon very much at ease and chummy with his European audiences. He was conversant in French, had learned some Danish fairly quickly, knew a few sentences of Swedish, liked to joke with the clubgoers in between numbers in their own language, and the music was never short of superb.

Still, Gordon commuted back and forth across the Atlantic quite regularly, as almost all his studio albums for Blue Note were recorded in Van Gelder's New Jersey studio. Just as Ralph Ellison's invisible man is listening in time *and* space, the tenorist was *playing* in time and space. The title—and the music—of Dexter Gordon's 1965 album also serves as a trope of the first of two theoretical concepts that inform my critical analyses, namely Afro-kinesis. The act of getting around, constitutive of any manifestation of transnationalism, is made audible in and by the jazz solo, which travels across, and sometimes well beyond, the harmonic structure of the song being performed. Representative of this kind of mobility are Gordon's solos, which traverse a musical territory marked by Western harmonic conceptions but which are simultaneously propelled by a distinct Afro-kinesis that gets Gordon around the changes, as it were.

Afro-kinesis informs both jazz rhythm and jazz melody. Blue notes, for instance, defy the conventions of musical notation and resist exact localization on the staff. Listen to the glissandi of Billie Holiday on the 1957 version of "I Wished on the Moon," whose trajectory is definitely not charted by NASA as the singer's voice, buoyed by Ben Webster's equally slurry-breathy tenor, barely recognizes the evenly spaced five staff lines as suggestions.[10] But it's in jazz rhythm, notably swing, where Afro-kinesis is perhaps most readily audible. To be sure, jazz is not the exclusive province of Afro-kinesis: blues and other blues-influenced genres also contain Afro-kinetic elements to varying degrees. After all, syncopation entails a displacing of the regularly spaced meter, a rhythmic—that is, temporal—disruption that appears to both delay and advance the musical pulse. While syncopation and swing aren't identical, the latter resounds in jazz and jazz-related genres with much higher frequency than elsewhere. Swing can be heard as the kinetic elasticization of time, but a more concrete definition has long eluded musicologists: Joachim Ernst Berendt came to the "final" conviction that "swing cannot be put in words." Still, he tried—and figured that if anybody was privy to the secret of swing, it would be the drummer of the Count Basie orchestra, perhaps the swingingest big band of all time, Jo Jones: "It's a real simple thing," Papa Jo told Germany's Jazz Pope, "but there are some things you can't describe, some things that never have been described. [. . .] The best way to say what swinging is, is you either play with a feeling or you don't. It's just like the difference between receiving a genuine handshake and a fishy one." Berendt was left to derive from this only that "Music is art in time," but this in turn raised the question "which time—psychological or ontological time, relative or absolute time, lived or measured time?" The sole, tentative answer he was willing to tender was that "Swing relates to both planes of time—to measured, objective time and to psychological, lived time. It relates simultaneously to an African time feeling on the one hand, to a European one on the other."[11]

Gordon's sense of time, his rhythmic phrasing, was quite unusual, often hanging back behind the beat, especially on ballads, which paradoxically created a tension that appeared to push things forward. Consequently, not every rhythm section managed to "click" with the tenorist—there are in fact quite a few live recordings where even otherwise superb accompanists cannot adapt to Gordon's style. A most telling anecdote in this regard comes from Danish newspaper cartoonist and hobby drummer Klaus Albrectsen, who sat in with Gordon one night: "I sat behind the drums and tried to keep time, and

I felt this enormous toughness, how far behind he floated, how he, consciously and all the time, put his own beat in relation to the beat, tightened, pulled tugged, I was sitting in the middle of a hurricane, trying desperately to hang on to the beat, dammit how I admired Alex Riel at that moment!"[12] Swing, like Afro-kinesis in general, is therefore also a form of motion that is attuned to other stories, other histories, an *inter*play whose direction is informed by close *listening*. After all, even Long Tall Dexter will have problems making your foot tap without an empathetic rhythm section with big ears. Albrectsen's attempts at a meaningful, swinging—that is, Afro-kinetic—interplay with Gordon coincide with the discovery of what the invisible man calls "a slightly different sense of time": "you're never quite on the beat. Sometimes you're ahead and sometimes behind. Instead of the swift and imperceptible flowing of time, you are aware of its nodes, those points where time stands still or from which it leaps ahead. And you slip into the breaks and look around." As Ellison's protagonist journeys into Louis Armstrong's sonic breaks, "I found myself hearing not only in time, but in space as well."[13] The invisible man's location is narrowly circumscribed: hibernating in his Harlem basement, his is a quintessentially American story. And yet, precisely because Satchmo provides the soundtrack to his narrative, it is a story that has ramifications far beyond the borders of the United States: Afro-kinesis slips into the jazzy breaks of the Black Atlantic as well as its neighboring territories, looks around, and listens to a wide variety of stories, including their dissonances. Afro-kinesis is a form of motion that traverses preordained borders, extemporizes modalities of exchange with and in new-old sonic geographies, and in the process limns an aural modernity that constantly reinvents itself. Happening in the moment, it remains attuned to both the historicity and futurity of its current trajectory and is therefore antiphonal in nature.[14]

Berendt ventures that swing "creates intensity through friction and overlapping of time planes."[15] While the experiential effect of swing is a seemingly inexorable forward momentum—that "thing" which makes your foot tap—the complex dynamics at play in linking up individual notes within the collective totality of musical performance requires an acute awareness not only to what is happening in the improvisational moment but also to what has just happened, and what might be about to happen. Or, as drummer Max Roach puts it, "After you initiate the solo, one phrase determines what the next is going to be. From the first note that you hear, you are responding to what you've just played: you just said this on your instrument, and now that's a constant. What follows from that? And then the next phrase is a constant. What follows from that? And so on and so forth. And finally, let's wrap it up so that everybody understands that that's what you're doing. It's like language: you're talking, you're speaking, you're responding."[16] Musicologist Matthew W. Butterfield also turns to the drummer in his efforts to define swing—and, tellingly, to scansion: he points to anacrusis as one of "Multiple features of syntactical structure" that "interact with subsyntactical timing processes to generate varied qualities of motional energy that either drive the groove or temper its flow."[17] Thus, swing elasticizes different planes of time to allow them to intersect—and then make you dance. Lubed by swing, Afro-kinesis is the elasticization of time, musical as well as cultural, historical, and socioeconomic time.

Historically, the Afro-kinesis of jazz as proto-world music is inescapably the sonic byproduct of the Middle Passage and its aftermaths. With emancipation, writes Ellison, the former chattels

> were now the owners of their own bodies and had the freedom to express something of their aspirations as individuals. As slaves they had long been aware that for themselves, as for most of their countrymen, geography was fate. Not only had they observed the transformation of individual fortune made possible by the westward movement along the frontier, but the Mason-Dixon line had taught them the relationship between geography and freedom. They knew that to be sold down the Mississippi River usually meant that they would suffer a harsher form of slavery, and they knew that to escape across the Mason-Dixon line northward was to move in the direction of greater freedom. But freedom was also to be found in the West of the old Indian Territory. Bessie Smith gave voice to this knowledge when she sang of "Goin' to the Nation, Going to the Terr'tor," and it is no accident that much of the symbolism of our folklore is rooted in the imagery of geography. The slaves had learned through the repetition of group experience that freedom was to be attained through geographical movement, and freedom required one to risk his life against the unknown.[18]

The trajectory Ellison limns here to the tune of Bessie Smith, the Empress of the Blues, is that of an Afro-kinesis historicized in modern(ist) sound. Or, as Angela Davis heard it, "Movement backward into the African-American historical past becomes movement forward, progressive exploration."[19] While Afro-kinetic propulsion strives toward freedom, it is multidirectional; jazz extends Ellison's and Davis's New World cartographies of blues beyond national and continental borders.

In jazz music, these various temporal planes intersect in a specific space, the stage or the studio. At the same time, the music's Afro-kinesis expands these specific performance locations into overlapping figurative territories. Afro-kinesis thus leads to the second critical trope, Afropolitanism—for Blue Note, and for the American jazz fan, Dexter Gordon was, again, *Our Man in Paris*. The popularization of the term is usually credited to West African novelist Taiye Selasi's essay "Bye-Bye Babar," which begins in a London dance club where the crowd is grooving to a Fela Kuti remix spun by a DJ who is half-Nigerian, half-Romanian. Afropolitans are "dispersed across Brixton, Bethesda, Boston, Berlin" and are "not citizens, but Africans of the world," writes Selasi. Though they may sometimes feel "lost in transnation," more often than not they "belong to no single geography, but feel at home in many."[20] The term has also rapidly gained currency in academic circles, largely thanks to Cameroonian political theorist and historian Achille Mbembe. For Mbembe, the Afropolitan traces "a transnational culture," a "cultural, historic, and aesthetic sensibility" that stems from an "awareness of this imbrication of the here and the elsewhere, the presence of the elsewhere in the here and vice versa, the relativization of roots and of primary memberships and the manner of embracing, in full knowledge of the facts, the foreign, the foreigner, and the faraway, the ability to recognize one's face in the countenance of the foreigner and to value the traces of the faraway in the nearby, to domesticate the unfamiliar, to work with that which has all the expression of the opposite."[21]

Though related to the ongoing debate over the contested meanings of the term, the concept of Afropolitanism proffered here derives from "Négropolitaines," a composition penned by Mbembe's compatriot, saxophonist Manu Dibango, the godfather of Afropop. Born Emmanuel Dibango N'Djocke in 1933 in Douala, Cameroon—a region that constitutes the buckle of what Gerhard Kubik has designated "the swing belt of Africa"—little Manu came into contact with all kinds of music early on.[22] When the French navy made port in Douala, the sailors also brought Western music, and Dibango remembers that as a boy he could not get enough of Glenn Miller. Later, the early infatuation with the slick sounds of Miller's polished big band became, in French exile, something else once he had decided on a career in music. Dibango says that it was his immersion in American jazz that eventually turned his ears back to Cameroon and allowed him to reconstitute the pop music of western Africa—bikutsi, soukous, high-life, assiko, and especially makossa—in new ways. The music of Duke Ellington, Louis Armstrong, Bud Powell, and, most importantly, fellow expat Sidney Bechet showed him how he could find his own voice combining diverse musical languages and paved the way for his greatest success, 1973's "Soul Makossa." Afropop's first global super smash hit wasn't really "jazz" per se, but it was indeed born of jazz's inherent Afro-kinesis, the same kind of sonic mobility that allowed Gordon to traverse time zones and national borders in "Three O'Clock in the Morning." "So when I did 'Soul Makossa,'" remembers Dibango with some exasperation still, "Americans said I was doing African music, and Africans said I was doing Western music, and Europeans said I was doing American music."[23] Sharing Ellington's allergy to categories, Dibango posits the portable label "Afro-quelque chose," Afro-something, against territorializing taxonomies of sound.[24]

Recorded in France in 1989 and 1992, respectively, the two-volume *Négropolitaines* is therefore very much an Afropolitan affair. Conceived as a tribute to African pop standards, it contains among a few Dibango originals also cover versions of Miriam Makeba's "Pata Pata" and Joseph Kabasele's "Indépendance Cha Cha," for example. The title track, however, written and arranged by Dibango, begins quite differently: the C minor mode of the first section takes up almost half of the seven-minute-plus tune, and its percussive scratch-guitar and electric slap-bass place the song firmly in the funk territory of a George Clinton. The only "African" touches that accompany the antiphonal exchange between Dibango's multitracked saxophones and Justin Bowen's piano are two brief interpolations of Bokilo "Jerry" Malekani's distinctive highlife guitar. After the break, things do take a decidedly "African" turn, with Pierre Didi Tchakouté's mbira (the African thumb piano) the only instrument audible for a few seconds. The harmony shifts to the A major mode, and the interweaving guitars, drums, and percussion create such a complex polyrhythmic web that it becomes difficult to tell where the beat actually is—Afro-kinesis at its most multidirectional. Still, Bowen's prominent synthesizer makes it clear that this section is not meant to orchestrate "authenticity," but sounds, quite literally, a call-and-response between tradition and modernity. The jazziest moment on the track is Peter Tholo Segona's solo on muted trumpet, heavily indebted to Miles Davis as it is. At the very end, the tune's underlying harmony shifts again, with an A minor/A major vamp that buoys the solo of Dibango's distinctive soprano saxophone. That "Négropolitaines" is firmly situated within a longer lineage of African appropriations of the jazz aesthetic, Dibango emphasizes by slotting it in between tunes by Nicolas "Docteur Nico" Kasanda and Joseph "Le Grand Kallé" Kabasele, respectively, the former the tremendously influential soukous guitarist, the latter the imposing leader of the pioneering outfit African Jazz, where the future Lion of Africa himself got his start.[25]

"Négropolitaines" is thus decidedly a product of the Black Atlantic. Recorded in the capital of the former colonial masters, it freely adapts American jazz and funk, but it also harks back to the musical heritage of west-central Africa; it pays homage to the pioneers of African jazz, but it is not averse, either, to availing itself of modern recording technologies and electronic instruments. Other songs in the *Négropolitaines* series incorporate French chansons, American spirituals, even a string quartet. "People must realize that you're not a prisoner of one music because you are African. You're a musician first. You're not a Cameroonian musician, you are a musician of Cameroonian origin," insists Dibango, but he also explains why there is such a liberatory, transnationalizing element in the jazz aesthetic: Dibango says that jazz brought him a "kind of freedom, fresh scope for the imagination. Jazz is the invention of a link between one continent and another—even if the story behind it is a terrible one. But the most beautiful flower can grow on a dunghill. [. . .] The dunghill is slavery and all its works. The flower is jazz, the fruit of what came from the West, on the one hand, and from Africa on the other. It is the twentieth-century music *par excellence*. It even introduces you to other kinds of music."[26]

Thus, Afropolitanism responds to the pressures and opportunities of urban, postcolonial existences by performing fluid, transnational identities that defy homogenizing taxonomies of nationhood and cultural or ethnic citizenship. It is aware that the desire for a *human* self requires the recognition of a "terrible" history that it seeks to deconstruct, but then Afropolitanism *re*-constructs history imaginatively to perform an experiential/experimental self emerging from the encounter with the other, across the border.[27] And so, what resonates in the transnational breaks of Afropolitan soundscapes is not necessarily the desiccation of "tradition," the disappearance of history and nationhood, or the alienation of the artist's self: instead, the ability to navigate, shape, and regulate the passage of time—to project an artistic self across geographical, cultural, and racial boundaries—which the Afro-kinesis in and of jazz affords, results in the creation of new identities, new authenticities. Clearly, Dibango the expat does not ignore the "dunghill" of history, but at the same time, the refusal to let the whiff of manure be the sole determining vector of his musical, transnational journeys allows him to "go from Miriam Makeba to Rachmaninoff."[28]

"Dislocated listening" is what Rashida Braggs has termed the North American version of this dynamic. Reading—and listening to—Baldwin's "Sonny's Blues,"

Braggs explains that dislocated listening entails "a more attuned listening to, and understanding of, African American experience. This understanding occurs when there is a dislocation, a separation or movement away from home. This movement creates distance that prompts disorientation, discomfort, vulnerability, and openness to new experiences. In the process of this distancing, one begins to accept [the] harsh realities of one's experience. [. . .] Instead of pulling away, the person is prompted to engage with more attuned listening."[29] Displaced listening oscillates in an Afro-kinetic field of push-and-pull, but for Dibango, as much as for Gordon, displaced listening becomes displaced *playing*. Like Ellington, Gordon preferred not to make overtly political statements with his music. At the same time, he met with Bobby Seale and Raymond "Masai" Hewitt in Copenhagen in 1969, gave several performances to benefit the antiwar and black revolutionary movements, and wrote "The Panther" as a tribute to the Black Panther Party.[30] The same Afro-kinesis that connected him onstage musically with Catalan pianist Montoliu or Danish drummer Riel also connected him culturally with the African diaspora and the freedom struggle at home.

Thus, it is the music itself that provides the foundation—the bass/base line, as it were—for the two concepts of Afro-kinesis and Afropolitanism: Gordon's *Gettin' Around* as representative of the African American jazz tradition, and Dibango's *Négropolitaines* as the tradition's transposition into a more explicitly transnational context. Accompanying these two critical concepts stemming from the music itself is the work of Walter Benjamin, particularly his figure of the flâneur. His beloved Paris, the birthplace of the flâneur, is a city full of sights but virtually no sounds, and Benjamin himself was essentially tone deaf: in his *Habilitation*, Benjamin relegated music to "the counterpart of meaningful speech."[31] Applying Benjaminian dialectics to jazz music thus might sound dissonant to some ears, but precisely because Benjamin heard in music the counterpart to verbal expression, sound was also intimately related to allegory. His entire body of work in all its various phases keeps circling back, almost obsessively so, to that which is ineffable in and about art—or, as Nathaniel Mackey would put it, to a "telling inarticulacy."[32] And it is this very aspect of Benjaminian theory that makes it particularly relevant to the art of jazz improvisation. Under the conditions of modernity, diagnoses Benjamin, our sense of self "is from minute to minute pure improvisation."[33]

To be sure, European theoretical concepts are not always conducive to an analysis of Afro-diasporic cultural expressions.[34] Still, Dibango positions himself as something of a transnational flâneur in the title of his memoir, *Balade en saxo*, figuring his life as a saxophonic stroll: "I am the man who, all his life, has promenaded his body and his sax in the sceneries of time and history. The piano is too heavy, the vibraphone too. So I chose to depart with the sax dangling from my neck." Playing with the French homonym, he asks "balade ou ballade"—stroll or ballad—and answers his own question right away: "certainly both."[35] His is an Afropolitan flânerie put in motion by jazz's iconic instrument, the saxophone. Dibango's hero Duke Ellington, too, linked jazz music to modern(ist) kinesis: "Jazz is like the automobile and the airplane. It is modern and it is American"—and couldn't help but add, "I don't like the word *jazz* but it is the one that is usually used."[36] And if jazz is the soundtrack to modernity and/as modernism, then Benjamin, among the foremost archaeologists of the modern(ist) age, can furnish a riff or two on how jazz and transnationalism engage in a call-and-response conversation. The two salient points between which Benjamin's dialectical thinking moves are destruction and construction (or, more precisely, *re*construction), a dialectic that is particularly pronounced in the modern metropolis. Consequently, his philosophy of aesthetics, like modernity itself, is concerned with the transient, the fragmentary, the ephemeral. It is precisely this dialectic, fleeting, transitory, and ever changing, that jazz as a modern and modernist music of the moment transposes into sound. Jazz improvisation is akin to Benjamin's Talmudic angels "who are born anew every instant in countless numbers, only to vanish into nothingness once they have sung their hymn before God"—unless, that is, there's a microphone and a recording machine present.[37] For Benjamin, modern art can exist only as long as it is facing its own temporality and dissolution. And even though he wasn't aware of it, his angels might as well have been scat-singing "Three O'Clock in the Morning": just as the lyrics situate the song at the threshold between the last waltz of the night and the dawning of a new day, so "the jazzman must lose his identity even as he finds it," as Ellison knew.[38]

This dialectic in and between Afro-kinetic time and Afropolitan space, between and within intersecting temporal planes and movement across and beyond the Black Atlantic, and jazz as the music that turns into sound the velocity of life in the modern metropolis, recalls Benjamin's figure of the flâneur. Flânerie means "To charge time, like a battery charges power," and "the interlacing of spaces" is "the spectacle to which the flâneur is inescapably drawn." The perceptive flâneur, always on the move, is at home anywhere and nowhere, his forays into the city turning him into "a kaleidoscope" that refractures the Baudelairean "multiplicities of life."[39] Attuned as he is to the striations of the modern city, his curious gaze is often drawn not to the monumental but to the transitory, the ephemeral, the fleeting. To be sure, Benjamin's Old World flâneur is no artist, but flânerie's dialectic between time and place finds its creative evolution in the Afro-kinesis of improvisation and the Afropolitanism of jazz. Flânerie thus often leads to what Ellison calls "the underground of [. . .] unwritten history."[40] To engage jazz music in a jam session of call-and-response with Benjaminian flânerie therefore effects, I hope, a transnational critical practice that hears in jazz also a world music refusing to be pressed into tightly delimited soundscapes vigilantly guarded by the jazz police. Yet for all its kinetic potential to cross any and all borders, the jazz aesthetic's Afropolitanism is one that remains keenly aware of the exigencies of history. After all, as Amiri Baraka reminds us, black music as we know it "could not exist if the African captives had not become American captives."[41]

Gettin' Around will therefore explore these transnational synergies, as well as dissonances, in a variety of scripted and unscripted texts and contexts. It begins by examining how jazz music works as a transnational narrative powered by Afro-kinesis and situated in an Afropolitan matrix. In Wynton Marsalis's estimate, "swinging is about coordination. It's about attaining an equilibrium of forces that many times don't go together. Someone who loves to swing is a great facilitator, and Duke Ellington is the very greatest of the great facilitators, because he played every style of rhythm that we know."[42] After all, the orchestra's theme song, "Take the 'A' Train"—penned by the Duke's musical alter ego, Billy Strayhorn—was all about swinging motion and became the very first composition Ellington registered with his new publishing firm, Tempo Music. The Afro-kinesis of his music the bandleader himself placed squarely in an Afropolitan site: in the preface to his autobiography, fittingly entitled *Music Is My Mistress*, Ellington asks rhetorically, "Where do I call home?" only to follow up with the deadpan answer himself: "I pay rent in New York City." The locale where he feels most at home he describes in the chapter "The City of Jazz." Populated by "all very nice human beings," this is a city whose walls were erected by King Oliver and Buddy Bolden but that has always been welcoming to musical flâneurs from all over the world. Statues of Sidney Bechet, Louis Armstrong, Coleman Hawkins, Chick Webb, and Fletcher Henderson can be found there just as easily as those of Bix Beiderbecke and even Paul Whiteman. But,

> This City of Jazz does not have any specific geographical location. It is anywhere and everywhere, wherever you can hear the sound, and it makes you do like this—

you know! Europe, Asia, North and South America, the world digs this burg—Digsville, Gonesville, Swingersville, and Wailingstown. There are no city limits, no city ordinances, no policemen, no fire department, but come rain or come shine, drought or flood, I think I'll stay here in this scene, with these cats, because almost everybody seems to dig what they're talking about, or putting down. They communicate, Dad. Do you get the message? Villesville is *the* place—*trelos anthropos!*[43]

The "crazy cats" based in this Afropolitan Swingersville revere the statues of Satch and Bean, but its mayoress is Madam Zajj. She is the protagonist of *A Drum Is a Woman*, an allegorical suite narrating the history of jazz music from its beginnings in Africa to the space age. Released first as an album, it was staged for television on CBS's *The United States Steel Hour* in the spring of 1957. Mostly neglected by critics and fans alike, Ellington himself always considered *A Drum Is a Woman* one of the most satisfactory accomplishments of his career. Given Madam Zajj's transnational, even interstellar journeys, it is among the composer's most heterogeneous works. From the beginning of his career, Ellington had always integrated musical elements stemming from beyond the borders of his native country—but, he said, "I want it to be reflection and not refraction."[44] It is certainly not happenstance either that during his 1964 presidential campaign, Dizzy Gillespie proposed that Ellington serve as his secretary of state. Consequently, *A Drum Is a Woman* declines to recycle the "jungle style" of the Cotton Club days that had propelled the bandleader to international fame. Tapping into calypso as much as big band swing, the allegorical suite is a transnational mélange of genres and styles. Still, Madam Zajj's birthplace is Africa, the cradle of humanity; it is therefore only fitting that when French bandleader and Ellington disciple Claude Bolling revived the suite four decades later, he tapped Manu Dibango to step into Duke's role as narrator of the story of the City of Jazz's mayoress. Since it has no city limits, as per Ellington, the City of Jazz as it becomes reflected in Madam Zajj's peripatetics verges upon Benjamin's Parisian arcades, "a city, a world in miniature." And since "the city is really the holy ground of flânerie," Madam Zajj's travels across the planet figure her as an Afropolitan flâneuse driven by Afro-kinesis.[45] Letting Benjamin's flâneur sit in on a jam session co-led by Madam Zajj and Manu Dibango delineates what Christian Moraru calls "the paradox of cosmodern authenticity," that is, how jazz is at once indubitably black in its lineage and yet—or precisely because of it—also "world music" long before we had a term for it.[46] Madam Zajj sashays to her twentieth-century audience "from way back," and Walter Benjamin in turn knew that "modernity always cites prehistory."[47] Jazz has always blurred the borders between the homeland and the *Ausland*—the "outland"—and thus, in the jazzy narratives of Ellington and Dibango, "Africa" becomes an Afro-kinetic signifier whose mobility does not devitalize localized traditions but reflects them in new, variegated "authenticities." Perhaps in this way, Africa, blackness, and jazz are all, to use Duke Ellington's favorite phrase, "beyond category."[48]

Still, for Ellington, jazz was and remained a quintessentially *American* art form, pioneered by *Americans* of African descent. At the same time, Ellington also understood—perhaps better than most—that the music to which he contributed so much had come into being precisely by bucking racialist, authenticating taxonomies, that its Afro-kinesis propelled the music in a centrifugal fashion, not a centripetal one. Categories are by nature normative, fixed, and stable, but the velocity of life in the modern metropolis, the City of Jazz, renders them perennially tenuous. It should therefore come as no surprise that one of the first stops Madam Zajj made after she left the United States was not London, not Paris, not even Douala, but Berlin. Perhaps her departure from American shores was also prompted by the elitism of many Harlem Renaissance leaders, who tended to hear in jazz light if risqué entertainment at best, a deplorable corruption of the cultural potential of the black tradition at worst. Thus, there was precious little synergy between jazz musicians and writers in the wake of World War I, with only very few exceptions. Bandleader Benny Carter later averred that "We in music knew that there was much going on in literature, for example, but our worlds were far apart. We sensed that the black cultural as well as moral leaders looked down on our music as undignified."[49]

In the Old World, by contrast, many intellectuals greeted the arrival of Madam Zajj with excitement. Writing for Berlin's influential periodical *Literarische Welt*, Paris-based poet Ivan Goll couldn't help but notice that "The Negroes are here. Already, all of Europe is dancing to their banjo. It can't resist. Some say, these are the rhythms from Sodom and Gomorrah. . . . Why shouldn't they be the rhythms from Paradise? Here, a decline and a beginning are intertwined."[50] Goll was ideally placed and may have noticed that in the roaring twenties, there were eighteen different record labels in Berlin that issued jazz music, producing twice as many original jazz recordings than in Paris. To be sure, Europeans didn't immediately understand the music Madam Zajj brought with her. To many citizens of the Weimar Republic, jazz sounded like "the intermediate product between jungle and skyscraper," and the syncope "the ringing characteristic for our mad, rushing epoch."[51] Moreover, much of the new music that both excited and enraged Germans wasn't really what we today would call jazz, but rather a lightly syncopated orchestral dance music of the homegrown variety. From this heady swirl of more or less syncopated sounds emerged what it proudly proclaimed to be "the first jazz-novel having unfolded according to the laws of jazz music," on either side of the Black Atlantic. Its author, Hans Janowitz, was Czech, Jewish, and a member of Berlin's cultural avant-garde. Titled after "the real program of the times," *Jazz*, his sole novel, follows the adventures of Lord Punch's Jazz-Band-Boys, a motley crew of amateur musicians crisscrossing western Europe.[52] Thoroughly cosmopolitan and highly kinetic, the novel curiously features only one African American character, and a seemingly peripheral one at that: Bibi Black isn't even a musician, but a dancer. Yet reading Janowitz's novel to the tune of John Coltrane's famous "sheets of sound" reveals that Bibi Black is indeed a second cousin to Madam Zajj. As A. B. Spellman has noted, Coltrane was concerned "with the development of a kinetic vernacular which facilitated the release of a kind of group energy"; similarly, Janowitz's polyvocal, fast-paced narrative is effectively propelled by "sheets of script."[53] Such a reading also amplifies what happens when the Afro-kinesis and Afropolitanism of jazz are transposed into a de-Americanized and seemingly deracinated context. And so, pairing Janowitz in a duet with Coltrane seeks to explain what we stand to gain when we "listen" to the literary text.

Coltrane's music demonstrates what instrumental jazz can contribute to critical practice, but it can also show how transnational resonances make the jazz aesthetic different from other musics by "listening" to the title of Langston Hughes's second autobiography, *I Wonder as I Wander*. Its wide-ranging flânerie concludes in a Parisian café on New Year's Eve of 1938, and the memoirist's final wonderment if his world would come to an end is the only allusion to the book's title, borrowed from the Christmas carol. The symbolic geography mapped out by "I Wonder as I Wander" and its contested origins finds its musical counterpoint in Coltrane's 1961 album *Africa/Brass*. The impulse for the entire project—recorded the same year construction of the Berlin Wall began—came from pianist McCoy Tyner's reharmonization of yet another traditional Christmas carol, the English folk song "Greensleeves." The autobiographer uses "I Wonder as I Wander" in much the same way that the tenorist reimagines "Greensleeves": the transmutational practices of Coltrane the Afro-kinetic seeker and Hughes the Afropolitan wanderer aim at a transnational reconstruction of ethical "with-ness" that plays on and over congealed divisions of ethnicity and nationhood but simultaneously strikes a posture of vigilance vis-à-vis the persistent constraints of history.

The Afro-kinetic journeys of *I Wonder as I Wander* and *Africa/Brass* thus resonate on different frequencies than the rock aesthetic as transmitted by the 2000 Hollywood movie *High Fidelity*. Benjamin may have been polemicizing when he insisted that "all problems of contemporary art find their definitive formulation only in connection with film."[54] But if "cinema was born under the natal sign of Wagner," as Jed Rasula declares flatly, then the melomania that shapes the worldview of *High Fidelity*'s Rob, Dick, and Barry gives Wagnerism a rock 'n' roll facelift.[55] Based closely on the novel of the same title by Nick Hornby, the characters themselves do not engage in either Benjaminian or Hughesian flânerie, but the plot does as it transposes the amorous misadventures of Rob, a rock aficionado and record store owner, from London to Chicago. Rob is, however, also the direct descendant of another type, closely related to the figure of the flâneur, to emerge in Benjamin's modern metropolis, the collector. The romantic comedy's dramatis personae assembles a multiracial and international cast, its soundtrack ostensibly helping to celebrate a harmonious amalgamation of styles, genres, and ethnicities. Yet the film's visualization of the rock aesthetic effectuates the expulsion of its sole Africanist presence halfway in. Without Madam Zajj's transnational Afro-kinesis, the very catalyst of Hughes's and Coltrane's Afropolitan forays, the film mutes almost completely the rich history of black music in the world's blues capital. To be sure, rock is likewise propelled in part by Afro-kinetic energy, but it tends to produce many fewer temporal nodes and Ellisonian breaks in and from which to look around.[56] And so the film actually rewinds the American "race record" of the twentieth century and replays it in the twenty-first.

Even if Madam Zajj has never visited *High Fidelity*'s Chicago, most everywhere else the Afro-kinesis of jazz improvisation resonates as a positivist force, most hopefully so in Ellington and Janowitz, a force that can circumvent or subvert even the most impregnable of borders. Of course, improvisation is not just a musical practice, but it is an activity paramount to human behavior. The tenor in jazz studies hears "improvisation as a positive model of cross-cultural exchange."[57] Yet in and of itself, improvisation is a neutral force, its multidirectional kinesis not by default uplifting or regenerative. Says Jamaican-born multi-instrumentalist Douglas Ewart, a member of the Chicago-based AACM, "we have to realize the magic of music—that it can bring good things, and it can bring bad things. We have to watch that."⁵⁸ Two such transnational narratives in which improvisation actually brings "bad things," where it cannot mediate the trauma of historical time, are Paule Marshall's novel *The Fisher King* and Steven Spielberg's film *The Terminal*. The catalyst for *The Fisher King*'s plot is the music of Sonny-Rett Payne, a jazz musician of West Indian descent who eventually settled in Paris, where he suffered a violent death in the *métro* at the hands of overzealous police. Years later, his former manager and lover, Hattie, travels back to Brooklyn with the pianist's grandson, Sonny, where she is to participate in the grand opening of a community center dedicated to the musical legacy of Sonny-Rett as well as to the urban renewal of the neighborhood. Their return, however, reveals that all the characters, including little Sonny, have their own scripts devised to take ownership of the pianist's legacy. These various scripts all seek to channel the Afro-kinesis of jazz improvisation in one specific direction or another in order to regulate the personal trauma of Sonny-Rett's premature passing, the familial trauma of the continuing feud between his family and that of his late wife, and the lingering traumata effected by the transatlantic slave trade. In the end, though, none of the characters manages to author a script that accomplishes the transposition of jazz's liberatory Afro-kinesis into a curative vision of an Afropolitan community that has negotiated trauma in positive ways. As a script itself, *The Fisher King* is unable to harness Afro-kinetic synergies and must therefore withhold closure from all its characters.

Big-budget Hollywood production that it is, Spielberg's *The Terminal* does provide closure for its characters. The romantic comedy is by no means a jazz film, even if Art Kane's famous photograph "A Great Day in Harlem" is eventually revealed as the MacGuffin. But the film is very much a tale about *social* improvisation: Viktor Navorski, a tourist from the former Soviet satellite nation of Krakozhia, ends up trapped in the international transit lounge of New York's John F. Kennedy Airport after a military coup in his homeland, staged while he was over the Atlantic, renders all his travel documents void. Though he is not a musician himself, Viktor improvises in and over the dizzying maze of U.S. immigration law and extemporizes for himself a life in the interstitial spaces of the transit lounge during his nine-month sojourn. Much like Marshall's novel, however, the film also symbolically pits sound against script: the improvised sounds of the jazz luminaries depicted in Kane's photograph are marshaled against the stabilizing scripts of U.S. immigration law. In the end, though, Hollywood's script ironically sides with the latter as it repatriates Viktor to Krakozhia and the rest of the characters of the multiethnic, multinational dramatis personae back to their designated places where they "belong." Fred Moten points out that "when the restructuring of capitalism dislocates nation and origin and when such dislocation is sped along by global and globalizing technicity," like the various *re*-location processes visualized in and by the Hollywood vehicle, this "secures, finally, the literal [or filmic] formulation of a 'world picture' that constitutes the final degradation of the illusory prefigurations of Enlightenment cosmopolitanism."[59] At the termination of *The Terminal*, with the unruly Afro-kinesis of jazz improvisation hermetically contained, the liberatory potential of social improvisation proves futile as it is subsumed eventually by newly reconfigured scripts of nationhood.

At the very end of *The Terminal*, Benny Golson has a cameo as himself. The tenor saxophonist and composer—whose "Stablemates" his contemporary Dexter Gordon played quite often on stage and recorded several times—also appears in "A Great Day in Harlem." As far as Golson is concerned, "music as likened to language" is akin to "a new nation where words are lined up and act musically."[60] Lining up such a discourse of musical nation-building requires precisely what the script of *The Terminal* fails to do: it presupposes *listening*. The art of Swiss saxophonist and composer Jürg Wickihalder is deeply invested in musical storytelling, particularly when it is improvised, where, as he underscores, it's important "to create in some kind of way an empathy with the other."[61] His duo with pianist Irène Schweizer on "Last Jump" sounds an empathy that extends not just to his partner on stage and the audience in the club but to a whole host of ever fluctuating interrelations fanning out across the entire planet, which along the way effects an alternative "worlding" in sound. For Moraru, transnational, planetary worlding constitutes an evolution of cosmodernism and designates "*a fluid, multicentric, plural, and pluralizing worldly structure of relatedness unfolding in the triple dimension of a geocultural space, discourse modality, and critical-imaginative framework or episteme, all of which are keyed to non-totalist, non-homogenizing, and anti-hegemonic operations existentially as well as culturally cognitive in nature.*"[62] Wickihalder's *Brandruf*, commissioned to commemorate the cataclysmic destruction in 1861 of his birthplace, Glarus, operates along such a planetary relatedness, its trajectories traveling not just to New Orleans, the mythical birthplace of jazz, but to Iceland, Australia, Pakistan, and Russia as well. In the process, Wickihalder's music amplifies what the ramifications for an ethically responsible transnational critical practice consist of.

For musicologist Daniel Fueter, "Making music and listening to it essentially entails a phenomenon of resonance, a peculiar kind of openness that could be described as attentiveness in the sense of empathy. In making music, we are taught to be open from 'one to the other,' and to be open for 'the one in the other'"—over there, across the border.[63] So, let's get going.

CHAPTER I

The Afro-kinetic Passages of Madam Zajj
Driving Jazz "Home" with Manu Dibango and Duke Ellington

One of the many conflicts raging in postcolonial Africa was the war between Libya and Chad. After Colonel Muammar Gaddafi's coup in 1967, Libya aspired to expand its influence in central Africa, and the military occupation in 1973 of the desolate but mineral-rich Aouzou Strip just beyond the border with its southern neighbor was a first move in escalating a long-simmering territorial dispute. Taking advantage of Chad's intensifying civil war that pitted the predominantly Muslim North against the Christian South, Gaddafi established an airbase and extended citizenship to the area's few inhabitants, resulting in the de facto annexation of the barren strip. Over the next few years, there were several attempts to expand the influence of the Gaddafi regime or to expel the Libyan garrisons from the Aouzou, prompting two military interventions by France, which succeeded only in consolidating the status quo, dissatisfactory to both sides. The last phase of the conflict began in January 1987, after most of Gaddafi's Chadian allies in the North, fed up with the dictator's meddling and suspicious of his motives, switched sides and joined the troops of president Hissène Habré. The Libyan units were heavily mechanized, but the defection of their allies deprived them of a nimble ground option. Perhaps the most effective weapon in the arsenal of the ragtag Chadian forces, on the other hand, was the Toyota pickup truck: its speed and dependability proved a decisive tactical advantage in the desert terrain of the Aouzou and helped deal the Libyans a series of humiliating defeats, culminating eventually in their expulsion and the restoration of the region to Chad. The sight of these technicals was so ubiquitous that the 1987 conflict was dubbed the Toyota War.[1]

The somewhat flippant moniker also pointed to the strong presence of the Japanese car manufacturer in the global economy. A major supplier of trucks to the Imperial Japanese Army during World War II, the company's postwar resurgence was also fueled by expansion into third world markets. From its hub in apartheid South Africa, where the company had built its first assembly line in 1962, Toyota targeted the newly independent nations to the north. Toyota's marketing juggernaut proclaimed, "La musique est un monde sans frontières. Toyota aussi." Ironically, it managed to enlist even the voice of Mama Africa herself, Miriam Makeba, on the promotional single "Toyota Fantaisie / Can't Stop Myself," a bouncy bit of Afro-funk in which Makeba praises the cars' unstoppable kinesis in French on the A-side, in English on the B-side. Toyota also approached the other superstar of Afropop, Manu Dibango, who delivered with "Toyota Makossa" another catchy promotional jingle. Toyota sponsored a tour through much of the continent, during which copies of the single were given away gratis by the thousands, making it a hugely popular song that everybody soon knew: Dibango remembers that through much of the 1980s, taxi drivers in Douala and Yaoundé would heckle him if they spotted him climbing into a different make of car. To maximize on Dibango's stardom, the title referenced the biggest record of Dibango's career, "Soul Makossa." While the global megahit is actually much closer musically to James Brown than to Douala, the Toyota jingle is indeed a prime example of makossa, the dance music popularized at midcentury in the urban areas of Cameroon that is characterized by a prominent bass line and horn section: here, a punchy yet spry electric bass, bubbly percussion, and Bokilo "Jerry" Malekani's filigreed guitar work create an irresistible groove over which both Dibango and the horns effusively approve of the female vocalists' claim that "Ma Toyota Corolla est fantastique, oh oui!"[2] And like the genre to which it claims allegiance, "Toyota Makossa" is very much a musical hybrid, with its only overtly "jazzy" element Dibango's extended solo on tenor saxophone. The jingle bears the fingerprints also of longtime musical director Malekani, who grew up with soukous, the Congo's guitar-centric equivalent of makossa, but achieved success as leader of Rico Jazz, a band comprised of fellow West African expats that became a sensation in the French Antilles in the early 1970s. Finally, "Toyota Makossa" also prominently features the synthesized pinging sample that signaled Dibango's growing involvement in electronica. And so, "Toyota Makossa" is a decidedly transnational affair resonating within a complex constellation of consumer capitalism and the global economy, technology, entertainment, and the bloody effects of postcolonialism from which black music was not exempt.[3]

Navigating this musical mélange—not to mention the sociopolitical and economic one—has not always been easy for Dibango. As he has recounted more than once, "There were two aspects to my fight. The first was in Europe, where people knew I played saxophone and piano but would say, That's not an African instrument. To be a musician you must play balafon or tom-tom. The other was in Africa, where you could not be a professional musician. Musicians were folk artists: People invited you to play and gave you food and drink. Not money. In between Europe and Africa was Manu Dibango." As allergic to categorization as his idol Ellington, the Cameroonian expat explains that "At first people in Africa said that I made Western music, that I was black-white. I carried that label around for a long time. In France people often told me that I made American music. And when I went to the United States, the Americans thought that I made African music. It's impossible to be more of a traitor than that!"[4]

This sense of "in-betweenness" is what Afropolitanism turns into sound. With the Afropolitan's quintessential background, it was jazz—African American jazz—that filled the musical interstices in Dibango's Black Atlantic identity. Still dividing his time between his saxophone and his studies when he got his start in Congolese Joseph "Le Grand Kallé" Kabasele's appropriately named outfit African Jazz, Dibango was part of the first generation of self-defined jazz musicians from sub-Saharan Africa. Guided through the music by a fellow student also from Cameroon, Francis Bébey, who in turn would go on to become one of the continent's premier ethnomusicologists, Dibango cites Duke Ellington's "Morning Glory" as the first jazz record he purchased.[5] And via the Duke, he discovered Count Basie, Charlie Parker, John Coltrane, and especially Sidney Bechet, to whom the Lion of Africa would devote an entire tribute album. These discoveries in turn would allow him to understand how he could negotiate the musical heritage of his native Cameroon in novel ways: "Take makossa: I treat makossa like people treat the blues here, or in Brazil samba. These kinds of differences are necessary. I'm not a Mississippi man. I don't drink Coca-Cola; I drink beaujolais. But in the total realm of jazz, you can bring something to it: You can be yourself. Jazz is also free, so you can do your thing with it. It's big enough to take a lot of ingredients. Bring your differences. Within jazz, everything is equal, but not the same."[6] Jazz is the stickum in this Afropolitan musical pastiche.

Over the course of his career, more and more influences accumulated in the trunk of Dibango's far-ranging musical Toyota Corolla. The saxophonist began to experiment increasingly with electronica; on his 1984 album *Surtension*, for example, the drum parts are all courtesy of a newfangled LinnDrum digital drum machine of the first generation, with only sporadic support lent by two human percussionists, an experiment that promptly got him branded as "a traitor."[7] Clearly, the Cameroonian expat headquartered in Paris has never had the intention of delivering traditional, somehow "authentic" makossa—especially not since the genre itself is a hybrid, of course. Just as clearly, if not always audible in prominent ways, the Afro-kinesis of American jazz continued to furnish the sonic protocols of Dibango's Afropolitan soundscapes. It is therefore no coincidence that when Duke Ellington's French protégé, bandleader Claude Bolling, planned a commemoration of the fortieth anniversary of his mentor's allegorical suite *A Drum Is a Woman*, he tapped the Afropolitan Dibango to narrate the saga of jazz and the passages of Madam Zajj, the music's mythical personification. Shortly before his death, Ellington himself had made plans with Bolling to revive the suite for a French-German television coproduction, but the project never came to fruition due to Ellington's precarious health. His "spiritual son," however, didn't forget his mentor's intentions, and when fragments of the original score of *A Drum Is a Woman* were discovered among the holdings of the Smithsonian Institute, the Frenchman revived the project to commemorate the fortieth anniversary of the suite's debut. Bolling's version is not an update of the original, but rather a faithful reproduction. Bolling and his associates painstakingly reconstructed the score from the original recording as well as from the newly rediscovered fragments. They even went so far as to transcribe the original solos—therefore, there was next to no instant improvisation to be heard when the suite was staged at the Théâtre national de Chaillot in the spring of 1996. The only marked deviation from the original was that Manu Dibango, the Lion of Africa, took on the role of the Duke of big band swing to narrate the adventures of Madam Zajj—in French.[8] Exact copy that Bolling's performance aspired to be, it ironically confined the Afro-kinesis of the original to a detailed script, somewhat akin to steering a souped-up Toyota Corolla through the turns of a closed race course instead of the off-road racing of the Paris–Dakar Rally.

Dibango's French narration is the only element that amplifies the polyglot Afropolitanism of Madam Zajj and the Lion of Africa both. Since "Rhythm came to Africa from way back," we have to trace the passages of *A Drum Is a Woman*'s heroine further back than that spring evening in Paris when Claude Bolling and Manu Dibango retold her story, and further back even than the first time Ellington accompanied her appearance onstage four decades before.[9]

The demise of the swing era in the postwar years, hastened by the ascendancy of bebop and rhythm and blues, found the Duke Ellington Orchestra in dire straits. Though one of the very few large jazz aggregations to survive the changing economic and musical landscape, it was rattled by the exit of several key members, perhaps most crucial that of Johnny Hodges, whose creamy alto saxophone had been a signature sound of the orchestra since its Cotton Club days, and the extended leaves of absence Billy Strayhorn was taking from his arranging and composing duties. Strayhorn in particular was missed dearly by the Duke: "He was not, as often referred to by many, my alter ego," Ellington would later write. "Billy Strayhorn was my right arm, my left arm, all the eyes in the back of my head, my brainwaves in his head, and his in mine."[10] But in the mid-1950s, two events signaled the sudden resurgence of Duke Ellington. First, both Strayhorn and Hodges returned to the organization after finding the going economically unfeasible and artistically unsatisfying. Strayhorn, who rarely performed in public anyway, realized that it was ill-advised to sever his ties to Ellington; and Hodges's only hit in the four years away from Ellington was "Castle Rock," which, ironically, featured fellow Ellington alumnus Al Sears's tenor saxophone instead of the bandleader's alto.

Second, Ellington's appearance at the 1956 Newport Jazz Festival instantly became one of the most legendary moments in jazz. It began inauspiciously enough when several members of the band were not yet present for the first set (the Ellington orchestra was notorious for its lack of discipline, and it was a common sight to see musicians casually stroll onstage well after a concert had already commenced). Beginning shortly before midnight, the second set finally had the full band assembled. Things took a sudden and entirely unexpected turn with "Diminuendo and Crescendo in Blue," two blues Ellington had first recorded separately back in the 1930s and rarely revisited since. At Newport, the two sections were bridged by Paul Gonsalves's tenor sax solo, a marathon performance of twenty-seven choruses of volcanic energy. The savvy bandleader recognized the rare magic in the air that night, for he kept spurring his lead tenorist on by shouting—"Don't stop now! Don't stop!"—and pumping his fist. Before long, Jo Jones, Count Basie's drummer, who was standing in the wings, became infected with the galvanic Afro-kinesis and began pounding out the beat energetically with a rolled newspaper in his fist. Next, a striking, platinum-blonde woman in a black cocktail dress leaped from her chair and started to dance, prompting many others in the audience to do the same. With festivalgoers in a frenzy and angrily refusing to let the band end the concert, organizers feared that a riot would ensue and tried, unsuccessfully, to put an early stop to the show. On the unedited tapes, impresario George Wein can be heard arguing vociferously with Ellington in between numbers, who, following Gonsalves's explosive solo, attempted to placate the crowd's fervor with a couple of slower tunes showcasing Hodges's soothing alto. The national press reported widely on Ellington's and Gonsalves's exploits, and a gushing six-page cover story in *Time* magazine capped the media's heralding that the Duke was back indeed. It was simply "jazz at its jazziest," effused one who witnessed it all and would have known—Langston Hughes.[11]

The flurry of activity immediately following the historic night at Newport included a suite commissioned by Canada's Stratford Shakespeare Festival in Ontario based on the Bard's plays and characters and taking its title, *Such Sweet Thunder*, from Puck in *A Midsummer Night's Dream*, a new contract with Columbia Records, and plans for an extended European tour. Closest to Duke's heart, though, was an ongoing project he had tried to put onstage before. The idea had actually arisen with "Creole Rhapsody" in 1931; ever since then, an even larger historiography in sound had been on Ellington's mind: "I have gone back to the history of my people and tried to express it in rhythm. We used to have it in Africa, a something we have lost. One day we shall get it back again. I am expressing in sound the old days in the jungle, the cruel journey across the sea, and the despair of the landing. And then the days in Harlem and the cities of the States. Then I try to go forward a thousand years, when, emancipated and transformed, the Negro takes his place, a free being, among peoples of the world."[12] In 1943, finally, he premiered *Black, Brown, and Beige* at New York City's venerable Carnegie Hall, an extended work subtitled "A Tone Parallel to the History of the Negro in America." The "tone parallel" attempted to tell, in jazz, the history of black people in the New World, but its scope was so ambitious that the forty-plus minutes at Carnegie Hall presented only a truncated version of Ellington's elaborate, carefully researched scenario, and the complete suite was never performed or recorded in the composer's lifetime. The critical reception of *Black, Brown, and Beige* was lukewarm at best too, a serious disappointment to Ellington.

An earlier, more conventional production was the all-black revue *Jump for Joy*, which ran for three months in 1941 in Los Angeles before frequent production and directorial changes, massive overhead, and looming war with the Axis powers forced its close. Together with Strayhorn, Ellington had written the score for the musical, his orchestra performing it in the pit each night, and the show was the darling of Hollywood's liberal elite. In fact, Orson Welles approached the bandleader with the proposal of collaborating on a film documentary to be entitled *The Saga of Jazz*, and even though the undertaking never got far, the idea stuck with Ellington. Now, though, fresh off of his dramatic success at Newport and with newfound clout in the music business, he and Strayhorn revisited the song and story fragments they had tinkered with more than a decade earlier for what would become one of the most enigmatic and controversial projects of their careers, *A Drum Is a Woman*.[13]

Their timing was fortuitous in more respects than just Ellington's sudden prominence in the public eye and ear. The technology of color television was in its infancy then: CBS and NBC were experimenting with competing systems, and the two networks were in heated competition for official approval from the Federal Communications Commission. Hoping to outdo NBC's tube-based technology with their mechanical color-wheel concept, CBS executives were unusually receptive to programming experiments, and when they realized that Ellington was newly under contract with Columbia Records, their music subsidiary, they quickly acted to benefit from this potentially profitable constellation, especially since the network was already producing episodes in association with the prestigious Theatre Guild. Ellington in turn pitched to CBS a spruced-up version of the idea he and Welles had pondered in California almost two decades before, a multimedia spectacle on several platforms. This, the bandleader declared confidently, would be "the most ambitious thing we ever attempted artistically." Echoing the subtitle of *Black, Brown, and Beige*, Ellington went on to explain that "*A Drum Is a Woman* is a tone parallel to the history of jazz, and the heroine is called Madam Zajj, which is a funny way of spelling jazz backward. And she is the spirit of jazz, which comes about as a result of this tremendous romance that goes on between a musician and his instrument—and this is a big thing, and this is how we arrive at the statement that a drum is a woman."[14] Unlike *Black, Brown, and Beige*, this tone parallel was going to consist mostly of songs with lyrics as well as much narration, to be done by the Duke himself; like its predecessor, though, *A Drum Is a Woman* would have an explicitly transnational bend, incorporating African and European settings, but this time they would telescope the story of jazz even into space. The prospect of showing off in one fell swoop African jungles, Caribbean beaches, American metropolises, and distant stars to their viewership—and the FCC—sounded like a brilliant boon to the CBS brass. Willard Levitas, who would design the sets for the show, later scoffed, "The main thing for them was, 'Will it show off our color wheel?' [. . .] They didn't know very much about Duke Ellington except that he wasn't white, so there was more color for them."[15]

And color there was, already in early 1957, when Columbia Records released the album—even if the cover art showed a platinum-blonde white woman in a skin-tight red dress sitting with outstretched arms between two tribal drums. For example, the musical journey visits a Mississippi River "look[ing] like a puddle of pecan-blue pudding—pistachio and indigo—and the sun, a neon-rose lollipop, is being drawn up over the horizon into a fizzy bunch of grape-colored clouds." But the plot of *A Drum Is a Woman* opens on a Caribbean island, where Ellington, who serves as narrator and tour guide, introduces us to Carribee Joe: "One day, he found an elaborately fabricated drum. And when he touched it, it actually spoke to him, saying, 'I am not a drum. I am a woman. Know me as Madam Zajj, African enchantress. I can make you rich and famous. Together, we can travel and make beautiful rhythm for the world.'" Carribee Joe, however, "was in love with the jungle, the virgin jungle, God-made and untouched. And with the jungle he had to stay," but restless Madam Zajj is unwilling to linger. She leaves Joe in his jungle, and, after a brief stopover in Barbados and a dalliance with another, unsuitable Joe, she journeys on to New Orleans and Congo Square, the mythical birthplace of jazz. At the side of the legendary Buddy Bolden, crowned King of the Zulus that year, she officiates as first lady of Mardi Gras. Even though she cannot forget Carribee Joe, Madam Zajj travels up the Mississippi river to "Chicago—New York—San Francisco—London—Paris—the world." But "*real* swingin' chick" that she is, the world is not enough for her, and so she takes her act to outer space, to an "emerald rock garden just off the moon, where darkness is only a translucency and the cellophane trees grow a mile high. Come climb with me to the top of my tree where the fruit is ripe and the taste is like the sky. Star rubies are budding in my diamond-encrusted hothouse and the rhythm is melodic, the rhythm is rhapsodic—the rhythm."[16] But as she returns in her flying saucer to the ovations of the earthlings in New York City, she continues to dream of Joe. In her dream, she summons Joe to 52nd Street, the Broadway of bebop, and the man from the jungle transforms into a hipster with requisite goatee, beret, and sunglasses. Madam Zajj exhausts her powerful sorcery attempting to lure Joe out of the jungle, all to no avail. The two lovers are never actually reunited; Madam Zajj continues to travel the planet and galaxy from triumph to triumph, whereas Joe remains in his beloved jungle, talking to the animals and his ever-growing collection of drums.

The album was recorded during several separate sessions between September and December of 1956 prior to the television shoot, and Ellington confidently touted the release as "the mother of all albums."[17] He and Strayhorn had done some extensive window-shopping in the bazaar of world music, and the title song that opens the suite signals already that this would not be a conventional retelling of the story of jazz in that it owes much more to opera than to swing. Other genres and styles tapped to score the travels of Madam Zajj include the calypso of "What Else Can You Do with a Drum," the Las Vegas lounge stylings of "You Better Know It," the New Orleans trad-jazz of "Hey, Buddy Bolden," or the nod to progressive bebop and its Afro-Cuban offshoots on "Rhumbop."

The TV adaptation aired shortly thereafter, on May 8, 1957, on CBS's *The United States Steel Hour*. Broadcast live and again narrated by Ellington, the orchestra, already augmented by Cuban-born percussionist Candido Camero and classical harpist Betty Glamann, was joined by a troupe of dancers, with the dazzling Carmen de Lavallade dancing the role of Madam Zajj and Talley Beatty in the role of Carribee Joe.[18] Back from the album sessions were Joya Sherrill and Margaret Tynes lending their voices to the heroine, and Ozzie Bailey sang all the male parts. While the storyline adheres largely to the itinerary traveled on the album, the broadcast version got shortened from four to three acts and a finale and omitted much of the narrative. Instead of the title song, *The United States Steel Hour* episode opens with an extended solo by Candido that accompanies Carribee Joe's discovery of the drum in the jungle, then follows Madam Zajj from Joe's island to Barbados and to Mardi Gras in the Crescent City, where the sorceress endows Bolden's trumpet with jazzy sounds. Act 2 begins with lonely Joe in his island jungle, while Zajj is living it up in a Chicago nightclub. There, she enchants Johnny Hodges's alto saxophone and briefly indulges the flirtations of a third Joe but soon zooms on to New York, "the metropolis around which the entire world revolves," as Ellington reminds the viewing audience. From the corner of Broadway and 52nd Street, she makes a quick dash to the club where the Duke holds court and Sherrill sings "Rhumbop." Zajj, however, is sitting by herself in a corner, overcome with longing for Joe when she sees a palm tree painted on the wall.

It is in the final act where the script begins to deviate from the album's story line. The hopelessly lovesick heroine "conjured herself right back to Carribee Joe's island," where her lover sings "Pomegranate" to her—in contrast to the lyrics, the two are indeed in each other's arms as the final strains of the song ebb—and offers her the titular fruit. Searching all over the world for a place of cohabitation amenable to Joe the homebody, she finally succeeds with "the most out-of-this-world offer: she offered him the moon, or a little place just off the moon." After "The Ballet of the Flying Saucers," the camera cuts back to Duke Ellington sitting at the piano in front of his orchestra: "Aha! Madam Zajj, a real swingin' chick. She drew on all of her resources of interplanetary sorcery to get her man, and get him she did. Was, is, and always will be a *real* swingin' chick. You know, why doesn't everybody get a drum? A drum's an awful lot of fun and—say, hey!" The bandleader bends down to pick something up from the floor, and as he lifts a small drum into the camera frame, he asks coquettishly, "Whose pretty little drum are you?"[19] After one last commercial interruption and an announcement of the next episode of *The United States Steel Hour* (an aviatic adventure called *Shadow in the Sky*, again in association with the Theatre Guild), the finale is different, too. On the album, the "Finale" is a percussive fanfare, where the singers simply chant the suite's title again. On television, Tynes sings the full version of the title song, flipping the album's script, where "A Drum Is a Woman" figures as the opener. Ellington is standing at the piano and directs his orchestra with the gravitas of a classical conductor; as the last notes fade, the maestro sits down on the piano bench with a beaming smile and immediately leads the orchestra into an instrumental rendition of "You Better Know It" as the credits begin to roll.

That the TV extravaganza shortens the international stages of Madam Zajj's world tours or bypasses some altogether and also concludes with (ostensibly) a happily-ever-after ending is surely in part due to the constraints, both technological and temporal, of the format. But it is also a concession to commercial, corporate exigencies converging with national interests in the Cold War era. The authoritative voice at the very beginning of the broadcast that makes sure viewers not only see the sponsor's name, but hear it as well, assures them that "Only steel"—that is, *American* steel—"can do so many things so well." To drive home the superiority of American-made steel, the first commercial break takes viewers to U.S. Steel's research center in Monroeville, Pennsylvania. The visually dramatic tour is narrated by radio journalist George Hicks, who had worked as a war correspondent during World War II. At the start of the second commercial break, Hicks announces "news on a colorful subject: today's kitchens." Actors Sheila Jackson and Byron Carlson then show viewers around "a kitchen styled in steel" and urge them to order U.S. Steel's *Kitchen Planning Book* if they too want to enjoy culinary delights among "smart, decorative colors," a pitch Jackson repeats in the third and final commercial break.[20] The image of upper-middle-class domesticity begotten by consumer capitalism and American-style democracy cannot tolerate Carribee Joe's uppity, renegade sputnik on the loose in the cosmos, especially since U.S. Steel was of course a major contractor for the U.S. armed forces.

Even so, the black press and other African American artists (Ellington's erstwhile collaborator Langston Hughes among them) largely applauded the production, recognizing that a full hour of color television conceived, written, and performed by black people constituted a coup of truly historic proportions. Other reviews were mixed, however. The American viewing public apparently didn't know what to make of the show either, as the ratings were dismal. And to add insult to injury, shortly after the program aired, the FCC opted for NBC's tube system as the national broadcast standard for color TV. Consequently, in his sprawling autobiography—as meandering as Madam Zajj's own forays—Ellington devotes only one brief paragraph to *A Drum Is a Woman*, even though he continued to think of the suite as one of the major achievements in his artistic career. Ellington blamed the bad press on music critics who believe "that jazz can't be written, and then when you combine it with voices, and you make a fanfare like Madame [sic] Zajj coming out of the flying saucer, well they don't think this is jazz."[21]

But the project had been beset by problems from the beginning. Even before *A Drum Is a Woman* aired on TV, none other than Barry Ulanov, Ellington's first biographer, griped in his review of the album that "Such banality, such inanity, such a hodgepodge does not stand up either to close reading or close listening."[22] True enough, the music does not rank among the best of Ellington-Strayhorn collaborations. Ellington's penchant for singers of questionable talent was once again audible on *A Drum Is a Woman*, whose title song features the vocals of Tynes, an operatic soprano who had never before performed in a jazz context. Moreover, in Strayhorn's own estimate they were extremely rushed, even more so than they were wont to be as they worked feverishly on the commissioned suite *Such Sweet Thunder* at the same time, and while the bandleader kept up his relentless touring schedule. The pair soon resolved to recycle snippets from the abandoned *Saga of Jazz;* still, it took five separate recording sessions to put *A Drum Is a Woman* on tape. A sixth session on March 7, 1957, a mere two months before air date, was necessary to record "Pomegranate" in order to have some musical material that could accommodate the rerouting of Madam Zajj's roving to its happy conclusion.[23]

The new song's lyrics, however, placed the heroine "On some far isle in the sea" where "she sits beneath a blue tree" instead of reposing in an embrace with her lover. Thus, with planning for *The United States Steel Hour* episode well underway, "Pomegranate" did little to alleviate the executive producer's puzzlement: "Do whatever the hell you want, because the thing doesn't make any sense," Marshall Jamison told set designer Levitas and the rest of the production staff.[24] The story, or what is left of one, seems even more erratic and cursory on TV. In addition to director Norman Felton, Will Lorin credited for the screen adaptation, and Paul Godkin's choreography, the credits include William Herman as story consultant and Ralph Norman Wilkinson as musical director. As a result of this many cooks in the stainless-steel kitchen where Madam Zajj's travels were warmed over from the vinyl for the camera, and with so much of Ellington's narrative from the album grated away, the crucial part—that the protagonist was supposed to embody jazz music itself—was probably lost on many in the viewing audience. And those who did make the connection, reminded perhaps by the promotional material circulated widely by CBS and U.S. Steel both, were likely confused why the story would open on a Caribbean island instead of Madam Zajj's birthplace in Africa, or in New Orleans—except that it afforded Ellington and Strayhorn the opportunity to capitalize on the calypso craze that was just then sweeping the country in the form of Harry Belafonte's "Day-O (The Banana Boat Song)." The suite's song lyrics, too, can be thoroughly pedestrian and sometimes simply don't make sense, as even on the broadcast version the imagery that defines Carribee Joe remains puzzling:

> Tooth, claw, and petal,
> Feather-thin every limb—
> Joe loved the jungle, and the jungle loved him.[25]

Talley Beatty's bare-chested Joe wears no accessories and is wiry rather than "feather-thin." But both Ellington and Strayhorn were primarily composers after all, not lyricists. As Ellington once conceded, "You can say anything you want on the trombone, but you gotta be careful with words."[26]

Even though audiences in the mid-1950s didn't appear to mind much, many later listeners of *A Drum Is a Woman* have taken exception also to the bizarre misogyny of the governing trope, particularly in the song "What Else Can You Do with a Drum?" The tune occurs toward the beginning of the story, after Carribee Joe declines to accompany Madam Zajj on her world tour. The "African enchantress" has little patience, and so she embarks on the search for "another Joe," narrates Ellington. On the bouncy, cheerful calypso, Ozzie Bailey then sings,

> There was a man who lived in Barbados.
> He saw a pretty woman one day.
> He took her home, and when they got there she turned into a drum.
>
> It isn't civilized to beat women,
> No matter what they do or they say—
> But will somebody tell me what else can you do with a drum?[27]

Among many others, jazz poet Jayne Cortez, assisted by the percussion of her son, Denardo Coleman, asks angrily,

> if the drum is a woman
> why are you pounding your drum into an insane babble
> why are you pistol whipping your drum at dawn
> why are you shooting through the head of your drum
> and making a drum tragedy of drums
> if the drum is a woman
> then don't abuse your drum, don't abuse your drum, don't abuse
>   your drum[28]

Ellington himself didn't help matters very much: "Any real jazz cat is in love with what he plays," he declared. "A cat says to his wife, 'Here's $2, chick, go out and have a ball.' He says it so he can be with what he loves, his horn or whatever it is. [. . .] Maybe he doesn't drink or gamble or play around with the chicks. But he can be real dirty and mean when he gets alone with what he's in love with. He's a schizo. That's why a drum is a woman."[29]

"What Else Can You Do with a Drum" can indeed be taken as a manifestation of what some have seen as a latent misogyny in its composer.[30] But the overall portrayal of Madam Zajj herself presents a rather different character than simply an object of desire, let alone a victim of sexual battery. On the contrary, throughout the album version of *A Drum Is a Woman*, its protagonist is anything but passive or submissive. Even after she has fallen for Joe in his island jungle, she is not "'lifed' by love" or turning into "a restless ghost, finding peace nowhere and in nothing" like so many of Toni Morrison's characters, for example.[31] Though she pines for her lover, she is beholden to no one, not Carribee Joe, not Buddy Bolden—not even to Ellington himself. "Roaming through the jungle, the jungle of 'oohs' and 'ahs,' searching for a more agreeable noise," the composer would recognize in his autobiography that "Music is my mistress, and she plays second fiddle to no one." Even an ardent admirer like Ellington must concede that

> Music is the woman
> You follow day after day,

but then

> Music is the woman
> Who always has her way.[32]

Madam Zajj's various suitors might serenade the object of their desire, convinced that

> You belong to me,
> And you'd better know it,[33]

yet Zajj, true Afropolitan that she is, does not "belong" to anyone or anything. She is beholden to but one overriding principle, her inherent Afro-kinesis: "the rhythm is melodic, the rhythm is rhapsodic—the rhythm. Come with me. Rhythm. Rhythm. Rhythm. Rhythm."[34] Rhythm, Afro-kinesis, therefore emerges as a *female* principle, with Madam Zajj as the original and most important ambassador of Mother Africa.

Despite the apparent closure provided at the end of the CBS telecast, Madam Zajj's gendered self-determination is actually amplified on screen, where Ellington explains at the outset that although the heroine loves Carribee Joe deeply, "she had a craving for the big time," and consequently, "This was always to be a big love affair. Maybe a little one-sided, but—big." After quickly ditching "the wrong Joe" in Barbados, she meets a clarinet-playing pirate with eyepatch and bandana on another island and rebuffs his advances with repeated blows to the head. Later, in the Chicago nightclub, she does respond to the flirtations of a third Joe—played, ironically, by the homosexual Bailey—and even accepts coyly the ring he offers her, though she arches her eyebrows a few times. But just after Joe number three has confidently looked straight into the camera to assure the audience that he plays "for keeps," he turns to his right only to discover that Zajj has vanished, leaving behind the ring. Eventually, the lovesick heroine does return to Carribee Joe's island to be serenaded with "Pomegranate," but Ellington ventures that their story came close to a tragic one of the Romeo-and-Juliet kind: "After all, Zajj just couldn't stay in the jungle; she'd become too, much too sophisticated."[35]

Finally, the title song's new placement in fact undermines the script's intimation that the two lovers lived happily ever after in their "little place just off the moon." While "A Drum Is a Woman" opens the album, on television it is slotted as the grand finale after the final plug for the *Kitchen Planning Book*. Echoing the invisible man in his Harlem coal cellar, Tynes's concluding lines inform viewers that *A Drum Is a Woman* is a story

> With no end,
> No middle,
> No start.[36]

Obviously, Madam Zajj is not content with the conventional role of housewife and already left her kitchen in outer space once, to visit Duke Ellington in the CBS studio. If hers is truly a story without an ending, then Madam Zajj indeed "always will be a *real* swingin' chick" continually roaming the galaxy, never tarrying long in one place, not even at the foot of the Duke's grand piano.[37] Moreover, her open-ended itinerary undermines the conventional ending not only of the script but also of the Cold War narrative, constructed by the show's corporate sponsorship and commercial breaks, that extols American industriousness, capitalist enterprise, and the prosperous domesticity (white) U.S. citizens can therefore enjoy among their stainless-steel kitchen appliances.[38]

Thus, *A Drum Is a Woman* operates on a reversal of traditional gender roles. It is Carribee Joe who exhibits many of the attributes of the ingénue: ignorant of or, rather, innocent in the ways of the world, sheltered, and isolated, Joe lives in harmony with his natural environs, speaks with the forest's denizens "in their jungle slang," and is incapable of transplanting himself elsewhere on the planet.[39] Content with his drums, the only time he ever leaves his pastoral island paradise is in his lover's dream on the album, and on the screen in the final elopement to space—where, given his partner's busy travel schedule, it is *he* who is left manning the stainless-steel kitchen at home. Madam Zajj, on the other hand, both restless and resolute, shape shifting and determined, is the very personification of Afro-kinesis: she is a "swingin' chick" indeed. Joe betrays none of the drive, curiosity, and adventurousness that propel Madam Zajj around the world and into the cosmos. Her means of transportation include not only a Mardi Gras float but also a stretched-out limousine with an eighty-eight-cylinder engine as well as a flying saucer. No wonder, then, that she doesn't stick around Barbados too long (even if it is the ancestral home of Irving Burgie, the man who penned "The Banana Boat Song") and does not care to wait until the "other" Joe figures out the answer to the question, "What Else Can You Do with a Drum?" Via Sam Woodyard, Madam Zajj delivers the answer herself: on that song, Woodyard's sticks barely touch the skins at all; instead, they gently tap out the distinctive calypso rhythm on the cymbals. "When he is playing," Ellington would say of Woodyard, "he just about has an affair with his drums, an observation that was the inspiration of *A Drum Is a Woman*."[40]

Historically, Madam Zajj's inherent Afro-kinesis is clearly circumscribed by the Black Atlantic:

> Rhythm came to America from Africa,
> From overseas—
> Africa—
> To the West Indies,
> America.
> Rhythm came to Africa from way back.[41]

Placing the very origins of rhythm, and therefore humanity, in Africa, Madam Zajj's story is not confined to the map of the Black Atlantic, however. Even though "she's from way back, as far back as way back goes," she has also "been way out, as far out as way out goes." Her Afro-kinesis makes her an international, even interstellar jet-setter: "Madam Zajj picked up many influences along the way," and even "Though her past was shady, Zajj was a lady," Ellington informs us. "They dressed her in woodwinds and strings; she was seen in the company of kings, but still spoke her mother tongue fluently."[42] Thus, Cortez's catalog of demands

> I mean, if the drum is a woman
> then understand your drum, understand your drum
> your drum is not docile

> your drum is not invisible, no
> your drum is not inferior to you, no way
> your drum is a woman[43]

describes exactly the credo by which Madam Zajj herself lives and travels. She embodies a *gendered* energy principle, an Afro-kinesis that transgresses common social expectations of female comportment—as well as, significantly, Ellington's own misogynist notions.

☾ ☾ ☾

How the story of Madam Zajj orchestrates a transnational Afro-kinesis always on the go is amplified when brought in dialogue with Benjaminian flânerie. Not quite coincidentally, perhaps, the only reference to jazz music in Walter Benjamin's critical publications occurs in "The Return of the Flâneur," a review of his friend Franz Hessel's *Spazieren in Berlin*. Designating it "the holy grove of flânerie," the city's Tiergarten Park was a place where "one can see the leaves sinking to the ground even more melancholically during the jazz than usual."[44] The stereotypical reduction of jazz to bluesy melancholia tells us less about Madam Zajj than its association with flânerie does. For Benjamin, the figure of the flâneur embodies metropolitan modernity. Building on his reading of Hessel and especially Charles Baudelaire's *Les fleurs du mal*, the francophile Benjamin locates the birthplace of the flâneur not in his native Berlin but in the capital of the Second Empire. There, the flâneur—much like Madam Zajj—assumes many guises, but as a connoisseur of the streets, he also represents a counterhistory to the monuments of empire:

> The type of the flâneur was created by Paris. That it wasn't Rome, this is the wonder. But in Rome, doesn't even dreaming move along streets that are too well-paved? And isn't the city too full of temples, enclosed squares, and national shrines to be able to enter undivided into the dreams of the passer-by along with each paving stone, each shop sign, each step of a stair, and each gateway? The great reminiscences, the historical thrills—these are to the true flâneur but junk that he gladly leaves to the tourist. And all his knowledge of artists' quarters, birthplaces, or princely domiciles he trades away for the scent of a single threshold or the felt touch of a single floor tile, that which any old dog carries away.[45]

As "the high priest of the *genius loci*," the flâneur's perambulations take him invariably to the ephemeral, the fleeting, the common—the quotidian and "pedestrian." It is "the habitus of the flâneur [. . .] to botanize the asphalt" of the modern metropolis, and, exactly like Madam Zajj, "He snatches things in flight."⁴⁶ This habitus that initially appears to be concerned with the material world of the present can nevertheless also open up to a different kind of history to the attentive flâneur:

> The street leads the flâneur into a vanished time. For him, each street is precipitous. It leads downward [. . .] into a past that can be all the more spellbinding because it is not his own, private past. [. . .] In the asphalt over which he passes, his steps awaken a surprising resonance. The gaslight that streams down on the floor tiles throws an equivocal light on this double ground. [. . .] The walk takes on greater forced momentum with each step; ever weaker grow the temptations of shops, of bistros, of smiling women, ever more irresistible the magnetism of the next street corner, of a distant cluster of leaves, of a street name.⁴⁷

The flâneur's perpetual kinesis can reveal a hidden counterhistory of the metropolis that to most others is obscured by its grandiose architecture and the diversions of consumer capitalism. Under the meandering steps of the flâneur, the city's "double ground" yields intersecting, interacting planes of time—not necessarily "swing" time, but intersections nonetheless of the here and now with the then and there; his world, both spatial and temporal, is therefore characterized by an "interpenetrating and overlapping transparency." To the perceptive flâneur, the city becomes a vast palimpsest of stories and histories.⁴⁸

To be sure, the kinesis of Benjamin's flâneur is no *Afro*-kinesis. Both Madam Zajj and the flâneur are *in* the metropolitan crowd, but not *of* it, a peculiar dynamic de Lavallade performs brilliantly in the extended dance scenes during Mardi Gras or in New York City, for example.⁴⁹ Benjamin's flâneur, though, remains confined to the city limits of the capital of the Second Empire, with its arcades as his base of operations. As perceptive as he may be, he never arrives at a position from which to observe the metropolis as a whole; his vantage point is never panoramic, never all-encompassing. In sharp contradistinction, Madam Zajj is the ultimate jet-setter: "Transportation is no problem for Madam Zajj: she simply hops a trade wind, and off she goes," explains Ellington.⁵⁰ Always on the move—but, like the flâneur, never rushed—she is also a *flâneuse* who actively resists attempts at normative socialization. Other than his perpetual movement, Benjamin's flâneur, always a male figure, remains a largely passive observer of the striations of the modern metropolis. Madam Zajj's gendered flânerie makes her not just an active participant in and major inspiration for the music she embodies. As a flâneuse, she contests the male historiographies of jazz: "If gender is a kind of doing, an incessant activity performed"—as for example in the dancing of de Lavallade's Zajj—"it is not for that reason automatic or mechanical. On the contrary, it is a practice of improvisation within a scene of constraint," writes Judith Butler.[51] Benjamin also likens the flâneur's perpetual movements to that of a timepiece: "The figure of the flâneur, as if impelled by a clockwork mechanism, proceeds on the street of stone with the double ground."[52] Madam Zajj first appears to Carribee Joe in the shape of a drum, certainly the most important, as well as polyrhythmic, timekeeping piece in jazz music. She clearly marches and roams to the beat of a different drum—her own—refusing to submit to the timekeeping authority claimed by the controlling, collecting percussionist Carribee Joe. As Afropolitanism's designated timekeeper, she is, to borrow Langston Hughes's terminology, "the eternal tom-tom," standing on top of the world free within herself.[53] And so, Madam Zajj's Afro-kinetic interventions deconstruct the African diaspora as a collection of quasiprimitive cultures and reconstruct it as a proudly and unapologetically Afropolitan enterprise.

Madam Zajj's forays from her homeland were not Ellington's first engagement with Africa—but, ironically, parts of the music to *A Drum Is a Woman* are more "African" than the so-called "jungle style" that had propelled the Ellington orchestra to national and international prominence three decades earlier. The music is among the most percussive Ellington and Strayhorn ever wrote, with the orchestra's regular drummer, Woodyard, joined by percussionist Candido and even a second drummer, Terry Snyder. The jungle style that had so enraptured the white audiences at the racially segregated Cotton Club three decades prior was characterized not so much by rhythmic experiments but rather by the innovative techniques of the brass players. While Sonny Greer's gleaming battery of percussion instruments—sponsored by the Leedy Drum Company in one of the music's very first endorsement deals—was the visual centerpiece of the orchestra, his bass drum adorned with the silhouettes of a couple kissing in the moonlit jungle night, James "Bubber" Miley and Joe "Tricky Sam" Nanton were the two band members most crucial in forging the jungle style. Miley was a cornetist who doubled on trumpet, Nanton a trombone player, and both were known for experimenting with a wide array of plungers and mutes, sometimes approximating the human voice in uncanny ways. "Bubber didn't *play* the blues on his horn," adjudged Greer; "he sang them."[54]

How central the Caribbean was to Ellington's jazz cosmos, something that the opening scenes of *A Drum Is a Woman* depicted, is also highlighted by the special role Ellington accorded Nanton in the band: the composer always wrote with specific members of the orchestra and their individual sounds in mind, and what the trombonist "was actually doing was playing a very highly personalized form of his West Indian heritage. [. . .] Tricky and his people were deep into the West Indian legacy and the Marcus Garvey movement. A whole strain of West Indian musicians came up who made contributions to the so-called jazz scene, and they were all virtually descended from the true African scene." Reminiscing back on the Cotton Club days, Ellington writes in his autobiography that vocalization "was very important in that kind of music. Today, the music has grown up and become quite scholastic, but this was *au naturel*, close to the primitive, where people send messages in what they play, calling somebody, or making facts or emotions known. Painting a picture, or having a story to go with what you were going to play, was of vital importance in those days. The audience didn't know anything about it, but the cats in the band did."[55]

As allergic as Ellington was to labels, he wasn't immune to them; as far as he was concerned, the word *primitive* was by no means a derogatory epithet. Dancing at the center of Congo Square, Madam Zajj herself, for example, is "the most primitive woman. This, of course, does not mean simple or elementary: she is an exciting, ornately stimulating seductress with patterns of excitement and the power to hypnotize and innovate the will toward total abandonment."[56] On one hand, Ellington panders to what he knows are the expectations of the white audience. At the same time, he also attempts to undermine these selfsame expectations: "of course," he insists, neither Madam Zajj's primitivism nor the jungle style's vocalizations are to be equated with inferiority or childishness or innocence. Still, Ellington's relationship with the white power brokers of the music business was not unlike that of Langston Hughes with "Godmother" Charlotte Osgood Mason. Racialized exoticism and eroticism were at a premium in the 1920s musical marketplace. For example, for the *Cotton Club Revue*, Ellington had written what would become the classic "I Let a Song Go out of My Heart," but his manager, Irving Mills, felt that the show lacked spice and instructed the composer to come up "with something that had to do with Hawaii"—and so "I Let a Song Go out of My Heart" was replaced with the ditty "Swingtime in Honolulu."[57] Writes Emily Bernard, "Baker's bananas, Ellington's jungle rhythms, as well as the Cotton and Plantation clubs were all inspired by colonialist fantasies that lay at the heart of the primitive craze. Primitivism upholds immutable distinctions between the teller and the tale. Ultimately, primitivism is a story about the power of the West to dominate in language as well as in might." Therefore, primitivism "was, irrefutably, a concept central to modernism. Desire for the other defined the moment. Primitivism was the avant-garde; it offered artists in a variety of media an exciting new way to think about culture."[58] And so, as long as the modernist pastiche of cultural references that made up the Cotton Club floor shows was deemed sufficiently sexy and exotic, the engagement paradoxically afforded the composer the opportunity, too, to experiment, to hone his compositional and arranging skills and forge what would later come to be known as "the Ellington sound."

Establishing the pattern he would adhere to for the rest of his life, Ellington the artist and public figure preferred subtle subversion and persuasion to overt confrontation and protest. "I think," he mused, "a statement of social protest in the theatre should be made without saying it, and this calls for the real craftsman."[59] Thus, the Afro-kinesis of the jungle style was often more than just Greer thrashing away on his drums with Miley and Nanton inserting plungers into their horns and bleating away to the gyrations of a chorus line of scantily clad high yallers. Take, for example, one of the more memorable Cotton Club skits, one that impressed, and puzzled, a young Harvard undergraduate who enjoyed going uptown for a break in his studies:

> I recall one where a light-skinned and magnificently muscled Negro burst through a papier-mâché jungle onto the dance floor clad in an aviator's helmet, goggles, and shorts. He had been forced down in darkest Africa, and in the center of the floor he came upon a "white" goddess clad in long, blonde tresses and being worshipped by a circle of crying "blacks." Producing a bullwhip from heaven knows where, he rescued the blonde and they did an erotic dance. In the background, Bubber Miley, Tricky Sam Nanton and members of the Ellington band growled, wheezed, and snorted obscenely.[60]

Unfortunately, Marshall Stearns fails to mention which tune the Cotton Club Orchestra played: "Jungle Nights in Harlem," maybe, or "Echoes of the Jungle"—or perhaps "That Lindy Hop." But he unwittingly proves Ellington's point about "telling a story" with his jungle music. For one thing, the figure of the black aviator embodies both Afro-kinesis and modernity. Moreover, the "obscenely" growling, wheezing, and snorting horn section is indeed "calling somebody, or making facts [...] known" as the skit signifies upon Hubert Fauntleroy Julian, "the Black Eagle of Harlem." The gregarious Julian, a native of Trinidad, became a celebrity as a stunt pilot and parachutist in the air shows wildly popular in the Jazz Age. Among his more spectacular stunts, many performed over the skies of Harlem itself, was one from 1923, when he leaped from an airplane playing "Runnin' Wild" on a saxophone on his way down. If the young Stearns had heard of Julian, he failed to make the connection to the (to him) garish Cotton Club skit—but, as Ellington says, it is safe to say that most certainly "the cats in the band did."[61]

To be sure, Ellington's Afro-kinesis did not always incorporate a subversive assertion of Afropolitanism, and in this regard the jungle style was not a direct precursor to, say, *We Insist! Max Roach's Freedom Now Suite*. Still, the composer was acutely aware of the difference between his own aspirations as an artist and the perceptions of the Cotton Club management and audiences. In fact, the label was affixed to the music ex post facto: to white audiences, it *sounded* as if Miley's trumpet and Nanton's trombone, aided and abetted by Greer's battery of exotic percussion instruments—not to mention by the raffish set designs—came from somewhere deep within the African forests. Club management as well as the wily Irving Mills gladly obliged the thirst of visitors elegantly slumming in Harlem for salacious, exotic "blackness." Greer later recalled that it was actually George Gershwin who had coined the term "jungle music." As the Ellington drummer tells it, the young Gershwin and his running buddy Paul Whiteman (the false "King of Jazz") were "in awe of the things Duke used to do, so they were sitting up at the Cotton Club and George Gershwin said to Paul, I know what that is, that's jungle music. And it stuck with us."[62] On that note at least, Ulanov was correct in insisting that "All of Duke's jungle nights have been spent in Harlem."[63]

Ulanov's ostensibly paradoxical mapping of the Ellington sound's provenance delineates the soundscapes of *A Drum Is a Woman* as well. On the one hand, Madam Zajj indubitably hails from Africa. At the same time, *A Drum Is a Woman* lacks not only closure but also a concrete point of origin. To be sure, the careful elision of any references to the Middle Passage or the peculiar institution can be ascribed to the production's design as entertainment for the masses. On the other hand, the narrative structure of Madam Zajj's adventures also moves her story close to myth. Moreover, the absence of a concretely demarcated *genius loci* of Madam Zajj's rhythm, reinforced on the album by the operatic introduction, allows Ellington to present jazz music as a transnational hybrid rather than a "tribal" or national essence. Madam Zajj's restless flânerie thus also slyly subverts the teleological narrative of (African) American nationhood purported by the U.S. State Department as well as, in this case, the industrial conglomerate U.S. Steel and its corporate sponsorship of *A Drum Is a Woman*, which touted jazz as the culmination of the journey from Phillis Wheatley's "*Pagan* land" to the freedoms liberally dispensed in and by American democracy, and shored up by industrial capitalism.⁶⁴

Once again, the unknown starting point of Madam Zajj's journeys returns us to Walter Benjamin. Benjamin conceives of the notion of origin as a process rather than a fixed point on a linear, historical timeline. The origin of any aesthetic expression can only be approached by studying the traces it has been leaving over time. In this dialectical play of before-and-after, the concept of origin is likened to "an eddy in the stream of becoming" whose centripetal "rhythms" swallow up all the various elements that, together, form the idea of "origin." Thus, "origin" really is a *process*, a process of coming into being and fading away: "That which is original never reveals itself in the naked, manifest existence of the factual; its rhythm opens itself up only to a dual insight."⁶⁵ We can analyze the Benjaminian traces Madam Zajj has been leaving along her journey—on Barbados and other Caribbean islands, in New Orleans, in New York City, in Paris, as well as in space—but the exact geographical determination of her place of birth, the reduction of her genesis to a localized, "tribal" essence, remains impossible. Thus, Madam Zajj's planetary flânerie turns "Africa" into an Afro-kinetic signifier whose oscillations resist mooring to any nationalizing cartography.

The story of Madam Zajj therefore challenges metaphysical claims to the primacy of the authentic and the original; the "mockingly creative" Ellington may have conceived *A Drum Is a Woman* also as a satire on the racialist paradigms imposed on him by the many jazz critics who, often quite vociferously, exhorted the composer to return to the jungle style of his Cotton Club days.⁶⁶ A skit in *Jump for Joy*, the 1941 revue for which Ellington scored much of the music, depicts in all likelihood fairly accurately how "the cats in the band" and their boss felt about the "authentic" origins projected onto their "jungle music." The sketch shows the stately king and queen of an ancient African nation in their state room daintily enjoying a glass of brandy after dinner, she wearing the latest French designer clothes, he clad in a tuxedo. When servants inform them of the impending arrival of yet another expedition from the United States in search of the authentic origins of jazz, the queen's impulsive reaction is, "Oh, damn." In sympathetic consternation, her husband sighs, "Yes, my dear [. . .] we shall have to get out our leopard skins again."[67]

Thus, it is no surprise that the musical leopard skins remained in the closet for the *Togo Brava* suite, which echoes the Afro-kinetic perambulations of Madam Zajj and which was, along with the Liberian suite, one of the few tone parallels to African nationhood in Ellington's oeuvre. Situated at the eastern end of Kubik's African swing belt, the Republic of Togo—formerly a German and then a French possession, like its neighbor Cameroon three doors to the east—became independent in 1960 in a peaceful transition brokered by the United Nations. Seven years later, to celebrate the twentieth anniversary of UNESCO, the country issued a series of four stamps bearing the likenesses of Beethoven, Debussy, Bach—and Ellington. Ellington repaid the favor by composing the *Togo Brava* suite and premiering it at the prestigious Newport Jazz Festival in July 1971. He had never been to Togo—the orchestra's first African trip had been to Senegal back in 1966—but as he always did with his extended works, he researched this project carefully: he had already amassed some eight hundred books on black art and history in his personal library and even interviewed acquaintances who had actually visited the country.

The suite retraces Madam Zajj's journey in more ways than one: in its original conception, it was supposed to be a trip by sea landing first at Togo's beaches before heading into the interior and the jungle, where a strikingly beautiful woman is encountered. Those who might have expected to hear a return to the jungle jazz of the Cotton Club days were sorely disappointed though. In fact, the suite does not contain any (overt) West African references at all but is brimming instead with musical imports from elsewhere. For example, the very opening movement, "Soul Soothing Beach" (or "Mkis" originally), is a bossa nova, signaling the arrival at "a hundred miles of beautiful, silver, sand beach with a southern exposure, facing the equator, on the western bulge of Africa," as Ellington would explain to the audience.[68] Apparently, Togo's beaches are a favorite vacation spot for girls from Ipanema as well as Madam Zajj. "Tego" had made its first appearance as "Limbo Jazz"—a title that highlighted it as a calypso—the opening track on a 1962 small-group recording featuring the legendary Coleman Hawkins, a native of Missouri, not Trinidad.

Even more intriguingly, for a brief time Ellington also envisioned "Tego" as the opening movement of another extended piece of programmatic transnationalism, *The Afro-Eurasian Eclipse*. Ellington's introductory remarks that open the studio album are noteworthy not only for their debonair humor but also for the ways in which, yet again, the composer sought to undermine some listeners' expectations about what "real," "authentically black" jazz was supposed to sound like:

> This is really, this Chinoiserie—last year, we, about this time, we premiered a new suite titled *Afro-Eurasian Eclipse*, and of course the title was inspired by a statement made by Mr. Marshall McLuhan of the University of Toronto. Mr. McLuhan says that the whole world is going Oriental and that no one will be able to retain his or her identity—not even the Orientals. And of course we travel around the world a lot, and in the last five or six years we too have noticed this thing to be true. So as a result we have done a sort of a thing, a parallel or something, and would like to play a little piece of it for you. In this particular segment, ladies and gentlemen, we have adjusted our perspective to that of the kangaroo and the didgeridoo. This automatically throws us either down under and/or out back; and from that point of view it's most improbable that anyone will ever know exactly who is enjoying the shadow of whom. [Tenor saxophonist] Harold Ashby has been inducted into the responsibility and the obligation of possibly scraping off a tiny bit of the charisma of his Chinoiserie immediately after our piano player [Ellington himself, of course] has completed his rikki tikki.[69]

Similarly, not even Togo grooves to the jungle style. "Naturellement," initially titled "Tugo & YoYo," does sport a jungle-istic break, but its rather involved arrangement alternates between 3/4 and 4/4, with drummer Rufus Jones pounding out a rock rhythm in the beginning that is much closer to Tupelo, Mississippi, than to Lomé, West Africa. In fact, this is also the only tune in the entire suite where the brass section uses plungers, and very briefly at that. "Afrique" (aka "Toto") does not use the Miley-Nanton growls and effects that are associated with the jungle style, either.[70]

As was customary with Ellington, the various elements as well as the sequence of movements of the *Togo Brava* suite were in constant flux. The first recording of the work in June 1971 comprised seven movements but was clearly never intended for commercial release, landing directly in Ellington's stockpile of rehearsal tapes. At that time, the musicians were not yet very familiar with the work, most noticeable in the trombone section and in a Paul Gonsalves solo that is not only mostly off mic but also rather rote. By the time of its official premiere at Newport the very next month, Ellington had tightened the musical narrative into four movements. Over the next few months, he continued to tinker with the sequencing of the four individual movements. By mid-

1973, the suite had acquired its final form, which remained in the repertoire until the Duke's death. Whittled down to three movements, the suite now presented a different narrative arc than its predecessors: "Soul Soothing Beach" remained the opener; it was followed by "Right on, Togo" and bookended by "Amour, Amour." Dropped entirely was "Naturellement," which Ellington would introduce with "And now, into the jungle," and which had been slotted originally either as the second or third movement and also briefly figured as the suite's closer when performed in concert.[71]

Thus, the final version of *Togo Brava* eliminated entirely the sonic tableau of the jungle. Instead, it articulated a sublimely confident Afropolitanism, presenting in sound the idealized vision of a multicultural, multiethnic nation taking its rightful place among the modern countries of the world, not a latter-day Cotton Club phantasmagoria. The thoroughly transnational soundtrack to Togo may not have reflected the political, social, and cultural realities of the newly independent country, but it did present an idealistic vision of what that country, what any country, *could* be like. This, therefore, was the Togo of Duke Ellington's artistic *mind*, very much like the Africa of "Soul Makossa"—or, for that matter, even "Toyota Makossa"—was one of Manu Dibango's artistic mind. The Duke, said his trumpeter Clark Terry, "wants life and music to be always in a state of becoming," and so in his mind was the Republic of Togo.[72] After all, "La Plus Belle Africaine" had been written "in anticipation of our first visit to Africa—after writing African music for thirty-five years," the maestro would tell his audiences in typical ducal fashion.[73]

Ellington's transnational flânerie in sound, in the *Togo Brava* suite and elsewhere, is not to be confused with some kind of aural tourism. Yes, the composer did research on Togo prior to putting together the suite, but his compositional style was anything but the result of a tourist's raid on the gift shop. If the artist panders "to the audience according to geography, nationality, race, or creed, he is condescending, and this is the world's worst social offense," he explained, and added, "I am neither a tourist nor a sightseer, so what is observed is easily digestible—when I look. I always love to hear the music of my hosts, and hope we shall be in mutual (and total) agreement, so that we can *both* say, 'Encore!'" A propos of *The Far East Suite*, he elaborated:

> As one who dares to title pieces of music in direct association with countries I visit, I explain to them, I always must be on guard against condescension, for that is the vilest of offenses. And that was why Billy Strayhorn and I, after having been in the

> Middle East, India, Iran, and Ceylon for fifteen weeks, decided not to write any "Eastern" music until we had been away from it for three months—to avoid the re-echoing of those native sounds we had absorbed and the identical retracing of traditional melodies. The titles, nevertheless, were impressions indelibly inscribed in our minds at the moment of exposure to the splendors of the East.[74]

The snapshot-like "impressions indelibly inscribed in our minds at the moment of exposure" echo the experience of "shock" that for Benjamin characterizes life in the modern metropolis in general, and the perambulations of the flâneur in particular, for "in flânerie, distant countries and times interpenetrate the landscape and the present instant."[75] According to Benjamin, we recall, the true flâneur bypasses the symbols of nationalism—the statues, the palaces, the birthplaces of national heroes and heroines—and leaves them to other visitors as "junk," preferring instead to navigate the streets far away from the tourist sights, the dross and dregs of day-to-day life in the metropolis.

Much like the flâneur's perambulations augur modernity and all it entails, so does Madam Zajj's jet-setting herald the age of intercontinental air and even interstellar space travel. Madam Zajj's flânerie thus positions Africa and the African diaspora as a constitutive element of modernity and the space age. *A Drum Is a Woman* flickered across American television screens five months before the *Sputnik* crisis and almost two decades before David Bowie's Major Tom and George Clinton's interplanetary *Mothership Connection*. Madam Zajj already knew that space was the place before the most visionary jazzman of them all, Sun Ra, first set foot in an earthly recording studio: "The real aim" of his interplanetary music, the expat from Saturn wrote in the liner notes to his 1957 debut album, "is to co-ordinate the minds of peoples into an intelligent reach for a better world, and an intelligent approach to the living future. By peoples I mean all of the people of different nations who are living today."[76]

Ellington, too, had always been intrigued by kinetic technologies—not only did he have a lifelong fascination with trains, but he was an avid follower of the space race as well. He didn't live long enough to experiment with musical electronics, but his admirer Manu Dibango did. Although "Soul Makossa," Afropop's first worldwide hit, was inspired in part by a traditional makossa rhythm, subsequent versions of it became more and more hybridized. On *Afrijazzy*, "Soul Makossa" appears as "Makossa '87" in a dub version produced by Bill Laswell; on *Past Present Future* a quarter-century later, "Soul Makossa 2.0" appears as a slick techno production with a rap by British-Jamaican producer

Wayne Beckford. Dibango's use of synthesizers and high-tech postproduction technologies has garnered him much criticism over the decades; he says he is still waging the same kind of "cultural combat" as when he first came to Europe to face audiences puzzled by the fact that he didn't play the tom-tom.[77]

The resistance to Dibango's Afropolitanism bucking Western impositions of authentic blackness recalls uncannily the acerbic exchange in the pages of *Down Beat* between Ellington and John Hammond, who felt that the experiments with "symphonic jazz" that began to preoccupy the Duke after his Cotton Club engagement ended were patently "un-negroid."[78] But to Dibango as much as to Ellington, "Africa" is not a site of primitivistic authenticity but a deterritorialized Afro-kinetic signifier that connects the nodes of transnational (post-)modernity. And when he insists that, as a resolutely Afropolitan artist, "I must compose the music of my time, not yesterday's music," he positions himself as an "Afro-tricknologist" for whom "Africa" is not the originary source of "authentic" blackness but a field of sonic discourse imbricated with digital modernity.[79] Thus, the Lion of Africa echoes another great musical innovator accused of betraying the jazz tradition when he went electric, Miles Davis: "All these purists are walking around talking about how electrical instruments will ruin music. Bad music is what will ruin music, not the instruments musicians choose to play," scoffed the Dark Prince.[80]

Taking their cue from restless Madam Zajj, all these artists hear in Afro-kinesis the propulsion that powers an Afropolitanism resisting the racialist taxonomies of postcolonialism that persist beneath the blithe platitudes of twenty-first-century "postracial" discourses. Says trombonist George Lewis, "No music has been judged and sentenced as harshly as Black Music—sentenced to authenticity, accuracy, and to the confines of its prescribed borders. I'd like to say it very emphatically: jazz is the symbol for the ability to be free. But such a precious position is constantly threatened. It's about the necessity to reinvent yourself in any given moment. It's about mobility. If you don't move, you're dead."[81] Stasis is death, kinesis is freedom—or, at least, the possibility to lay claim to freedom. Madam Zajj knows this best of all. And so, as she makes her way from the cradle of jazz on Congo Square to the Windy City, she pilots

> the longest automobile you've ever seen: 88 cylinders. She came through town doing 440 miles per hour; she stopped for a green light, cop came up, gave her a ticket and says, "Lady, that will be five dollars' fine." She gave him a ten-dollar bill and while

he was looking for change the light changed. And when she saw that red light she said, "Keep the change, officer, 'cause I'm comin' back just as fast as I'm going." She blew her horn, pushed the throttle to the floor, and zoom—Chicago![82]

Walter Benjamin never had the chance to visit this particular intersection, but it could just as easily have been Madam Zajj's arrival there that prompted him to jot down in his notes that "The flâneur sabotages traffic."[83] And if he had indeed witnessed this scene, he may also have noticed that, waiting right behind Madam Zajj's high-powered ride at that same green light, was Manu Dibango's Toyota Corolla, poised to come back just as fast as it's racing on.

CHAPTER 2

Sheets of Jazz

Hans Janowitz Takes the Coltrane

Duke Ellington's grueling touring schedule was legendary, and he kept it up until the end. Among the many memorable concerts abroad was one he gave near the town of Menton in France on July 31, 1970. Menton is the last town before the French-Italian border, the two border posts being connected by the Saint Ludovic bridge. There, in this picturesque setting of the Mediterranean Alps, the Ellington orchestra's performance caused the border to shut down completely for several hours. In the audience was also a correspondent for the *Washington D.C. Afro-American*, who cabled a gushing review to the home office back in the States: "A pity that Duke Ellington isn't invited to perform on the Israeli-Jordan border, or along that Suez Canal, so that peace could be enhanced. Come to think of it, the same thing would be marvelous along the demilitarized zone between the two [Vietnams]. And it just might be possible [that] foreign armies would pack up and go home."[1]

The fates of jazz and war have been inextricably intertwined ever since James Reese Europe's regimental band and the rest of the famed Harlem Hellfighters of the 369th made port in Brest on December 27, 1917, and were deployed to the battlefields of France.[2] For many European avant-garde artists, jazz delivered both the excitement of discovering an entirely new sound that appeared to accompany perfectly *"die wilden Jahre"*—the wild years—of the decade ushered in by the armistice signed in a railway car parked in the woods outside of Compiègne. The wild new music for those wild years heralded the promise of a return to a more intensely felt humanness after the deadly mustard gas clouds of modern warfare at Ypres and elsewhere had wreaked havoc not just with human bodies but also penetrated in profound ways Western man's sense of what it meant to be alive. For Europeans, the protojazz of the man bearing the continent's name sounded like "skyscraper primitivism incarnate, its atavistic energy lubricating the machine age," as Jed Rasula puts it.[3] Many among Europe's intelligentsia tended to hear a more futuristic undertone in this new music than their American counterparts, but just as many, if not more, heard exotic otherness. The brash, undomesticated sounds of jazz felt threatening, too. In 1927 Herman Hesse had his world-weary Harry Haller pause in front of a dance hall during one of his nocturnal walks. Assaulted by the rambunctious sounds of jazz, "hot and raw as the steam of raw flesh," the Steppenwolf confesses,

> This kind of music, much as I detested it, had always had a secret charm for me. It was repugnant to me, and yet ten times preferable to all the academic music of the day. For me too, its raw and savage gaiety reached an underworld of instinct and breathed a simple honest sensuality. I stood for a moment on the scent, smelling this shrill and blood-raw music, sniffing the atmosphere of the hall angrily, and hankering after it a little too. One half of this music, the melody, was all pomade and sugar and sentimentality. The other half was savage, temperamental, and vigorous. Yet the two went artlessly well together and made a whole. It was the music of decline. There must have been such a music in Rome under the later emperors. Compared with Bach and Mozart and real music it was, naturally, a miserable affair, but so was all our art. [. . .] This music was at least sincere, unashamedly primitive and childishly happy. There was something of the Negro in it.[4]

The flâneur's ambivalent reaction to this riotous new music permeating his phantasmagoria, wavering between repulsion and fascination, distills precisely the reception of jazz in the Weimar Republic. Jazz was the music of the Other: it was foreign and different, and it was raw, savage, primitive, sensual—and black. To be sure, the syncopated music resounding throughout Europe in the roaring 1920s was often not really the kind of jazz that we today would categorize as such; Cornelius Partsch, borrowing Adorno's terminology, calls it a "metropolitan *Gebrauchsmusik*" and "degraded, second-rate jazz."[5] In Germany, Ernst Krenek's hugely successful "jazz opera" *Jonny spielt auf* (*Jonny Strikes Up*) was *the* musical sensation of the decade, but its creator would later confess,

"Real jazz was unknown in Europe. We gave the name jazz to anything that came out of America."[6]

Berlin was right alongside London and Paris when it came to its seemingly insatiable appetite for such jazzy entertainment as the foxtrot or the Charleston or when, with compliments of Ma Rainey's Georgia Jazz Band, the black bottom took the city by storm. Even Ada Beatrice Queen Victoria Louise Virginia Smith, better known as "Bricktop" and the reigning queen of the City of Light's *les années folles*, confessed about the capital of the Weimar Republic, "I loved that city. It was a circus. Compared to it, Montmartre, even at two o'clock, was a sleepy little town. [. . .] At night the sounds of music and singing and laughing made a steady, joyful din, and there were so many lights that you could hardly see the sky. Anything went in Berlin, and I mean anything."[7] In Germany, as elsewhere, the equation of the decal *jazz* with blackness signaled both sexual liberation and exotic-primitivistic rejuvenation, on one hand, as well as Dionysian chaos, moral decadence, and a threat to national identity on the other. This dialectic, so salient in Harry Haller's musings, is also mirrored in the handful of novels from the period that portray jazz. Bruno Frank's *Politische Novelle*, Vicki Baum's *Stud. chem. Helene Willfüer*, or René Schickele's *Symphonie für Jazz*—like Hesse's *Steppenwolf*—are concerned less with the music than with cultural decline, social fragmentation, moral incertitude, and political turmoil, and jazz seemed to furnish the perfect soundtrack for life in the chaotic Weimar Republic. Echoing the reception of jazz (in whatever form) by German consumers, these literary texts figure the music as the sonic sign of an Afro-kinetic blackness bridging the New World civilization of the victors unburdened by the moral, economic, and cultural failures of the Old, with a sub-Saharan Africa unleashing a primitivist, primal black force unsettling the racial authority of Europe.[8]

But 1927, the year of the Steppenwolf, when Josephine Baker had already become a superstar trading on European fantasies of blackness, also saw the publication of a very different kind of book with a very different take on jazz. Penned by Hans Janowitz, the slender novel was simply titled *Jazz*.[9] Janowitz, a native of Bohemia, had studied in Prague, where he met Franz Kafka, Max Brod, and Karl Kraus, and began to publish essays and poetry. After the Great War he moved to Berlin, where, in collaboration with Carl Mayer, he wrote the screenplay for the box office hit *Das Cabinet des Dr. Caligari*, creating a high demand for his screen and stage work. He associated with other young artists like Kurt Tucholsky, Bert Brecht, or Friedrich Hollaender and headquartered at Trude Hesterberg's Wilde Bühne, for which he also wrote satirical lyrics. Berlin's swirling cultural atmosphere also introduced the Czech expat to a recent import from the New World—jazz. In 1924, however, he was compelled to return to his hometown of Poděbrady to take over his recently deceased father's business. His years in Berlin, though, and especially the music he had heard in the cabarets and dance halls, left an indelible impression, and so he began to write *Jazz*, which would remain his only novel.[10]

The "head" of *Jazz* introduces us to Lord Henry, a young English gigolo and wannabe jazz musician, and Madame Mae R., a foxy upper-crust flapper. Their accidental encounter on a train from Liverpool to London is brief, indeed, but just long enough for the two to be smitten with each other instantly. In the sprightly tale springing from this chance contact, Janowitz's narrator tracks Lord Henry's rise to stardom in Paris as the charismatic front man of "Lord Punch's Jazz-Band-Boys" and Madame Mae's attempts to find Henry. This underlying plotline—if it can be called one—is accompanied by sundry other subplots involving a panoply of offbeat characters: among them are Astralagus, known to the secret police as "the dice man," a Russian painter and serial killer who likes to produce nude studies of dying models; Baby, an aspiring jazz dancer with big, blue eyes and a serious crush on Henry; Mr. Roberts, a snub-nosed private eye and militant nonsmoker; or Dr. Curel, a celebrity lawyer to London's aristocratic elite. In a book that declares itself proudly "the first jazz-novel having unfolded according to the laws of jazz music," there is one curious elision, an absence that sets it apart from almost all other writings on jazz to come out of the Weimar Republic.[11] Whereas, for example, Hesse's "Negro Orchestra" is comprised of "enraptured and ecstatic" musicians who "hung over" their instruments with "blissful intoxication" and "a childlike radiance," the music resonating in Janowitz's novel is notably disengaged from any images of blackness.[12] In fact, although the narrative voice recognizes the blues as the main tributary to the music of Lord Punch's Jazz Band, there is only one African American character, and a seemingly ancillary one at that, in Janowitz's dramatis personae.[13] Bibi Black, though bearing an eponymic name, isn't even a musician but a dancer. What Toni Morrison might call an "Africanist presence" in the novel is at once Janowitz's nod to the origins of jazz (as music and dance) but also serves to dissociate the music from essentialized concepts of racial identity predominant in the discourse of the era.[14]

In sharp contrast to Hesse's *Steppenwolf*, Janowitz's jazz as "the real program of the times" elides any racialist conflations of the music with blackness. As the disembodied narrative voice follows the adventures of Lord Punch's Jazz-

Band-Boys, its transnational kinesis frequently digresses, conjectures, imagines, swinging back and forth between the capitals of France and England, abruptly interposing new characters and guessing at their intentions. "The world," the narrator insists, "had become jazz, surely, no doubt about it," and the first chapter, consisting of a single sentence, sets the tone for what is to follow:

> A European chronicler in the year 1999 relating the time around 1925 would have to begin,
>
> It was the time of the "bob," it was the time of "miniskirts," of "flesh-toned stockings," it was the time of absconded sons and abducted daughters, it was the time when the fatherlands, instead of demanding goods and blood from their poor participants as in the murderous years 1914–1918 (where one wasn't only allowed to die, but was asked to murder too), were content with the worldly possessions of their taxable subjects escaped from the World War, it was the times when radio waves in an increasing rush washed around the globe more and more densely, a whirlpool whose effect on the constitution of the patient was then still entirely uncertain, it was the time of the first zeppelin flight across the Atlantic Ocean, the funny time when the "United States of Europe" appeared as a utopia of idealistic dreamers and were jeered by the so-called *Realpolitiker* [pragmatic politicians] as fantasy—unbelievable, but true!—; it was the time of historic dissonances between East and West: the first decade of Communism in Russia was soon endured, a new mankind had grown up under the Soviets in one half of the world, strictly demarcated from the bourgeois West of the impoverished, discordantly split Europe, from the West-West of the all over overgilded America, a chasm of heretofore unprecedented depth was ripped open between the two halves of humanity, straight through the former civilization of democracy its red borderline went, behind which the proletarian culture built its future empire; this dissonance between East and West sounded shrilly through all life on earth, yes, it was the time of just this shrill dissonance, of stirred-up contrasts, it was the time of wild kiddie games, but shadowshapes of the tragic wilderness yet to come, it was the time of wild joy in wild pranks, in wild mischief in the area of law and order, in short: the real program of the time was:
>
> **Jazz,**
>
> and it's of course jazz that we shall be dealing with here.[15]

True to the program of the times, the disembodied narrator, impatient and nosy, eschews traditional modes of storytelling, oscillating instead between various times and places, introducing new voices, bumping into and then expanding new motifs, concocting scenes and dialogue. It is, in short, a narrative voice engrossed in a performance of improvisational storytelling. It suspends time and again the main story line unfolding from Henry and Mae's chance encounter "because it brings me delight to disrupt syncopationally the so-called course of action once again and always again. For do not forget, ladies and gentlemen: it is a jazz novel that is developing here. After all, the jazz character must finally erupt somewhere. And because much has been ruptured in this chapter already, it shall therefore erupt in the next one."[16] Reminiscent of Dexter Gordon's uncanny ability to create the illusion of intensifying musical velocity by playing behind the beat, *Jazz* here creates a sense of intensifying narrative velocity by deferring, postponing, suspending.[17] Like the jazz musician, the narrative voice, too, leaves the head of the tune behind to extemporize on anything and everything, from the foibles of Hungarian *Eintänzer* to the joys of chewing gum, for example. It is the jazz soloist's high-wire act of creation that Janowitz's narrator is engaged in, following serendipitous turns, doubling back when necessary, and even getting lost when the connection between the improvised line of the solo and the roadmap of the underlying changes snaps. *Jazz*'s narrative voice is that of the cosmopolitan flâneur. As Benjamin writes, "The sensation of the newest, most modern is thus just as much as the eternal return of all sameness. The spatial perception corresponding to this temporal perception is the penetrating and overlapping transparency of the flâneur's world."[18] While Janowitz's narrator, quite unlike Madam Zajj, is rather disinterested in historicity, he shares the flâneur's preoccupation with intersecting temporal and geographical spaces. Playing with polyvocal effects, rhetorical riffs, call-and-response—and, of course, with the one device paradigmatic of the times, syncopation—the language itself is a language aspiring to become music as it emulates the rhythms of jazz.[19]

In these Coltranesque "sheets of sound," Bibi Black is the sole black character. Even though Bibi is considered "a rare dance temperament," we never actually see her perform—nor do we hear her voice.[20] The only glimpse we get of her finds her on a train from London to Liverpool in the company of private investigator Mr. Roberts, Madame Mae's chauffeur Bob and maid Ann, and limns her as almost the exact opposite of the usual personifications of blackness:

> Dinner began in the dining car. Our party occupied a table and devoted itself silently to the four courses. Of course, the black lady dined with them, and there

was no hint of her attracting any attention. Because only Englishmen dined in the car, and with an Englishman attention, too, remains an affair unnoticeable on the outside, one that rightfully occurs behind the façade and nowhere else. The black lady, by the way, dined with perfect sophistication and partook from the plates with great discretion, even though Mr. Roberts urged her to dig in because they would have to remain awake through the night and there was a curious interaction between sleep and food, to wit, that sleep deprivation could often be counteracted by a surplus of nourishment. [. . .]

"True," Bob opined. "When I stay up through the night, I can gorge on a whole mutton if the beer supply isn't lacking . . ."

Bibi only smiled and commented that she felt completely up to any and all challenges that might yet be posed to her today.[21]

Not only does the narrator, here as elsewhere, refer to Bibi as "the black *lady*"; her characterization undercuts the negrophilia rampant in other German texts of the era, amplified implicitly by the reference to British restraint in matters of race. Bibi's blackness does not draw any (noticeable) attention whatsoever, as her blackness is also characterized by perfection, sophistication, discretion, and composure. Bibi's blackness is not an exotic atavism to be consumed for titillating entertainment purposes; on the contrary, the black lady is depicted as an urbane, discriminating consumer herself. Moreover, during her London engagements "Demoiselle Bibi" resides at the Hotel Falstaff in the notorious Soho district—and yet, it is chauffeur Bob who reenacts the gluttony of Shakespeare's character when Falstaff and his revelers indulge in eating mutton (during Lent, no less) in London's Boar's Head Tavern.[22] Recalling Carmen de Lavallade's graceful enactment of Madam Zajj, Bibi's character is the "anti-Josephine Baker" in a way: no banana skirts for Madame Bibi Black.

Lastly, Bibi is the only one among the characters the narrative voice assembles in the dining car who is acting in her own interest. The party is hot on the trail of the mysterious Russian Astralagus, the sinister "dice man" suspected of being responsible for the disappearance of Madame Mae. Bob and Ann are servants, while Mr. Roberts is in the employ of Mae R.'s lawyer. A year earlier, as it turns out, Astralagus had attempted to paint—that is, kill—Bibi, then as now in town as a member of a highly successful "Negro revue."[23] Yet the dancer is not only the sole female character to resist his wily if deadly charms, but after the assault she also filed suit against parties unknown. Now, she espies the nefarious painter in a London bar and immediately contacts Dr. Curel again, who also happens to be Madame Mae's lawyer, to refile proceedings against the offender, but, she hopes, this time with more urgency. The character of Bibi here is reminiscent of another new type closely related to the flâneur that the modern metropolis engenders: the detective. Attuned to the phantasmagoric double grounds and striations of the city as the flâneur is, "the unsettling and menacing aspects of urban life" can cause him to become a "detective against his will."[24]

In contrast, Curel's junior partner in the law firm is not too keen on reopening the old case and tracking down the elusive dice man: "Abstruse, this case. All of this doesn't even amount to a real charge of . . . is this maybe a threat? A threat to do bodily harm? That's really nothing—nothing, I say. Abstruse, this case. An incomprehensible offense. Not an offense at all, really. But this, you see, such an adventurer, he consorts with Lady Douglas R. Well, yes! I'm telling you—too much money, the people have too much money! Playing games like foolish children—sports and jazz—'playing-with-fire'—this they do."[25] Here again, the British upper class surrenders to the temptations of the phantasmagoric city and is associated with moral abandon, lack of judgment, juvenile foolishness—and jazz. In sharp contradistinction, Bibi Black is censored for being perhaps a little *too* prudish as she is juxtaposed to the jazzy recklessness in which white European women often indulge. But the most important tip leading to the apprehension of the notorious serial killer comes from her, as she is the one whose transnational flânerie "allows the intellect to penetrate this emotion-laden atmosphere."[26] Astralagus, on the other hand, is the creature whose deadly actions are governed by pathological, perverse impulses beyond his control—his character is clearly influenced by Cesare, the somnambulist murderer in *Caligari*—as are the European women like Madame Mae who seem incapable of resisting, as Bibi did, his pernicious attraction.[27]

The novel accordingly refuses to regurgitate stereotypical images of blacks. Even the music itself, jazz, is divorced from blackness as Lord Henry and the four other "jazz-band-boys" likewise subvert racialist explanations and definitions of jazz music. The quintet's multicultural personnel is comprised of Henry, the disgraced English lord; Siegi Winter, the Jewish shoe manufacturer; Tobby, the seasick sailor; Punch, the clown who makes his audiences weep; and Tino, the Italian street singer with a strong aversion to Neapolitan beauties. What all five have in common, the narrative voice discloses, is that they were "born to be jazz-band-boys." From the cradle, future jazz-band-boys "already sport the mark of the sonic somersault on their forehead: they form a secret order that has syncopation on its escutcheon and wicked sounds in its arms. While the claim of the intellectual in diapers to horn-rimmed spectacles is not necessarily manifest, the claim of the jazzbandist in diapers to make syncopationally fractured, atonal, and disharmonic noise necessarily is."[28] Anticipating uncannily Steve Lacy's description of the jazz musician as "a combination orator, dialectician, mathematician, athlete, entertainer, poet, singer, dancer, diplomat, educator, student, comedian, artist, seducer, public masturbator, and general all-around good fellow," the five jazz-band-boys become so good at their craft that they eventually embark on a tour of America, the very home of jazz. The fact that this "secret order" of "jazzbandism" is all white was in and of itself not unusual in Weimar Germany; the fact that race (blackness) is not among the order's initiation requirements was extraordinary, though.[29]

But before their triumphant U.S. tour, Lord Punch's Jazz-Band-Boys, now augmented to "Lord Punch's Jazz-Band-Boys and Dancing-Girls," hone their chops in Paris's premier entertainment hall, the Château d'Or. The narrator's description of their climactic performance reveals how little their music has to do with the jazz of, say, Sidney Bechet, Louis Armstrong, or even the Original Dixieland Jazz Band:[30]

> Punch's saxophone sweeps through the witch's cauldron of the room with its capricious blare or grunt, with the effect of an invisible ladle that swirls everything in the pot into a jumble, the bottom to the top and the top to the bottom; but a whole bushel of small and larger ladles stirs the pot's contents into an even more frantic whirl, so that the top in turn comes to lie again at the bottom and the bottom at the top, only to be whirled anew from top to bottom and right to left and left to right, crosswise up and crosswise down. There are the violins and the piano, the drum, vocals of male and female timbre, there is the "flexatone" in the hands of Siegi, the step-board beneath the feet of Henry and the girls. Horns and children's trumpet, castanets and bursting balloons, sound dispensers all, which, each after its own fashion, prove their mettle as hefty ladles.[31]

The instrumentation is decidedly unjazzy and serves mostly to highlight the carnivalesque attributes of jazz music (or what Janowitz and his contemporaries would label as such), a recurrent motif in the novel. The passage also reflects fairly accurately how German combos simply integrated elements perceived to come from American jazz into existing traditions of salon and ballroom entertainment but retained the core repertoire and instrumentation demanded by waltzes, marches, or polkas. For example, most outfits purporting to play jazz retained the so-called *Stehgeiger*, a solo violinist who sometimes doubled as vocalist or on another instrument. And we recall that Henry, the actual bandleader, plays the violin, like the black protagonist in *Jonny spielt auf*. Many combos also sported a conductor, a function Siegi fulfills in the band before he branches out to the flexatone or an accordion, Tobby's primary instrument.[32] Accentuating the playful amateurism of Lord Punch's Jazz-Band-Boys, Tino the Neapolitan street singer has apparently now become a versatile multi-instrumentalist. The band's multicultural, multiethnic personnel speaks to a democratic, transnational egalitarianism "that whirls everything in the pot into a jumble": it is no coincidence that the nominal leader of the band is the hapless clown Punch, granted lordship possibly due to his mastery of the "jazziest" instrument of them all, the saxophone.[33] And it is the saxophone that early on sounds the novel's profound hope, "a utopia" though it may be, of "a United States of Europe" after the carnage of the Great War:

> The gipsy, who had violined a little something into the word's ear until 1914, was relieved by the fiddler roaming the trenches of the International Fratricide Combine for four years. But then arrived his brother Fool, *the man of the syncope*, the violin of death was relieved by the saxophone of life, the drum of the henchman by the percussion of the dancer, the machine gun by the beat of the stepper. Radical rejuvenation of the world through flourishing nonsense! The time had found its Offenbach. It was called: Jazz![34]

The prelude to a transnational, pan-European reharmonization to which jazz gives voice thus also accounts for the fact that Janowitz's novel is set not in Berlin but oscillates contrapuntally between London and Paris, the capitals of the former enemies. Its sonic vagabondage, traversing a rapidly changing political and economic map as it does, replaces the concept of nationhood and national belonging with the need for perpetual roving.[35] *Jazz*'s syncopational storytelling thus brings to mind Gunther Schuller's aphorism of swing as "the 'democratization' of rhythmic values."[36]

Janowitz himself left Berlin in 1924, right around the time the Dawes Plan stabilized the *Reichsmark* and gave German consumption of jazz and of other forms of entertainment a tremendous boost. He therefore missed Sam Wooding's band, the first African American jazz outfit of note to play Berlin as part of the *Chocolate Kiddies* revue in late 1925, Josephine Baker in *La Revue Nègre* the following year, or the implementation of the world's first jazz course at the Frankfurt Hoch Conservatory in 1927. While the Bauhaus students had latched on to the music early on and even went on tour with their own combo, jazz fever reached its apex in the second half of the 1920s with the spectacular success of Krenek's *Jonny spielt auf* and Kurt Weill's *Dreigroschenoper*.[37] Still, encounters with "real" African American jazz, recorded or performed, were relatively few and far between and underscored the fact that German professional musicians, more so than their neighbors, relied more often than not on sheet music and concocted a sound that was based partly on legends, lore, and hearsay, partly on lightly syncopating the existing repertoire of salon dance music, and partly on the café tradition of the *Stehgeiger*, whose music in turn drew on the tradition of improvisation in gipsy music. Weimar jazz was in fact a barely syncopated and rarely improvised update of commercial entertainment hits, popular standbys, and light classics, punctuated by vagarious percussive explosions, car horn bleats, and other sonic novelty effects, played by ensembles sometimes derided as *Radaukapellen*, "racket bands."[38] At least also in part due to musicians' demands for "real" jazz and the original's relative dearth in Germany, the 1920s saw an astonishing slew of musicological how-to guides to the music. The most influential of these was Alfred Baresel's 1925 *vade mecum:* his *Jazz-Buch* was in such high demand that it went through four printings in less than twelve months, and its author published an expanded and revised edition four years later. All these instruction manuals also reflected the general reception and performance of jazz—or what was perceived as such—throughout the decade. Writing in 1932 about the era, composer and musicologist Hans Heinz Stuckenschmidt perceptively identified three characteristic elements of Weimar jazz: "the proximity to European entertainment music" accompanied "the trivialization of Afro-American culture through the exotic perspective" and contributed to "the ostensible desire of jazz to present itself in musically respectable guise." Nevertheless, this trivialized "racket," with its indelible association with black otherness, sounded particularly unsettling in a country that had just lost the costliest war in its history, and whose musical *Übervater*, Richard Wagner, had been dead but little more than a generation.[39]

Although the music of these racket bands—a term surely befitting Lord Punch's Jazz-Band-Boys—was perceived as radically new, German audiences had not at all been strangers to black music. The famous Fisk Jubilee Singers gave their Berlin debut in November 1877 to gushing reviews: anticipating the reception of later forms of African American music, the *Berlinische Zeitung*, for example, swooned at "the magic effects of beauty" the vocalists managed to conjure and even counseled that the Singers' art might very well have the power to rejuvenate Germany's own culture, a culture that was "beginning to decay."[40] In Berlin as elsewhere, the Fisk Jubilee Singers opened the doors for black performers. For the year 1896, the German weekly *Der Artist*, a publication for traveling performers, actually listed well over one hundred entertainers of African descent touring all over Germany. Audiences flocked to ragtime dances, minstrel performances, and so-called pickaninny shows, and Germans proved as susceptible to ragtime fever as their fellow Europeans. Which is not to say that all these performers, or even most of them, were African *American:* especially after World War I, many black artists "passed" as African American in order to capitalize on the commercial windfall promised by *Amerikanismus* and by anything and everything labeled "jazz." For example, the popular Wild West Bar—Sidney Bechet's employer—advertised as "authentically American" jazz "The MacAllan Blackband," a quintet led by drummer William "Willi" MacAllan, son of a German mother and a Somali father.[41]

American or not, for any musician touring the continent, Berlin was a logical stop on the itinerary, also because early in the twentieth century, the German recording industry was a veritable international juggernaut: in 1906 alone, the monthly production output amounted to one-and-a-half million tons of cylinders and discs, much of which was destined for export.[42] This dominance came to a temporary halt with the outbreak of the Great War, but not even the postwar occupation of the Rhineland by colonial troops from French Africa, an affront quickly decried as "*die schwarze Schmach*" (the black disgrace) that lingered for years in the country's cultural memory, diminished German audiences' fascination with black music.[43] And so, jazz as *Zeitgeist* quickly pervaded virtually every nook and cranny of Berlin years before "La Baker" strutted her stuff for Berliners for the first time. Irrespective of the homegrown particularities of the German versions of the music, what the public discourse surrounding the decal *jazz* shared with its counterparts across Europe was its association with an eroticized, primitive blackness by the time the first international ambassador of jazz, New Orleans legend Sidney Bechet, finally made it into town in 1926 as a member of Baker's *La Revue Nègre*. Bechet would often jam at the "Wild West Bar" in the Haus Vaterland, the city's premier entertainment complex, where he occasionally sat in with a local ensemble billed as the "Tom Bill Nigger Band."[44] Thus, even though part of the music's allure—and threat—was its perceived radical newness, the arrival of African American jazz musicians in the Weimar Republic merely reaffirmed a set of assumptions about race and culture, elements of which had been part of the public discourse since the Fisk Jubilee Singers had first performed for German audiences half a century earlier.

In this context, the uniqueness of Janowitz's maverick take on jazz that decouples it from fetishized (or demonized) blackness is amplified by its juxtaposition to a 1921 column in the *Berliner Börsen-Courier*, one of the most highly respected cultural arbiters in the city, by journalist Joseph Roth, whose report on a visit to a jazz cabaret is emblematic on several levels. The fact that Roth intended to satirize the insatiable negrophilia of his fellow citizens only enhances how pervasive the conflation of jazz and blackness already was three years before Janowitz returned home, and four years before Wooding and the *Chocolate Kiddies* came to town. It also, inadvertently, demonstrates Roth's own ignorance and Eurocentrism—he calls the music itself "jazzband" consistently (like many of his compatriots did, too) and sums up the whole affair as "not barbaric, but anti-cultivated, so to speak," and simply "childish." "Jazzband," he clucks, "is no 'composition,' but an eruption. It isn't invented, but born. And it has the melodiousness, the wild, the *divinely ordained* rhythm. For in the souls of the Negroes, you see, slumbers the lawless, arbitrary music of a chaos not yet coalesced into the community of peoples. The whites in America and Central Europe call this: 'Jazzband.'" He pities the customers in this "*Jazzbanddiele*," "who know nothing of the culture of the Negro" but who "believe that Expressionism is an African business." The performers appear to Roth just as patently ridiculous as the dancers: "Sometimes a musician put the trumpet on his head, spun in a circle three times, and sat back down. The drummer sang. He sang an American song, deficiently. He sang like Negroes sing who, having just arrived from their songless home, begin to comprehend the culture of the whites at their apex—the chanson." In short, scoffs Roth, what had assembled at the club that night was a coterie of "pseudo-Niggers" representative of "the hypocrisy of these times: liveried niggerdom and niggerized Europeanness."[45]

Even though Janowitz's jazz betrays some affinities with Joseph Roth's excursion to a jazz dance—the recurrent childishness of the sounds of jazz and the musicians who play it, the discombobulating "frantic whirl" characterizing the whole experience—the context in which these sounds reverberate is noticeably different. The band playing for dance-crazed urbanites that Roth described for the readers of the *Berliner Börsen-Courier* may have been comprised of white Germans in blackface, a phenomenon not unknown in postwar

Germany: the musicians he saw and heard in the "*Jazzbanddiele*," "they say, are Americans. They look like movie stars. But during intermission they speak German. I heard it."[46] After all, the Lechner company marketed a product called "Neger-Schwarz (Negro-Black)," makeup that was easy to remove but still wouldn't rub off even on white gloves, the ads proudly assured, and Friedrich Hollaender landed a minor hit with "*Ich lass' mir meinen Körper schwarz bepinseln*" (I'll have my body painted black).[47] The tableau Roth paints leaves the national and ethnic identity of the musicians ambiguous, yet to him, the synesthetic spectacle immediately conjured an indisputable "niggerdom." The discursive blackening of all sounds and sights jazzy reveals a deeply racialized perception shared by performer, consumer, and critic alike.[48]

In glaring contrast, *Jazz*'s "rejuvenation of the world through flourishing nonsense" is *not* coupled to a parasitic, minstrelized appropriation of blackness. Paris's Château d'Or is a site almost completely devoid of any Africanist presence. The jazz-band-boys as well as their five female dancers are all white, as is the merry throng of partiers. Professional performer Bibi Black never sets foot in the Château d'Or; she is on the train to Liverpool at that very moment, her apparently sole stand-in at the club (and the only other Africanist presence in the book) being "a tall black man" seen dancing with Mae R.[49] This "tall black man" is, like Bibi, portrayed as a consumer discriminate in taste: the Château d'Or is the City of Light's hottest nightspot, Lord Punch's all-white Jazz-Band-Boys and Girls are considered to provide the most exciting jazz on the continent, and Madame Mae is a beautiful woman indeed.

This consistent decoupling of jazz from blackness does not, in turn, mean that Janowitz's is a deracinated text. Rather, the inclusion of transnational flâneuse Bibi, "the black lady," suggests that she acts as a figure who satirizes the racialist and often racist discourse surrounding black people (regardless of their provenance) rampant in the Weimar Republic and reveals her to be a relative of Ellington's Madam Zajj. Moreover, her role actually turns out to be indispensable for the development of the novel's narrative structure, for Bibi Black is the character whose actions eventually cause *Jazz*'s many parallel plotlines to coalesce. Without the crucial clue she provides as detective-flâneuse, and without her directive to Dr. Curel to reactivate the search for Astralagus, the plot's climax at the Château d'Or that brings together all the principal players would not be possible. Bibi Black sets in motion the events that not only lead to the arrest and incarceration of the painting serial killer but also to Lord Henry's epiphany that his true love is the dancer Baby, to Mae R.'s reunion with her husband, and to the "graduation" of all the jazz-band-boys to successful, respected "jazz-symphonists."[50]

To be sure, as the ascension of the five jazz-band-boys to "symphonists" indicates, Janowitz's jazz is not completely free of Eurocentric stereotypes. The music of *Jazz* is basically "fractured, atonal, and disharmonic noise" from misfits and outcasts, if a joyfully subversive noise. Also, Janowitz's decoupling of jazz from blackness results in the book's sole black character being deprived of a voice of her own, the effective silencing of the Africanist presence. Bibi Black, as crucial as she is to the plot structure, never performs, nor do we ever hear her voice—the price the novel pays for its satire of European negrophilia and negrophobia, for its refusal to equate blackness with otherness. *Jazz*'s kinesis is no *Afro*politan kinesis—not necessarily because the majority of its characters are white, but because they show no awareness of Benjaminian *Geschichtlichkeit*. In the homeland of jazz itself, the Africanist presence, be it acknowledged or suppressed, "is the vehicle by which the American self knows itself as not enslaved, but free; not repulsive, but desirable; not helpless, but licensed and powerful; not history-less, but historical; not damned, but innocent; not a blind accident of evolution, but a progressive fulfillment of destiny," according to Toni Morrison's perceptive diagnosis. Clearly, the dynamics of blackness in Janowitz's *Jazz* are fundamentally different, and Bibi's voicelessness is not at all a result of demands of white identity formation and "the parasitical nature of white freedom."[51] The novel is not engaged in compulsive whitewashing, not the kind anyway practiced by the aptly named Paul Whiteman, also tremendously popular in Berlin. Rather, the novel's somewhat problematic silencing of the Africanist presence is partly dictated by its satire of European discourses of blackness, and partly a result of a lack of familiarity with the historical exigencies of the black experience in the New World. As Partsch correctly points out, "The paradoxical status of jazz as *the* symbol of American culture, represented in Germany primarily by a shallow, second-rate German variant, demonstrated a lack of knowledge even among Germany's intellectuals about jazz's outsider position in the United States and its function in the musical avant-garde."[52] And let us not forget either that in the homeland of the original "*Radaukapellen*," a *New York Times* review once snootily referred to Duke Ellington as "the djinn of din."[53]

Even so, what sets Janowitz's jazz apart from that of his contemporaries is that for him, jazz is not the music of the racial Other. This, perhaps, is also the reason why Siegi's Jewish ethnicity is barely alluded to, and certainly never highlighted, even if *Jazz* makes a passing reference to "swastikaesque" discourse.⁵⁴ As a Jew himself, Janowitz was without a doubt intimately familiar—and Benjamin was most certainly so—with the kind of marginalization that, for example, Hesse's Harry Haller merely cultivates among the rising tide of anti-Semitism in the Weimar Republic.⁵⁵ The same music that had become synonymous with stereotypes of blackness the novel instead offers as the ideal instrument for transnationalizing ethnic, cultural, and civic identities. Thus, jazz can redraw the map—or, rather, reconstitute it altogether in the wake of the moral and political bankruptcy that had crawled out of the trenches of the Somme and Verdun.

(((

Regardless of how far removed the music Janowitz heard in Berlin's cabarets and nightclubs was from "authentic" jazz, his literary adaptation incorporates with uncanny keenness the dynamics of the music. How prescient *Jazz*'s literary transposition of distinctive elements of jazz music really is—and how crucial the character of Bibi Black is for the book's narrative structure—emerges if we read Janowitz's text to the tune of John Coltrane. In the second half of the 1950s, Coltrane began to emerge as *the* force in jazz to be reckoned with. Having honed his chops "walking the bar" as a member of various rhythm-and-blues bands in and around Philadelphia, the tenor saxophonist put in high-profile stints with Miles Davis and Thelonious Monk while recording a string of albums under his own name. His *Traneing In* from 1957 concludes with a veritable tour de force on "Soft Lights and Sweet Music," taken at such a ridiculously high tempo that it prompted critic Ira Gitler to joke in the liner notes that the song title, "in this case, is more apt to mean the headlights of a Maserati and the music of wheels taking a curve."⁵⁶ In the new style Coltrane had been perfecting, Gitler heard an "excruciatingly exhilarating intensity of rapid, exigent runs with their residual harmonic impact" and coined the famous and subsequently often overused phrase "sheets of sound" as shorthand for the tenorist's seemingly endless phrases played at breakneck speed on his follow-up on the Prestige label, the 1958 *Soultrane*.⁵⁷ Specifically, Gitler referred to Coltrane's solo on "Russian Lullaby"—coincidentally, like "Soft Lights and Sweet Music," a tune penned by another Jewish refugee from Europe, Irving Berlin. Taken at a blistering 360 beats per minute, this rendition of the show tune will not rock anyone to sleep. The breathless intensity with which Coltrane rushes through the changes recalls *Jazz*'s rapid-fire tour de force of the opening chapter in particular: consisting of a single sentence, it appears as a solid-block paragraph that reads very much like the literary equivalent of Trane-ish sheets of sound as it zaps from bobbed hair and short skirts to world war to radio waves to zeppelins to communism until it finally comes to rest—the narrative voice, like Coltrane, must take a breath at some point after all—on the word "**Jazz**." To put it differently, the root of the chord of *Jazz*'s first chapter is "the program of the times," that is, "**Jazz**," and all the notes of the related scale are crammed into its one run-on sentence. And just like on the musical staff the root is the lowest note of a chord, "**Jazz**" is at the very "bottom" of the first chapter.[58]

In this heady swirl of Janowitz's sheets of words, Bibi Black is the structural equivalent of the "residual harmonic impact" discernible in Coltrane's solos. As random as the saxophonist's mind-bogglingly fast runs may sound to the lay listener, they are in fact closely related to the scalar properties of each chord.[59] As Coltrane himself would later explain what he was trying to do at that stage of his career,

> About this time, I was trying for a sweeping sound. I started experimenting because I was striving for more individual development. I even tried long, rapid lines that Ira Gitler termed "sheets of sound" at that time. But actually, I was beginning to apply the three-on-one chord approach, and at that time the tendency was to play the entire scale of each chord. Therefore, they were usually played fast and sometimes sounded like glisses [glissandi]. I found there were a certain number of chord progressions to play in a given time, and sometimes what I played didn't work out in eighth notes, sixteenth notes, or triplets. I had to put the notes in uneven groups like fives and sevens in order to get them all in. I thought in groups of notes, not of one note at a time. I tried to place these groups on the accents and emphasize the strong beats—maybe on 2 here and on 4 over at the end. I would set up the line and drop groups of notes—a long line with accents dropped as I moved along. Sometimes what I was doing clashed harmonically with the piano—especially if the pianist wasn't familiar with what I was doing—so a lot of times I just strolled with bass and drums.[60]

This high-velocity Afro-kinetic flânerie of "stroll[ing] with bass and drums" is not quite the same thing that Gitler heard: where the critic heard Coltrane's solos hurtling *away* from the underlying harmonic structure of the song, the tenorist explained that it was in fact more like the exact opposite, cramming as many notes of any given chord's scale into his torrential lines. And yet the effect on many listeners is indeed that of a merely "residual harmonic impact" amidst a massive sonic turbulence—not unlike what Punch's whirling, swirling "invisible ladle" of a saxophone must have sounded like to the dancers at the Château d'Or. Gitler's formulation nonetheless limns another connection between Janowitz's novel and Coltrane's music: Madame Bibi Black, then, embodies the residual *Africanist* impact within *Jazz*'s sheets of words. Not only that, she personifies the Afro-kinesis without which the plot simply could not exist: she provides the Afropolitan spark indispensable for the structural development of the plot, just as the underlying harmonic chord progression is indispensable for the development of Coltrane's solo on "Russian Lullaby."[61] Moreover, the rhythmic implications of Coltrane's sheets of sound also pertain to the narrative structure of Janowitz's novel: the "uneven groups" of notes in place of the standard triplets or sixteenth notes correspond to the "uneven" structural development of *Jazz*'s many plotlines. Written language, like the saxophone, is after all a monophonic "instrument" that, unlike a piano or guitar, can sound only one "note" at a time.[62]

In concert, then, Janowitz's *Jazz* and Coltrane's "Russian Lullaby" amplify each other's Afropolitan flânerie. The novel's Afro-kinesis may not have a voice of its own—but the Afro-kinesis of Trane's horn certainly does as it dances across the changes. "I want to cover as many forms of music as I can put into a jazz context and play on my instruments. I like eastern music," the saxophonist said, and "music with a Spanish content as well as other exotic-flavored music."[63] In the novel's opening chapter, the narrative voice expresses Janowitz's personal hope that "the translation of the world into jazz music" would sound the prelude not only to a "United States of Europe" but also sound a call to "idealistic dreamers" to take over from the "*Realpolitiker*" and forge a world free of war. In his memoir *Balade en Saxo*, Manu Dibango shares a very similar dream, one in which music, transnational music, clears the path to a united Africa. Of course, we know that Janowitz's dream was illusory then, and continues to be elusive now. But Dibango's dream, at least, reminds us of the reason why the book's urge to "translate the world into jazz" remains as valid and urgent early in the third millennium as it was in Janowitz's Weimar Republic.[64]

CHAPTER 3

High Fidelity on the Black Atlantic

Rocking Out with Langston Hughes and Nick Hornby

Hans Janowitz passed away in 1954, the same year Johnny Hodges fired a young Coltrane due to the tenorist's escalating heroin habit and began to contemplate a return into the Ellington fold. Nine years later, the Afro-kinesis of his endless searching had taken Trane to an entirely new musical as well as personal plateau. After Amiri Baraka went to hear him at the famed Village Vanguard, he wrote, "If you can hear, this music will make you think of a lot of weird and wonderful things. You might even become one of them."[1] And even if Janowitz himself might have declined to take the Coltrane, his *Jazz* reminds us that the stakes that this music amplifies, still, are nothing more and nothing less than our common humanity. Baraka's experience at the Vanguard that night also echoes Langston Hughes's travels around the world, where time and again he came face-to-face with these same stakes. Unlike Janowitz, Hughes felt compelled to let Bibi Black's own voice, the voice of Madam Zajj—the *human* voice of blackness, in other words—be heard, even and especially in places where no African American had heretofore visited.

In the famous opening scene of *The Big Sea*, the aspiring poet stands at the railing of the S.S. *Malone* en route to Africa and, in an act of literary emancipation, throws his entire personal library into the Atlantic ocean.[2] Not just the beginning of his international adventure, but the entire autobiography is in many ways also a narrative of divestment: among the other "baggage"

Hughes discards along the way is the revivalism of Auntie Reed, the dominance of his stern father, and, at the very end, the equally controlling interference of his patron, Charlotte "Godmother" Osgood Mason. How different, then, the traveler who, some years later, heads to the pier in New York City, "loaded down with bags, baggage, books, a typewriter, a victrola, and a big box of Louis Armstrong, Bessie Smith, and Ethel Waters records" about to cross the Atlantic yet again, only not to Africa, but this time bound for Russia. Throughout *I Wonder as I Wander*, the "Harlem victrola" is not only Hughes's most constant traveling companion, but the race records it spins become the instant connection to the *human* race everywhere he goes, from the capital of the still-young USSR to the windswept steppes of Uzbekistan to the bustling metropolis of Shanghai.[3]

To Hughes, of course, African American music is perhaps the most profound expression of the human spirit in a world that often questions, and even threatens, that very humanity. *I Wonder as I Wander* ends in Paris on New Year's Eve, 1938, with the world on the brink of war. Even so, Hughes reports, "All over Paris that winter was Negro music [. . .] and French jazz bands all over town were trying their best to beat it out like the Negroes."[4] But the last evening of the year finds him with an old acquaintance, Japanese theater director Seki Sano, in the Café de la Paix—an at once hopeful and defiant symbol of transnational harmony and brotherhood.[5] The autobiography concludes with the poet on his way back to his hotel, musing about his travels over the previous few years:

> The year before, I had been in Cleveland. The year before that in San Francisco. The year before that in Mexico City. The one before that at Carmel. And the year before Carmel in Tashkent. Where would I be when the next New Year came, I wondered? By then, would there be war—a major war? Would Mussolini and Hitler have finished their practice in Ethiopia and Spain to turn their planes on the rest of us? Would civilization be destroyed? Would the world really end?
>
> "Not my world," I said to myself. "My world will not end."
>
> But worlds—entire nations and civilizations—do end. In the snowy night in the shadows of the old houses of Montmartre, I repeated to myself, "My world won't end."
>
> But how could I be so sure? I don't know.
>
> For a moment, I wondered.[6]

This final scene, then, ironically juxtaposes two contesting visions of the world: the volkish nation-state's rapacious quest for *Lebensraum*, on one hand, the roaming of the individual artist who dares to imagine human dignity in the face of history on the other. The ontological posture the poet assumes here—there are, after all, one world war and one genocide between the conclusion of the memoir and its publication—also echoes Walter Benjamin's take on Paul Klee's *Angelus Novus*, the angel of history, whose gaze is fixed upon the pain and suffering of the past while his outstretched wings carry him resolutely to the future.[7] The Benjaminian intersection of different planes of historical time resonates in the memoir's penultimate line, where sureness is rendered in the past tense, uncertainty in the present. Moreover, Hughes's final musings are also the only allusion to the autobiography's title, borrowed from the traditional Christmas carol. And although neither *The Big Sea* nor its successor is a "jazz text" as such, the very source for the title of *I Wonder as I Wander* amplifies how the memoir's transnationalism is orchestrated with an artistic sensibility born of an Afro-kinetic jazz aesthetic. Reading Hughes's *I Wonder as I Wander* to the tune of John Coltrane's album *Africa/Brass* elucidates this sensibility: both sound a creative transformation of indurated ethnic and national borders, yet their Afropolitan stance is nevertheless grounded in the understanding that the newly reconfigured self (both individual and communal) that may emerge from the encounter with the other, across the border, ultimately cannot—and perhaps *should* not—transcend the exigencies of historical time.

The memoir's final juxtaposition, one that pits artistic imagination against national socialism, is also refracted in the contested history behind the song that lends the autobiography its title. Margaret Walker, for one, adjudged that what became known as a Christmas carol had its roots in the sorrow songs of African American slaves and their direct descendants: it was, she insisted, an expression "taken from Black folklore and is part of the folk-song or Negro spiritual."[8] "I Wonder as I Wander" thematizes a spiritual quest occasioned by worldly disenfranchisement, retracing the flight of Benjamin's angel of history:

> I wonder as I wander out under the sky
> How Jesus the savior did come for to die
> For poor on'ry people like you and like I;
> I wonder as I wander out under the sky.[9]

However, there is also a very different account of the origins of "I Wonder as I Wander." White folklorist, performer, and composer John Jacob Niles copyrighted the song under his name and first published it in his 1934 collection *Songs of the Hill Folk*. He later contended that the song

> grew out of three lines of music sung for me by a girl who called herself Annie Morgan. The place was Murphy, North Carolina, and the time was July, 1933. The Morgan family, revivalists all, were about to be ejected by the police, after having camped in the town square for some little time, cooking, washing, hanging their wash from the Confederate monument and generally conducting themselves in such a way as to be classified as a public nuisance. Preacher Morgan and his wife pled poverty: they had to hold one more meeting in order to buy enough gas to get out of town. It was then that Annie Morgan came out—a tousled, unwashed blond, and very lovely. She sang the first three lines of the verse of "I Wonder As I Wander." At twenty-five cents a performance, I tried to get her to sing all the song. After eight tries, all of which are wonderfully recorded in my notes, I had only three lines of verse, a garbled fragment of melodic material—and a magnificent idea. With the writing of additional verses and the development of the original melodic material, "I Wonder As I Wander" came into being. I sang it for five years in my concerts before it caught on. Since then, it has been sung by soloists and choral groups wherever the English language is spoken and sung.[10]

Subsequently, Niles was so protective of "his" song that he even filed multiple lawsuits to consolidate his claim of primary authorship. Niles's assertion that he shepherded the song from under the shadows of the Confederacy, a nation no longer in existence, into a transnational anglophone phenomenon is problematic on multiple levels. For one thing, Niles was dogged throughout his career by accusations of simply appropriating his songs from others, not composing them himself—the hillbilly version of love-and-theft, perhaps.[11] Moreover, not only did he furnish different accounts of how many verses young Annie actually sang to him, this particular version also amounts to an exercise in "whitewashing," given the symbolic landscape in which it takes place: the Confederate memorial in conjunction with Murphy's location in Cherokee County—formerly the home of Fort Butler, a starting point of the Trail of Tears and part of yet another bygone nation—assures a lineage of "I Wonder as I Wander" that is ethnically cleansed. The figurative territory in which Niles's account plays out thus also highlights its fundamental difference from Hughes's Café de la Paix: "To articulate the past historically," insists Benjamin, "does not mean to recognize 'how it really was.' It means to seize a memory as it is flashing up in a moment of peril."[12]

Although the Morgans are about to be evicted from the town square, Niles's account bathes their plight in a warm light of Appalachian quaintness, an aura of the picturesque, where any sense of Benjaminian *Geschichtsbewusstsein* is cloaked by the sight of drying laundry hanging from the memorial to the Confederacy and by the sounds of cute little Annie's endearing if futile efforts to sing a complete version of what eventually would become "I Wonder as I Wander." The entire tableau is quite Benjaminian—the town square as the Morgans' living room, the Appalachian version of the Parisian arcades, where outside becomes inside, "the street [. . .] as the furnished, lived-in interior," and where Niles pays two dollars in quarters for Annie's musical fragment and thus reenacts the kind of flâneur who has become deaf to "the surprising resonance" of the "double ground" over which he is gallivanting, "who no longer understands anything of production" but instead "aims to become an expert on the market (on prices)." And so, the pseudoanthropological flânerie of Niles in effect "takes the concept of marketability itself for a walk."[13] Where and how Langston Hughes first heard the song, he does not tell us. Walker maintains that he had known "I Wonder as I Wander" as a sorrow song all along. While one might be inclined to side with Walker, the two divergent backstories of the song portend the contesting visions of the world with which the autobiography ends, juxtaposing the national-socialist ideology of *Blut und Boden* and the humanistic imagination of the individual artist. Yet in and of itself, Hughes's choice of title expresses, as R. Baxter Miller puts it, "the creative delight of being an African American modern who reconfigures the map of human freedom."[14]

The transnational reconfiguration at play in the symbolic cartography of *I Wonder as I Wander* is amplified if we read the autobiography to the tune of another African American modern and fellow sojourner, John Coltrane, specifically his *Africa/Brass* sessions. John William Coltrane—named after his grandfather, a minister in the AME Zion Church—was born in North Carolina, his hometown of High Point about 260 miles east of Murphy, where Niles would hear "I Wonder as I Wander" some years later. The unexpected commercial success of *My Favorite Things*, recorded in 1960, intensified Coltrane's quest for a new sound and a new concept. The title track features the saxophonist on soprano, an instrument that had fallen into disuse after its prominence in early New Orleans jazz, but was resurrected by Coltrane also because its nasal, exotic timbre echoed the classical Indian music in which he was beginning to immerse himself. But on the heels of his heretofore best-selling record, the saxophonist moved from Atlantic Records to the newly formed Impulse! label.

His very first project there was by far his most ambitious to date: in addition to the "classic quartet" with pianist McCoy Tyner, bassist Reggie Workman, and drummer Elvin Jones, *Africa/Brass* featured a fourteen-piece orchestra including French horns and euphoniums. Recorded on two separate dates in Van Gelder's Englewood Cliffs studios, in May and June of 1961—the same year Hughes's *Black Nativity* made its debut (with Madam Zajj's Carmen de Lavallade in the cast); the same year the Freedom Riders in the United States were tearing down a wall, and the Ulbricht regime in the GDR began construction of another—the album appeared to have an Afro-centric slant to it: the majestic "Africa" was inspired by Coltrane's recent encounter with traditional West African musics, particularly the recordings of Dahomean percussion duo Albéric and Frédéric Glélé; the defiantly titled "The Damned Don't Cry" with its blueslike A section was a composition of Cal Massey, whose song titles in the 1960s began to voice the concerns of radical black liberation politics; and "Song of the Underground Railroad" was the saxophonist's take on the spiritual "Follow the Drinking Gourd." While it was Impulse! producer Creed Taylor who came up with the album title, Freddie Hubbard, who helped deliver the titular brass, averred that the tenorist "wanted that African sound."[15]

Although "Africa" would be the album's centerpiece, the catalyst for the entire project was a completely different one: strangely enough (or so it would appear), it was another Christmas carol, "Greensleeves." Coltrane had been intrigued by Tyner's comping over the age-old English folk song and told the pianist to rearrange his voicings for orchestra. For that task, multi-reedist and frequent collaborator Eric Dolphy was brought in, who transcribed Tyner's characteristic block chords in his arrangement of the seventeenth-century *romanesca* for an eighteen-piece orchestra.[16] The pivotal role of "Greensleeves" for the *Africa/Brass* sessions is also underscored by the fact that it was the first tune to be recorded, and the only one Coltrane insisted on rerecording during the initial session on May 23, 1961, despite limited studio time. Moreover, "Greensleeves"—not "Africa"—became a staple of the classic quartet's live performances, caught on tape twice during the famed Village Vanguard recordings that following November, and revisited the year after for the *Ballads* sessions. As Coltrane explained his attraction to the English folk song,

> There's a lot of modal music that is played every day throughout the world. It's particularly evident in Africa, but if you look at Spain or Scotland, India or China, you'll discover this again in each case. If you want to look beyond the differences

in style, you will confirm that there is a common base. [. . .] Certainly, the popular music of England is not that of South America, but take away their purely ethnic characteristics—that is, their folkloric aspect—and you'll discover the presence of the same pentatonic sonority, of comparable modal structures. It's this universal aspect of music that interests me and that attracts me; that's what I'm aiming for.[17]

Consequently, the saxophonist had not only begun to listen to field recordings from Africa but to folk music from India, South America, China, and Europe as well. At the same time, what allowed these variegated elements to congeal into an artistic whole were Coltrane's roots in the blues as well as Elvin Jones's polyrhythmic drumming.

In fact, the Afropolitan aesthetic at work in Coltrane's music overlaps with Hughes's literary artistry to such an extent that Miller's observation on the poet's memoir might as well appear in the liner notes to *Africa/Brass:* Coltrane, too, as much as Hughes,

> translates one nation to another and then reinterprets the reception by the second nation back to the originating one. Hence, the autobiographer becomes a two-way mirror whose brilliant adaptation of the diverse national lights it receives enables it to speak to varying nations expressing diverse cultures. Since each national expression is an adaptation, however, neither one is completely the same. However much the globe may seem to approximate Harlem, an inspirational and distinctive quality of the community persists.[18]

In this sense, *Africa/Brass* and *I Wonder as I Wander* both anticipate Moraru's cosmodernism in that they pose "being-with as a formula of authentic—because authentically self-conscious—being. 'I know and am myself "with," because I am and am known with and by an other.' 'I can bear witness to myself and the world, because I have borne with-ness': this is the cognition, the cognition as self-cognition the cosmoderns attain and also the recognition they demand for themselves no less than for those with whom they gain this knowledge."[19] Jazz's Afropolitanism prefigures the cosmodernist response to late globalization because jazz, from its very beginning, was (not so) paradoxically both a distinctly African American art form and "world music." *I Wonder as I Wander*, in very much the same way as *Africa/Brass*, bears "with-ness": it articulates that "authentic" blackness actually thrives on hybridity, that it harnesses the possibilities inherent in the reconfiguration of individual and communal identities emerging from transnational encounters, without vacating the historical ritual ground of the black experience in the New World. The sonic with-ness occasioned by the Afro-kinetic crossing of literal and figurative borders results in a diasporic citizenship—that is, a mode of belonging that is fundamentally a *process* across time and place, a process that seeks to reconcile and/or reconfigure the terrors of history by creatively contravening received taxonomies of ethnicity, culture, and nationhood.

In contrast, Niles's and Walker's accounts of the origins of "I Wonder as I Wander" are each an effort to situate music in a putatively authentic, undiluted, and therefore stable context—that of quaint, isolated Appalachian mountain folk in one version, and that of the segregated space of the slave quarters in the other. But Hughes's autobiography isn't interested in this kind of authentication, nor is Coltrane's music: instead, *I Wonder as I Wander* transmits jazz music's inherent transnationalism into the world. Even in the faraway Turkmen capital of Ashgabat, the poet's Harlem Victrola sounds the bond of a common humanity that transcends culture, ethnicity, and nationhood: "Perhaps it was because of music that my room became a kind of social center. Everywhere, around the world, folks are attracted by American jazz. A good old Dixieland stomp can break down almost any language barriers, and there is something about Louis Armstrong's horn that creates spontaneous friendships." At the same time, "It's *my* music," the poet insists to Soviet apparatchiks, "and I wouldn't give up jazz for a world revolution."[20] And so, Hughes the wanderer and Coltrane the seeker share the same transformative aesthetics, one in which transnationalism does not somehow dilute the blackness of Afropolitanism but amplifies it. To the tune of jazz, both aspire toward an imaginative reconfiguration of a blackness—and therefore of a humanity—that flies alongside Benjamin's angel of history. Certainly, though, the poet's reconfiguring rarely, if ever, expresses the hieratic ecstasy of Trane's music: fellow tenorist Jimmy Heath said of Coltrane, "He had that eruptive feeling that [Charlie] Parker had—of exploding into chords."[21] That the saxophonist's spiritual quest sounded increasingly rapturous is therefore more a reflection of the different pace at which he tended to travel, but he and Hughes certainly processed the impressions they gathered along the way in strikingly similar ways as both of their journeys are propelled by the same Afro-kinesis.

The perambulations of Hughes's autobiographical persona and Coltrane's musical explorations are therefore a planetary extension of Benjamin's figure of the flâneur as archaeologist of modernity, whose roving is a localized activity of sensory accumulation. The Afropolitan flânerie of both the poet and the jazzman performs a creative traversal of indurated ethnic and national borders, yet its transnational trajectory is nevertheless grounded in the understanding that the newly reconfigured self that may emerge, however temporarily, from "with-ness"—the encounter with the other, across the border—ultimately cannot, and maybe *should* not, transcend the exigencies of historical time. As memory in motion, *I Wonder as I Wander*'s final scene concludes by assuming a narrative stance perpetually poised before the unknown; and so the book's transnational flânerie, mnemonic as it is, does not lead *away* from the black experience in the New World, or somehow desiccate or erase an "authentic" African American identity, but in fact amplifies it, and does so on a worldwide scale. The freedom and self-determination that is to be won by traveling, again and again, to the brink of the unknown is akin to the sonic travels of the improvising jazz musician in general, and of the freewheeling late-period Coltrane in particular: *Africa/Brass*'s "Song of the Underground Railroad" transposes Ralph Ellison's observation about geographical kinesis occasioning "the transformation of individual fortune" into Hughesian memory in motion.[22]

How Hughes wrote indeed as a jazzman, not only as a poet but as a memoirist too, is further underscored by the fact that he revisited the same trope to describe jazz that had produced the title of his first autobiography. *The Big Sea* concludes with the poet's realization that "Literature is a big sea full of many fish. I let down my nets and pulled. I'm still pulling."[23] Thus, the final two sentences turn a narrative of poetic divestment into a new resolve of artistic accumulation that anticipates *I Wonder as I Wander*. But a few years before the publication of the sequel, Hughes had given a talk entitled "Jazz as Communication." In it, he described jazz as

> a great big sea. It washes up all kinds of fish and shells and spume and waves with a steady old beat, or off-beat. [. . .] Some water has chlorine in it and some doesn't. There're all kinds of water. There's salt water and Saratoga water and Vichy water, Quinine water and Pluto water—and Newport rain. And it's all water. Throw it all in the sea, and the sea'll keep rolling along toward shore and crashing and booming back into itself again. The sun pulls the moon. The moon pulls the sea. They also pull jazz and me.[24]

The poet's big sea of jazz washes over all kinds of borders; it doesn't assimilate its innumerable stories and histories but carries them into the far-flung nets of curious, daring fishermen like Langston Hughes and John Coltrane. "Jazz is a heartbeat," Hughes concludes; "its heartbeat is yours. You will tell me about its perspectives when you get ready."[25]

❡ ❡ ❡

Hughes, the lone seafarer on the big sea of music, accumulates in his literary net impressions of people and places, mnemonic fragments that he subsequently assembles into an artistic jazz-vision of the world. In pulling in all kinds of objects in his net, the memoirist posing as Afropolitan fisherman combines oceanic flânerie with yet another figure with a close kinship to the flâneur, that of the collector. The "Happiness of the collector," writes Benjamin, is the "Happiness of the solitary: tête-à-tête with things. Is not this the bliss that sways over our memories: that in them we are alone with things that coalesce silently around us, and that even the people who then appear partake in this reliable, allied silence of things. The collector 'stills' his fate. And that means, he disappears in the world of memory." Collectors as "physiognomists of the world of things" become "interpreters of fate," and "for the true collector," all the many items in his possession come together "to form a whole magical encyclopedia, a world order, whose outline is the *fate* of his object."[26]

The record collection of Rob Fleming, the narrator of Nick Hornby's 1995 novel, *High Fidelity*, is just such a "magical encyclopedia," one that reveals "a world order" whose beat, or so Rob desperately hopes, will communicate to him the perspectives of his own heart. Unlike Hughes's memoirs or "Jazz as Communication," *High Fidelity* also delimits a rock aesthetic that is propelled by a different kind of kinesis than Coltrane's and Hughes's Afropolitanism. Musically, the rock aesthetic overlaps with the jazz aesthetic as they both share a common ancestor—the blues—but they also differ in significant ways. Rob is a postadolescent thirtysomething who runs Championship Vinyl, a gathering spot for rock music connoisseurs in London. He is given to rearranging his personal record collection according to his amorous misadventures, likes to put together mixtapes, and obsessively compiles "top five" lists: not just "five best side ones track ones of all time" but also "My desert-island, all-time, top five most memorable split-ups," for example.[27] Like *I Wonder as I Wander*, Hornby's novel is a story of accumulation; in marked contrast to Hughes's autobiography, *High Fidelity* revolves also around the process of canon-formation, an exercise of consolidation that determines who belongs and who doesn't. While the compilation of these top-five lists remains mostly a comical game of one-upmanship in arcane rock 'n' roll trivia between Rob and his two employees, the garrulous Barry and the introverted Dick, their arguments are fueled by the exact same disagreements that have accompanied the formation of literary canons, namely the debate over representative inclusiveness versus inherent artistic quality. More significantly, this dynamic also informs the transliteration from page—Nick Hornby's novel—to screen—the Hollywood movie adaptation—from analog to digital, and from London to Chicago. In the course of the plot's migration across the Atlantic, the romantic comedy's ostensibly multicultural, multiethnic inclusiveness is counteracted by a subtext that reinscribes the figurative American race record into the third millennium and the digital age. Moreover, the juxtaposition of Hughes and Hornby and their respective soundtracks also foregrounds how the jazz aesthetic is much more receptive to dynamic transnationalisms than its rock 'n' roll counterpart: in perhaps no other musical genre—certainly not in rock—is the tension between a respect for and knowledge of the tradition, on one hand, and the perennial demand for constant innovation and reinvention, on the other, so constitutive as in jazz.

One thing Hornby's protagonist does share with this jazz dialectic is that he recognizes the urgent need to reinvent himself. Rob feels as if life has passed him by. Running Championship Vinyl does not yield him much satisfaction anymore, and Barry's smug and uncompromising elitism, in particular, tends to turn potential customers away rather than attract them. So, Rob is brooding over where exactly his life went wrong, especially in terms of his relationships with women. Hurting from his most recent breakup with Laura, he reorganizes his personal record collection: "I often do this at periods of emotional stress. There are some people who would find this a pretty dull way to spend an evening, but I'm not one of them. This is my life, and it's nice to be able to wade in it, immerse your arms in it, touch it." This time around, Rob rearranges the sequence of his prized vinyls in the order he purchased them and concludes that "what I really like is the feeling of security I get from my new filing system."[28] Establishing a sense of order and control in an otherwise aimless, rudderless life is Rob's placebo. In reconfiguring his records into a newly meaningful interpretation of his past, he assumes the Benjaminian mantle of collector: the act of collecting, writes Benjamin, "is a grand attempt to overcome the wholly irrational of the object's mere existence through its integration into a new, expressly devised historical system, the collection. And for the true collector, every single object in this system becomes an encyclopedia of all the science of the epoch, the landscape, the industry, the owner from which it stems." And so "within this narrow field" of the record collection, its accumulator designates himself a physiognomist of the world of sound and an interpreter of the fates of others, especially that of his former lovers, as well as his own.[29] To Rob, the "irrational" Laura, just the latest in a long line of women whose thinking he has been at a loss to divine, is being subsumed into a new, encyclopedic order of his life that is not only legible but audible, too. Rock collector that he is, his "narrow field," however, has no place for Hughes's wide-ranging Afropolitanism or Coltrane's turbocharged Afro-kinesis.

Rob has no truck with flânerie either, Benjaminian or otherwise. Benjamin's flâneur is mobile and drawn to the "optical"; Rob, like Benjamin's collector, is stationary and drawn to the "tactile."[30] Moreover, the flâneur always harbors a certain disregard for hierarchies. In stark contrast, Rob, like all serious collectors, is obsessed with hierarchies and rankings about anything and everything. The periodic reorganization of his record collection as well as the compulsive compilation of top-five lists and mixtapes, the latter activity a "science" all its own, along with the constant and vociferous debates with Barry and Dick, amount to exercises in canon-formation, to determine who's worthy and who's not. For instance, Rob insists that Laura does not belong in his personal list of the top five most painful breakups: "Can you see your name in that lot, Laura? I reckon you'd sneak into the top ten, but there's no place for you in the top five; those places are reserved for the kind of humiliations and heartbreaks that you're just not capable of delivering."[31] In other words, Rob conceives his own personal canon of lost paramours as a means of self-empowerment and social control (no matter how illusory). To a lesser degree, so are the compilation of mixtapes and the arguments with Dick and especially Barry—and these debates, be they with others or in Rob's mind, are fueled by the exact same disagreements that have accompanied the formation of literary canons. Canon-formation, of course, is and has always been an exercise in power. John Guillory deems the conflict between conservative and liberal critiques of the canon "one of the more important events in the history of twentieth-century criticism," but he is quick to add that in order to understand the constitution of the canon, "we must see its history as the history of both the production and the reception of texts. We must understand that the history of literature is not only a question of *what* we read but of *who* reads and *who* writes, and in what social circumstances"—or, for that matter, who listens to the opening track of what album, or who ends a relationship with whom.[32] Therefore, in order to understand how exactly canons function, we must put their formation in a larger social and historical context.

That context changes dramatically in the movie adaptation of Hornby's novel, even though the basic plot remains the same, and even though the script reprocesses entire passages from the book verbatim. Directed by Englishman Stephen Frears, the film version of *High Fidelity* was distributed by Disney's Touchstone Pictures and came to theaters across the United States in the spring of 2000, netting a respectable $6.5 million on opening day as the fifth highest-grossing movie that weekend.[33] Rob still owns Championship Vinyl, where he employs Dick and Barry, still smarts over the recent breakup with Laura, and is still rearranging his record collection and debating all kinds of top-five lists with his buddies at the shop. The trajectory of the film's action follows closely that of the book, where Rob eventually comes to realize, after some more comic detours of the amorous kind—a fling with American folk-pop singer Marie LaSalle, the pathetic visits to his "top five" lost loves to find out what went wrong—that Laura is indeed the true love of his life. A maturing Rob reunites with Laura in the end and even manages to revive his dormant career as a disc jockey.

The single most significant change is the transposition of the novel's plot from the suburbs of London to the city of Chicago. For John Cusack, who not only stars in the role of Rob but also cowrote the script and served as coproducer, the transatlantic move to his hometown was "probably the simplest part of the whole process, 'cause when I read Hornby's book I could transpose it directly from London to Chicago. I mean, I knew where Rob would spin his records; I knew the record store, you know, from different areas in my life in Chicago; I knew when he got depressed he'd go to the Green Mill; I knew all the places he'd go."[34] This was further facilitated by the fact that the script was cowritten by D. V. DeVincentis and Steve Pink, who had worked with Cusack before on *Grosse Pointe Blank*. The trio had been collaborating since they first met in high school in Evanston, near Chicago. To director Frears, on the other hand, "The idea of it not being set in England was quite shocking" at first. After all, back in the Thatcher era of the 1980s, Frears was one of the most visible representatives of New British Cinema, a school of socially engaged filmmaking that also strove to emancipate itself from U.S. models. Moreover, he had witnessed firsthand the so-called lad lit craze that swept over Great Britain in the decade following, for which Hornby's books—*Fever Pitch* and *About a Boy* were also eventually made into feature films—were a significant catalyst. But after reading the script, the director, too, became convinced that it was "rather a good thing, taking it out of England" as it would enhance a "human predicament" that ostensibly "universalized the story."[35] At the same time, he notes, "We were able to film it in really nice neighborhoods that endlessly reminded me of London."

The second most visible alteration concerns the character of Marie. In Hornby's book, Marie, like all the other characters, is white by default as she is not endowed with any ethnic markers other than the generic "American": she is "some obscure American folk/country artist, someone with a cult following which could arrive together in the same car," Rob thinks initially. But when he sees her perform at the Lauder, a neighborhood pub, he volunteers that she is "pretty, in that nearly cross-eyed American way—she looks like a slightly plumper, post–*Partridge Family*, pre–*L.A. Law* Susan Dey." And it is this performance that reminds Rob of one of his fantasies: "All my life I wanted to go to bed with—no, have a relationship with—a musician: I'd want her to write songs at home, and ask me what I thought of them, and maybe include one of our private jokes in the lyrics, and thank me in the sleeve notes, maybe even include a picture of me on the inside cover, in the background somewhere, and I could watch her play live from the back, in the wings."[36] In other words, Rob thinks of Marie—of women in general—in much the same way as he does his record collection, and someone like Marie embodies the ultimate prize for any obsessive collector: the rarest of rare vinyls, only one pressing known to exist. For Rob, women and music are on obverse sides of the same LP.[37] Perhaps, then, he is the Old World counterpart of Carribee Joe and his collection of drums, stuck on his island of a record collection pondering over lost love.

In the movie, it is Dick who gives a very similar description of Marie to Rob—with one important addendum: "She's kind of Sheryl Crow-ish, crossed with a, uhm, post–*Partridge Family*, pre–*L.A. Law* Susan Dey kind of thing, but—uhm, you know, uhm, *black*." With *Cosby Show* alumna Lisa Bonet in the role of the suddenly blackened Marie DeSalle, Rob's canon-formation of music and women acquires a new dimension, especially since he avers early on that LPs are "fetish properties [. . .] not unlike porn." There is no equivalent line in Hornby's novel, even though the "vinyl addicts" who frequent Rob's shop are clearly fetish hunters as well: discovering that rare record one has been hankering after for years "is a prickly, clammy, panicky sensation, and you go out of the shop reeling."[38] Casting Bonet was apparently Frears's idea: "In this English novel, to have an affair with an American singer would be to an Englishman rather—extraordinary. It would be, you know, like meeting a film star or something. In his [Rob's] eyes, she is glamorous. So I eventually found

Lisa because I was looking for someone who had that quality and who had something exotic about her. But, uhm, she made sense in a way that nobody else did." In other words, for the British readership of Hornby's novel it is sufficiently "glamorous" that Rob sleeps with a white American singer-songwriter. But once Rob has become "Americanized" for the movie now set in Chicago, the best way to retain Marie's "exotic" allure is, apparently, to make her black. The seeming inescapability of the blackening of Marie is accentuatd even more when Frears commented that the role of Dick, who needs to be neither "glamorous" nor "exotic," could have been played by two or three actors other than Todd Louiso.

Other than Dick's halting description of Marie as a black Susan Dey, the movie does not make any other overt references to race. Nevertheless, racial allusions persist throughout, especially in the juxtaposition of black Marie with white Laura, Rob's true love. Laura is played by Danish actress Iben Hjejle.[39] Blond and blue eyed, Laura's ethnicity is subtly reinforced by a Nordic subtext: she drives a Swedish-made Saab, her mother (played by Anglo-American actress Laura Whyte) speaks with a Scandinavian accent, and on the mantle over the fireplace in her parents' house we spot two tiny flags of Denmark and the United States. Moreover, in the film the reviving of Rob's career as a DJ and his newfound joy in running Championship Vinyl is solely Laura's doing. In the novel, on the other hand, Marie plays a crucial role in putting Rob's life back on track: she gives a promotional concert at Championship Vinyl and later colludes with Laura to force Rob into DJing again. But Marie's movie counterpart is last seen outside of her apartment building saying goodbye to Rob after their tryst and walking down the street in the opposite direction. Thus, the romantic teleology of the movie abruptly exiles black Marie "stage left," as it were, and steers Rob inexorably toward Nordic Laura, the "proper" object of white sexual desire in Rob's romantic canon. Marie, the great-niece of independent Madam Zajj, is too disruptive in her self-determination: "That's how it works, right? I think it's okay if we feel horny and fucked up at the same time. Why should we be denied our basic human rights just 'cause we messed up our relationships?" Unwilling to budge on her opinion of sex as a basic human right, she adds, speaking of her ex-boyfriend James (a distant descendant of Carribee Joe, perhaps), "I won't let that asshole come between me and a fuck." No wonder the film banishes Marie's character halfway through as she is not at all shy about expressing the unruliness she inherited from her uppity relative.

This racially tinged form of canon-formation is also echoed by the film's use of music. Marie's solo performance at Championship Vinyl in the book is replaced in the film by the Kinky Wizards, a punk-rock group of underage "little skate fuckers," as Barry calls them, whom Rob signs on to his newly formed record label, Top-5 Records. The final scenes are set at the Double Door—an actual club in Chicago that features mostly alt-rock and other underground music—with Rob's comeback as a DJ paired with the release party of the Kinky Wizards' debut EP, *I Sold My Mom's Wheelchair*. Additionally, Barry and his band, Barry Jive and the Uptown Five (formerly known as the experimental rock combo Sonic Death Monkey), perform a cover version of Marvin Gaye's "Let's Get It On," which to the surprise of everyone is a very good rendition indeed. At the same time, though, the lead vocal performance by Barry—played by Jack Black—is clearly a parody, with comically exaggerated moans and movements. And, of course, his backup band, the Uptown Five, are all white.

With the Africanist presence in the form of Marie exiled from the film halfway through, the sole blackness that remains at the end are the strains of Stevie Wonder's "I Believe," which lead into the credits. Wonder's "I Believe" was later covered by both Peter Frampton and Art Garfunkel, an irony that contradicts the film's raciological canon-formation but is not sufficient to undermine it. Ultimately, the film admits African American music only if its black practitioners are rendered invisible or if it is appropriated by white musicians—in a way, the cinematic updating of blues singer Big Bill Broonzy's classic lines:

> Now, if you's white, it's all right;
> If you's brown, stick around;
> But if you's black,
> Oooh, brother:
> Get back, get back, get back.[40]

Broonzy's take on racialized canon-formation is particularly telling given that the Mississippi native got his start in the music business in the city of Chicago, still today the world capital of the blues.[41] In the movie, however, Chicago's storied musical past—which, after all, also includes Sun Ra's interstellar big band jazz and the avant-garde explorations of the AACM—is almost entirely invisible and inaudible. In fact, the only homage to the city's rich musical history is a brief snippet of Jean-Baptiste "Illinois" Jacquet's 1947 jump-blues recording of "Robbin's Nest," heard in the background of the scene in which

Rob has dinner with Penny Hardwick, the number two on Rob's list of the top five most painful breakups. "Developed as a way to make oneself heard within the city, South Side Chicago jazz" of the 1920s was, much more so than blues, "an object lesson in economic and cultural adaptation" and "served for many who heard it to affirm that a pluralistic urban society was possible," writes music historian William Howland Kenney.[42] Frears's film envisions this possibility in the character of Marie but ultimately rejects it in favor of the old homogenizing certainties and stabilities.

Representative of the movie's replication of Broonzy's racial stratification is the scene where a distraught and depressed Rob is pondering his recent breakup with Laura behind the counter at Championship Vinyl. An Asian American customer approaches him and asks, "Hey—do you have soul?" Rob's whimsical reply is, "That all depends . . . Back row, right next to the blues." In that very same scene in Hornby's novel, however, Rob directs the customer—whose ethnicity is not identified and is therefore, again by default, white—to the *front* of the store: "'Have you got any soul?' a woman asks the next afternoon. That depends, I feel like saying; some days yes, some days no. A few days ago I was right out; now I've got loads, too much, more than I can handle. I wish I could spread it a bit more evenly, I want to tell her, get a better balance, but I can't seem to get it sorted. I can see she wouldn't be interested in my internal stock control problems, so I simply point to where I keep the soul I have, right by the exit, just next to the blues."[43] Symbolically, the prominent placement of Championship Vinyl's blues records serves as a reminder that blues is the bedrock of *all* popular music, that blues is the source from which the entire rest of the store's musical stock springs. Though quite probably coincidental, the rearrangement of Championship Vinyl's interior layout in the course of its relocation across the Atlantic and from print to screen is nevertheless telling of the raciological stratification of the movie in general, which is a reprise of sorts of the British Invasion across a deracinating white Atlantic, and which ultimately banishes the Africanist, Afro-kinetic presence, quite literally, to the back of the store.[44] The film's Championship Vinyl is instead full of references to Chicago's *contemporary* music scene: flyers and posters announce such performers as Liz Phair, Urge Overkill, and others, all of whom have a Chicago connection. After Laura moves out, Hornby's Rob repeatedly contemplates having the logo of the legendary Chicago-headquartered Chess record label painted on his living room wall, acknowledging at least implicitly the central contribution of blues to contemporary popular music.

The legendary label had its heyday in the 1950s and 1960s and was instrumental in popularizing the electrified Chicago blues of Muddy Waters, John Lee Hooker, Howlin' Wolf, and many others. In signing the likes of Chuck Berry, Etta James, and house arranger Willie Dixon, the Chess output also chronicles the birth of rock 'n' roll.[45] Cusack's Rob Gordon, however, expresses no such awareness—there is no Chess logo to be seen in either his apartment or his store, not even in his daydreams. And so, Chicago's storied musical history suffers the identical fate as the Chess logo in the transposition from print to screen.

Toward the end of the film, with the two lovers happily reunited, Rob counsels Laura, "How can you like Art Garfunkel and Marvin Gaye? That's like saying you support the Israelis and the Palestinians." The musico-racial landscape of the movie purports to celebrate a late-capitalist commingling of styles, genres, and ethnicities, gesturing toward a cosmodern worldview of with-ness. In fact, it reinscribes the historical exigencies of the American "race record," even in the digital age, all over again. The seemingly irreconcilable conflict in the Middle East that Rob references to justify the sonic segregation of what he categorizes as distinctly and irrefutably "white" and "black" musics returns us, once again, to Langston Hughes's trusty traveling companions, his Harlem Victrola and record collection. The prelude to *I Wonder as I Wander*'s final wonderment finds Hughes as a newspaper correspondent in war-torn Spain. Reporting from besieged Madrid, he is headquartered at the Alianza hotel, which, like much of the rest of the city, is subject to regular shelling from Franco's Falangists. During intense bombardments, the guests and employees of the Alianza retreat to an adjacent building that they consider to be the safest spot in the entire complex. Hughes learns that in order to drown out the noise of exploding shells, its occupants have taken to playing records: Beethoven, Brahms, or, most ironically, Wagner. "But when I appeared with a box full of swing music," notes Hughes, "folks would call for Benny Goodman, Duke Ellington, [Jimmy] Lunceford or Charlie Barnet." During one especially heavy shelling, "The amplifier was turned up very loud—so loud in fact, that unless a shell had fallen in the courtyard, we could hardly have heard it. The automatic record player would repeat a disc innumerable times if one wished. So that night of the big bombardment, the Jimmy Lunceford record we kept going continuously until almost dawn was 'Organ Grinder's Swing.'"[46]

In contrast, the end of *High Fidelity*, both the book and the movie, shows an ostensibly wiser and chastened Rob compiling yet another mixtape for

Laura, engaging in yet another exercise in canon-formation, even though he claims that "Tonight, for the first time ever, I can sort of see how it's done."[47] The process of sonic selection and segregation is therefore still in place, as *High Fidelity* simply cannot conceive of a world where Marvin Gaye and Art Garfunkel *do* appear back to back on the same mixtape. The rock aesthetic of *High Fidelity* differs from the jazz aesthetic of *I Wonder as I Wander* and *Africa/Brass* in a kinetic sense: the former, despite the more advanced, more portable sound reproduction technology of magnetic audio tape, is all about drawing and enforcing sonic boundaries, which in turn stunts kinesis. In Hornby's novel, one of the many complicated rules Rob references for the making of a good mixtape is that "you can't have white music and black music together, unless the white music sounds like black music." Generally, Rob applies racialized standards of authenticity to popular music, in which "black" music is experienced as somehow more genuine, earthy, real. For example, to Rob, Solomon Burke is "authentic, and black, and legendary, and all that sort of thing."[48] Both of these lines are missing from the movie, perhaps because they were deemed too direct a reference to raciological taxonomies. The Afropolitan approach of both Hughes as well as Coltrane, on the other hand, requires a movement that traverses, circumvents, and blurs boundaries. Nor is this a distinction occasioned by the juxtaposition of artist and consumer. Like Rob, Hughes's persona is a *consumer* of recorded music, not its creator. But like Coltrane, Hughes heard in jazz a highly kinetic music whose Afropolitanism resonates on a transnational, planetary scale even as it signifies on its origins in the black experience in the New World—the blues.[49] Hughes's listening is *transformative:* the poet-memoirist listens with the ears of the Afropolitan jazzman. Rob's listening is merely *associative:* he listens with the ears of the jilted lover.

Coltrane had perhaps the biggest ears of any jazzer and voraciously consumed all kinds of musics from all over the world—except rock. This is not to suggest that jazz is "better" than rock, just that even Coltrane's catholic tastes apparently didn't hear in rock 'n' roll anything that might complement his Afro-kinetic explorations.[50] The stabilizing dynamics of rock in *High Fidelity* explain in part, perhaps, why this is so. Jazz *tends* to remain a process-oriented performance in the moment, even in the recording studio, while rock *tends* to be more end-product oriented. This distinction is most readily apparent in the disparate way jazz and rock albums are recorded. Take, for example, Gov't Mule, at its inception a bare-bones blues-rock trio of guitar, bass, and drums, and an offshoot of the Allman Brothers Band, the granddaddy of the 1990s jam band scene. The Mule had been instrumental in creating that scene, and still rightly prides itself on its improvisational agility and relentless tour schedule. Still, the demo tapes alone of what would become their self-titled debut album, released in 1995 and containing a seven-plus-minute paean to Coltrane entitled "Trane," had taken several weeks to record. Earlier that same year, young lion Eric Alexander, who had burst onto the jazz scene after winning second place in the Thelonious Monk International Jazz Saxophone Competition, recorded his sophomore album, *Full Range*, on the Dutch Criss Cross label with a sextet—in a single day. Some years later, on the other side of the digital revolution in the music business, Alexander would record his own tribute to John Coltrane, *Chim Chim Cheree*, with his regular quartet for the Japanese Venus label; once again the entire album was in the can in one day. Also in 2009, Gov't Mule, now augmented by a keyboardist to a quartet, took several months to put to tape their ninth studio album, *By a Thread*.[51]

Jazz, even more so than rock, is a music that puts a premium on the development of an individual, recognizable voice. The three rock 'n' roll aficionados at Championship Vinyl "agreed that what really matters is what you like, not what you *are* like."[52] In jazz, though, even a tribute album like *Chim Chim Cheree* undercuts *High Fidelity*'s ultimate postmodernist credo, as not very many lay listeners will confuse Eric Alexander's tone with John Coltrane's. As a tribute album especially, *Chim Chim Cheree* amplifies that even when jazz is harking back to the past explicitly, nostalgically perhaps, its Afro-kinesis does not result in an exclusively retroactive temporality since improvisation demands a musical storytelling that is interactive in essence and whose dynamics are not only shared but constantly renegotiated.[53] Thus, Alexander's tributary nod to the musical past is not a merely nostalgic or museal recreation, but one crucially dependent on the instantaneization of communicative creativity in that one moment, in that one measure in that particular song, in that single day in the studio. In this context, it is quite telling, too, that Rob and his buddies never reminisce about, let alone rank, the interactive communication (improvised or not) of any live concerts they, as lovers of music, surely must be attending often.

This is not to say that rock cannot be informed by Afropolitanism and Afro-kinesis—Paul Simon's seminal *Graceland* album certainly was. Though Simon's project has been attacked as just another instance of the great white antihero immersing himself in an indigenous culture, especially since the singer-songwriter circumvented the United Nations' cultural boycott of the apartheid regime in South Africa and his lyrics were deliberately apolitical, the actual dynamics of cultural exchange during the recording process were more complex than love-and-theft. Also, the South African pop music that inspired Simon had been hybridized by its own practitioners already, decades before the American singer-songwriter set foot in the racially segregated nation. Still, outspoken, all-black hard rock quartet Living Colour schooled Simon on the limits of rock's border-crossing kinesis when they pointed out on "Elvis Is Dead" that they, unlike Simon and his entourage on *Graceland*'s title track, had every reason to assume that they would not be welcomed at Presley's mansion, even and especially when accompanied by Little Richard and Maceo Parker—before offering up an alternate route with "Solace of You."[54]

"Elvis Is Dead" contains a rap by Richard and reminds us that by the turn of the millennium, hip-hop had succeeded jazz and rock as the most popular ambassador of Afro-kinetic transnationalism. The metaphor of fishing that Langston Hughes applies to both jazz and literature finds in hip-hop its complement in sampling and interpolation. Socially conscious hip-hop in particular has been helping itself regularly to snippets from the jazz archives. Activist-rapper Asheru, for instance, cofounder of the Hip Hop Education Literacy Program (H.E.L.P.), sampled Duke Ellington's "In a Sentimental Mood" for his 2003 collaboration with Talib Kweli on "Mood Swing." The entire track is built around the distinctive six-note vamp the pianist introduces on the 1962 version that opens *Duke Ellington and John Coltrane*. While the song is indeed a discursive exchange between Asheru and Kweli, elevating the original lyrics' ode to romantic love to a story of community uplift, the Ellington sample (and tenor saxophone interpolation of the theme's ascending beginning) remains simply accompaniment, a stationary carpet on which the rappers' message unfolds. The result, musically, is a diachronic conversation between the two emcees and technologically reproduced sound across time, between man and machine. The conversation taking place in Rudy Van Gelder's studio between Ellington, John Coltrane, plus Aaron Bell and Elvin Jones, is a synchronous conversation between *performing bodies*. Here, Afro-kinesis is compressed, happening in real time—and, once again, *Duke Ellington and John Coltrane* was recorded in a single day.[55]

In hip-hop, therefore, the process of music-making itself tends to be subordinate to the end product, much like in rock. Even in commercial rap designed to effect corporeal kinesis, and even at its most transnational, hip-hop's discursive scripts resound in a soundscape that is almost always scripted itself, relying on diachronicity also when it is performed with live musicians. One seminal hip-hop group that has been utilizing technologically transcribed sound less and less are Die Fantastischen Vier (the Fantastic Four)—Fanta 4 to their fans. Pioneers of German-language hip-hop, their megahit "Die da!?!" was the first rap song not in English to climb to the top of the charts in Germany, Switzerland, and Austria in 1992. Lyrically a comedy of errors vaguely reminiscent of the romantic entanglements orchestrated in Hans Janowitz's *Jazz*, the discursive script of "Die da!?!" is laid over an infectious groove that derives, transnationally, from two sources: similar to Asheru and Kweli's "Mood Swing," it is a keyboard riff that furnishes the musical carpet, an interpolation of the Fender Rhodes piano on "Mister Magic" by the godfather of smooth jazz, Grover Washington Jr. The riff is augmented by another interpolation, the bass line from Indian chanteuse Asha Puthli's cover version of J. J. Cale's "Right Down Here," which also provides the sampled horns. Puthli's claim to jazz fame, perhaps not quite coincidentally, is that she sang on two tracks on Ornette Coleman's *Science Fiction*. To be sure, there's not a whiff of harmolodics anywhere in Fanta 4's oeuvre, but musically "Die da!?!" is still a thoroughly Afropolitan affair, limning a planetary arc from the long since shuttered Bijou Café in Philadelphia, where Washington regularly held court, to Puthli's native Bombay, to the Stuttgart studio in Swabia where Fanta 4 hatched *4 gewinnt*.[56] The decision in the early days to rap in their native German rather than imitate their African American heroes came after a trip to the motherland of hip-hop in the late 1980s, when they realized that the 'hood of black rappers was a different world altogether than their snug middle-class existence in Stuttgart. Explains Michael Bernd Schmidt, aka Smudo, "the longer we traveled in the U.S., the better we understood the language and the country, the more absurd it seemed to us to rap in English. It had as much soul for us as if we were to make music in Latin."[57]

The commercial success of *4 gewinnt*, however, enabled them to tour with a nine-piece band and rely on samples only sparingly. Since then, the kinetic motor of the live band has been Flo Dauner, one of Germany's premier jazz drummers. For their twentieth-anniversary bash, Fanta 4 turned to tenor saxophonist Lutz Häfner, who was also put in charge of about half of the arrangements for the resulting triple album *Heimspiel*, recorded on the grounds of Stuttgart's Neckar Park in 2009—the same year Gov't Mule released *By a Thread* and Alexander whipped up *Chim Chim Cheree*. Häfner's task was formidable indeed, for in addition to Die Fantastischen Vier, the stage was also occupied by a seven-piece horn section, half a dozen background singers, and the full fifty-three-piece orchestra (including oboes, bassoons, and a decidedly unhip harp) of the National Academic Bolshoi Opera and Ballet Theatre of the Republic of Belarus, directed by Englishman Jules Buckley. While the new arrangement of "Die da!?!" hews close to the original, retaining all its signature elements, the opulent string section in particular reminds us that in Europe at least, disco never sucked. The only sample that remains is Luke Skywalker's line when he first espies Princess Leia in the German synchronized version of *Star Wars: Episode IV—Eine neue Hoffnung:* "Wer ist sie? Sie ist wunderschön!"[58] But despite the many jazz musicians on stage, despite the rearranged "Die da!?!" launching into outer space with a truly international crew alongside Skywalker's X-wing starfighter to cross, perhaps, Madam Zajj's flight path, there is almost no improvisation over the course of the entire show; the massive orchestra alone clearly required careful scripting and rehearsing. Save for a few drum fills here and there, a handful of heavy-metal guitar solos, and one long piano solo on the lounge-jazzy "Tag am Meer," the live performance is the end product of a long, diachronic dynamic of musical planning and sonic assemblage, not a process of extemporization in real time.

Still, "Die da!?!" too unfolds a soundscape that is thoroughly Afropolitan. It is precisely for this reason that Okie rocker J. J. Cale's *Really* might really be in Rob Fleming's record collection, but *Duke Ellington and John Coltrane* and "Mood Swing," let alone *4 gewinnt*, certainly aren't. For Rob, rock music is an instrument of demarcation, of canon-formation, something that jazz and hip-hop's transgressive, and transgressively transnational, energies cannot give him. Improvised musics in particular do not harmonize with Rob's melomaniac epistemology: "there is perhaps something singular about improvisation in that improvised performances are marked by and enable degrees of openness, mutuality, and collaboration that are heightened and intensified when compared with the interpretation of scored works"—or with the utilization of technologically transcribed sound snippets, as in hip-hop—"and that necessitate participants' real-time co-creation and negotiation of social-and-musical relationships," writes Georgina Born.[59] Consequently, jazz ranks right in between beer coaster tricks and "pretty desultory what-do-you-do kind of stuff" in the hierarchy of meaningless pub talk when all other subjects of conversation have been exhausted, while Rob's top-five list of dream jobs slots at number three "Any kind of musician (apart from classical or rap)."[60]

Whatever amount of kinetic energy rock may possess becomes utterly sublimated by the time the story of *High Fidelity* unfolds in the Windy City.

The film ultimately consolidates boundaries, instead of breaching them like *4 gewinnt* or *Chim Chim Cheree*. Its abrupt dispatching of Marie assures that the unruly potential of (Afro-)kinesis remains stunted. Musically, the most rebellious sounds are coming from the Kinky Wizards, but even the noisy neo-punk of *I Sold My Mom's Wheelchair* is co-opted to help launch a commercial enterprise—Rob's resuscitated career as a DJ and now as a label owner and record producer—and a healthy, long-term, monogamous relationship that does not violate the historical injunction against miscegenation—Rob's reunion with Nordic Laura. The only threat to the "establishment" emanating from the Kinky Wizards' CD release is that the young punk rockers are all underage and might cause the club to lose its liquor license, as Rob jokes. Society's and the law's moral precepts are to be upheld, and so the Kinky Wizards end up being more Justin Bieber than Sex Pistols. Nothing in *High Fidelity*, the movie or the book, is "beyond category" in the Ellingtonian sense; on the contrary, the dynamics between the characters and the music returns them all into pre-existing, socially sanctioned categories.

In stark contrast, Hughes and Coltrane are both all about crossing borders, propelled by the jazz aesthetic's inherent, and inherently transnational, Afro-kinesis. Certainly it is no coincidence that Langston Hughes's canon-formation of "top four artists to play when sheltering from enemy fire," as the guys at Championship Vinyl would put it, consists of Goodman, the Jewish Chicagoan of Polish ancestry; Ellington, the scion of black Washington aristocracy and pioneer of the "jungle style"; Lunceford, the Mississippi native from the land where the blues was born; and Barnet, the white New Yorker, who was among the very first bandleaders (together with Goodman) to integrate his orchestra. What even the guys at Championship Vinyl might appreciate, if they were only aware of it, is that *Africa/Brass* provided crucial inspiration to the members of the Byrds and the Grateful Dead.[61] And just as surely it is no coincidence that Hughes's multiethnic top four, the Alianza's *Brigadas Internacionales de Jazz* as it were, are marshaled not really for an exercise in canon-formation but are enlisted in the fight of true democracy against nefarious fascism, just the latest of humanity's struggles, epic and eternal, of justice and freedom against tyranny and oppression.

Here as elsewhere in the autobiography, jazz resonates from what Rashida Braggs terms "dislocated listening," that is, from a dialectic of distance and closeness that enables the attuned listener "to hear atop and beneath the surface of African American experiences," and that results in an ontological revelation in cultural time rather than geographical space. Dislocated listening, says Braggs, "disorients and discomforts, such that it prompts a vulnerability and more open reception to a new experience. In the process of this distancing, one not only moves away but toward harsh realities of African American experiences, specifically to a history of suffering"—and hence to an ontological stance strikingly similar to Benjamin's angel of history.[62] And so, when Hughes finally departs Madrid, "I took the night express to Paris, bags, banderillas, books, typewriter, shrapnel and all still intact. But," he adds laconically, "I no longer had any phonograph records to lug. Those I left with my friends in Madrid to play during the bombardments."[63] And so maybe, just maybe, we could learn something still if we download onto our collective iPod not the soundtrack to *High Fidelity* but Lunceford's "Organ Grinder's Swing" (or, indeed, Marvin Gaye's "What's Going On") and, say, Beethoven's *Eroica*—and play them back to back.

CHAPTER 4

"Good Morning, Heartache"

Sound, Script, and Improvisation in Paule Marshall's
The Fisher King and Steven Spielberg's The Terminal

In the Alianza Hotel, Langston Hughes's Harlem Victrola spins jazz as an improvised palliative against the traumata of history. But a palliative it is: Afropolitan jazz can remind us of our common humanity, a humanity that transcends cultural and national citizenship, but it cannot divert Falangist artillery shells or evade Toyota Land Cruisers converted to technicals. Hans Janowitz's hope that the kinetically jazzy sounds flooding the Weimar Republic would lead to a "United States of Europe" proved illusory: it took another world war and another genocide before his dream would be revived. And even when it was, jazz could not stop the cargo truck that killed eighty-six flâneurs and flâneuses on the beachfront Promenade des Anglais in Nice on July 14, 2016, a terrorist attack that in turn caused the venerable jazz festival, dating back to 1948 and France's oldest, to be canceled.[1] This, then, is also why *I Wonder as I Wander* resists closure and ends in wonderment. Despite the very different musical aesthetic (and emotional depth) that propels *High Fidelity*, Rob wonders exactly the same: "What came first—the music or the misery? People worry about kids playing with guns, or watching violent videos, that some sort of culture of violence will take them over. Nobody worries about kids listening to thousands, literally *thousands* of songs about heartbreak, rejection, pain, misery and loss. Did I listen to pop music because I was miserable? Or was I miserable because I listened to pop music?"[2] The fact that Langston Hughes's music consists of much more improvisation than Rob Fleming's does not mitigate either one's doubt. And if there is one jazz icon who embodies Rob's heartbreak and pain, it has to be Billie Holiday.

Among the songs Lady Day recorded at her fourth session for the Decca label on January 22, 1946, was a ballad expressly written for her entitled "Good Morning Heartache." When Holiday signed with Decca, her manager, Milt Gabler, had a specific vision for the singer's public image: "Every time I had listened to Billie, she was either with Teddy Wilson's band or one of the great bands that John (Hammond) put together. But I felt Billie a different way—as a pop singer. To me, when you went into a club and listened to Billie, she'd lovingly sing these slow ballads. She would sing for losers and really really read a lyric. So I wanted torch songs for Billie."[3] "Good Morning Heartache" is, in many ways, representative of the shift these sides amplified: the score modulates between minor and major keys, and the arrangement leaves no room for improvised solos, save for a few bars of Joe Guy's muted trumpet fills and Joe Springer's cocktail-piano stylings, pitting Holiday's by now slightly raspy voice against a small string section. The lyrics, too, are penned to fit Lady Day's new image and echo, quite fittingly, the standard blues stanza:

> Good morning, heartache, you old, gloomy sight.
> Good morning, heartache—thought we said goodbye last night.
> I turned and tossed until it seems you have gone,
> But here you are with the dawn.
> [. . . . .]
> Now every day I start by saying to you,
> "Good morning, heartache, what's new?"[4]

This ode to lingering trauma is exemplary of Holiday's image, gelling in the early 1940s, as the iconic embodiment of *l'artiste maudite*, "as a martyr to an uncaring world and to her own bad judgment," in the words of Francis Davis; ever after she recorded the sensational "Strange Fruit," Lady Day had "become an all-purpose Our Lady of Sorrows—embraced by many of her black listeners (and by many women and gay men) not just as a favorite performer but as a kind of patron saint. She touches such fans where they hurt, soothing their rage even while delivering a reminder of past humiliations, and the potential for more."[5] Or, as clarinetist Tony Scott explained it, "A singer like

Ella [Fitzgerald] says, 'My man's left me' and you think the guy went down the street for a loaf of bread or something. But when Lady says, 'My man's gone' or 'My man's left me,' man, you can see the guy going down the street. His bags are packed, and he ain't never coming back. I mean like never."[6]

Fittingly, then, Billie Holiday's recordings are a favorite with Hattie Carmichael, the former manager and lover of the late jazz legend Sonny-Rett Payne and guardian of his grandson in Paule Marshall's *The Fisher King*.[7] At the center of the novel is the musical legacy of Sonny-Rett, an expatriate pianist of West Indian descent who perished as a victim of police brutality in the Parisian *métro* in 1969. Fifteen years after his brutal death, Hattie returns Stateside with his grandson, Sonny, to help celebrate the opening of a community center in Brooklyn that is designed not just to revitalize the neighborhood and commemorate Sonny-Rett's music but also to resolve the long-standing feud between Sonny-Rett's family and that of his late wife, Cherisse. The center is but the latest project of the Three R's Housing Group of Central Brooklyn, headed by the pianist's older brother, Edgar, dedicated to "Reclamation. Restoration. Rebirth."[8] The group's motto accurately distills the "script" each character has for the pianist's legacy: they all attempt to appropriate Sonny-Rett's memory as a means to negotiate the personal trauma of his premature, violent death, the familial trauma of the ongoing discord between the Paynes and the McCullums—and underlying it all, the lingering historical (and transnational) trauma of the Middle Passage and diasporic rupture. Generally, the literary criticism on Marshall's oeuvre hears music as the salve to heal trauma, to "counteract cultural disintegration," where jazz "heals the wounds between the living and the dead" and is reconfigured as a "regenerative mode of African diasporic expression." Marshall's readers thus echo the tenor in jazz studies, which posits improvisation as sounding "ancient dreams of freedom communicated through the angular linguistics of urban experience."[9] *The Fisher King*, however, does not bear out these Pollyannaish takes on Marshall's use of music, as none of the characters' scripts succeeds in transposing the antiphonal synergies of improvised jazz into a healing vision of a familial, transnational, and/or ethnic community no longer fractured by trauma.

The novel's catalytic jazz moment occurs on October 12, 1947, when young Everett Carlyle Payne is invited to participate in the jam session that traditionally ends the Sunday concert at the Putnam Royal. He spent the previous few years on an army base just outside of Kansas City—birthplace of Charlie Parker—woodshedding on the piano and honing his chops. To the astonishment of all, when he takes the stand "of all things, he decided to play some hokey-doke, Tin Pan Alley tune called 'Sonny Boy Blue' from a Broadway musical at the time."[10] But under his fingers the song becomes, true to the transformative imperative of the jazz aesthetic, something else, something entirely new:

> Everett Payne took his time paying his respects to the tune as written, and once that was done, he hunched closer to the piano, angled his head sharply to the left, completely closed the curtain of his gaze, and with his hands commanding the length and breadth of the keyboard he unleashed a dazzling pyrotechnic of chords (you could almost see their colors), polyrhythms, seemingly unrelated harmonies, and ideas—fresh, brash, outrageous ideas. It was an outpouring of ideas and feelings informed by his own brand of lyricism and lit from time to time by flashes of the recognizable melody. He continued to acknowledge the little simpleminded tune, while at the same time furiously recasting and reinventing it in an image all his own.[11]

The performance, almost twenty minutes in length, leaves the audience in stunned silence until one of the Putnam Royal regulars leaps to his feet and rechristens the pianist "Sonny-Rett" on the spot. Thus, jazz music figures here once again as the sonic marker of African American identity and cultural practices: Sonny-Rett's improvisation frees the music from its mainstream, Broadway-authored script—the chord and note symbols on the musical staff, the lead sheet of "Sonny Boy Blue"—and reinvents it as a journey of Afro-kinetic self-determination at the conclusion of which Everett Carlyle Payne, the nondescript boy from around the block, is renamed and reborn as Sonny-Rett Payne, giant of jazz. The novelist's literary "transcription" of the pianist's solo also reflects most accurately the peculiar dialectics of Afro-kinetic time: what the improviser is doing in any given moment shall accrue meaning only in conjunction with what he is about to have done in the next.[12] To put it differently, any rhythmic-melodic figure the pianist instantiates "makes sense" only if it turns out to have been part of the transformation from Everett to Sonny-Rett.

Among the witnesses to this momentous renaming and rebirth in jazz are best friends Hattie Carmichael and Cherisse McCullum, sitting at a table in the back near the bar. Hattie, abandoned by her mother at an early age and brought up in a series of foster homes, is an aspiring singer as well as a jazz connoisseuse who works at the local record store, where she and Sonny-Rett regularly confer on all things jazz. Cherisse is the stunningly beautiful only child of Florence Varina McCullum-Jones, transplant from rural Georgia who climbed the social ladder to the very top of Brooklyn's black aristocracy. Cherisse has always been interested much more in boys and beauty products than in jazz, but hearing Sonny-Rett perform sparks something in her. "I'm not moving till he comes back here and tells me what he did to that song," she insists. Come back he does, but his return instantly dashes Hattie's own dreams and hopes: "She told herself it might not be as bad as it felt at the moment; that in fact, it might be the way things were meant to be, the three of them like the connected sides of the triangles she used to draw in geometry in high school, with her as the base, joining them to herself. It might be the way—the only way—to have them both."[13] The ensuing whirlwind romance between Cherisse and Sonny-Rett defers Hattie's dream, if only temporarily. It also flies in the face of the social and cultural scripts of Brooklyn's black community: bucking parental expectations and admonitions, the lovers elope to Paris and cut all ties to Brooklyn, especially after they are joined by Hattie and arrange themselves in a harmonious *ménage à trois*.

Sonny-Rett is the son of Ulene Payne, an immigrant from the West Indies who came to New York City after the Great War in search of a better life, "with nothing but a gripsack and two willing hands," as she still proudly proclaims. Amongst the clutter and trash filling her apartment is her most cherished possession, an old player piano. Above the piano is a large, framed photograph of young, unsmiling Sonny-Rett, when he was still Everett Carlyle, sitting at that same pianola with a music book of Bach sonatas behind him. From the beginning, Ulene felt Everett's interest in jazz, that "Sodom and Gomorrah music!" as she calls it, as a betrayal of the literal script of the paper rolls inside the pianola as well as the figurative script of her aspirations of upward mobility. She had paid for piano lessons, after all, so that her son could one day become a classical concert pianist playing Carnegie Hall. Still smarting over what she perceives as Cherisse's corruption of Everett, she now seeks to reinscribe her "script" onto her great-grandson. On his very first visit to her foreboding brownstone, Ulene directs little Sonny to the pianola: "For the longest time she repeatedly steered his hands back and forth across the keyboard, showing him how the game was played, while the huge sheet of paper with its hieroglyphic cuts and nicks rolled majestically down before his eyes, and the music soared. Finally, she released his hands, stood up from over him, said, 'All right now, you's to play till I say stop.'" The pianola is not just a symbol of gentrifying upward mobility; its mechanized script, the paper rolls controlling the keyboard apparatus, sounds a musical mobility aimed at exorcizing Afro-kinesis by mechanically reifying an irretrievable past desirous of an impossible future.[14]

Right across from Ulene on Macon Street lives her bitter rival, Florence Varina McCullum-Jones. Long since widowed like her enemy, also in failing health, she too clings to her own script of what should have been. She sought to mold her only child into a "milk-chocolate Shirley Temple girl," sending her to acting and dancing lessons as well as a weekly appointment at an upscale beauty parlor. For her, jazz is "crazy music," the Three R's Group a "gang of thieves" without regard for the historical importance of the McCullum mansion in particular and the neighborhood in general, "all those W.I.s" (West Indians) responsible for the community's demise. Florence's script is represented by and in the family Bible as well as the plaque on her brownstone that confirms the origins of the "Magnolia Grandiflora," the stately tree on her property, in (fictional) Varina, Georgia, in 1899. The McCullum mansion is now a regular stop on the historical tours organized by the Landmark Conservancy's Brooklyn chapter, the plaque and tree a tangible reminder to all of the McCullums' long-since-eroded superior social standing and leadership in the community.[15] Even young Sonny has his script: he has become fascinated with medieval fortresses and knights; he carries a drawing block with him everywhere he goes and, especially in times of stress, likes to draw elaborate medieval castles. As his signature, "he always drew a miniature version of himself in full armor, his visor down, in the bottom right-hand corner of the very drawing. Himself armed with a lance, a wicked-looking halberd, or a Sir Lancelot broadsword." Sonny has always kept the significance of this script sub rosa, until he explains it to Edgar's grandchildren, his cousins: "[. . .] his namesake grandfather lived inside the castles and fortresses, placed there by him for safekeeping. And not only was he safe, he was healed as well, all the bloody head wounds he had suffered in the Métro completely healed, his head, his face restored to that of his billboard image above the entrance to the Club Belle Epoque."[16] In other words, the script of Sonny—like the scripts of his two great-grandmothers as well as anybody else's—aims to reclaim, restore, and revive the legacy of Sonny-Rett Payne from the lingering trauma of his premature death in the belly of the Parisian *métro*.

The pianist himself initially experiences Paris as a place that liberates him from the racial exigencies of America, from the social strife caused by his love for Cherisse, and from the maternal expectations of assimilation and upward mobility. Like so many other artists of African descent, Sonny-Rett finds in Paris the veritable City of Light: "It was what he'd been hoping for all along [. . .], a place, a country, a continent where he could breathe and create without a lot of hassle." The titles of some of his signature compositions signal the transnational inspiration infusing his music, the Afro-kinetic "The Crossing" or the Afropolitan "Europhoria," for example. But he is soon disabused of his illusion of Paris as a multiethnic, multicultural refuge, and once again his song titles like "Continental Free-fall" and "Sodom and Gomorrah Days and Nights" reflect this change.[17] The general waning interest in jazz music is accompanied by rapid changes in the city's demographics, as more and more immigrants—some legal, many not—flock to the French capital from the former colonies in the wake of World War II and the escalating conflict in Algeria.

Even though Sonny had picked up a debilitating heroin habit while still Stateside, those who knew him believe that he was a victim of racially motivated police brutality, possibly because the French police suspected him of being a *sans papiers* himself—like the nameless, shadowy figure of his grandson's biological father, a transient street vendor who was soon deported back to his native Cameroon (coincidentally, Manu Dibango's country of birth). By the early 1980s, the *quartier* in which Sonny and Hattie now live is characterized by sharp divisions drawn along ethnic lines, by mistrust and antipathy, particularly toward "*les Algériens*."[18] The sociocultural dynamics that divided Sonny-Rett's native Brooklyn have been transposed onto his grandson's Paris: the people who fancy themselves guardians of communal identity feel threatened by the flood of newcomers, whom they view as wily upstarts at best, dangerous criminals at worst. This demographic process has been accompanied by a rapidly declining interest in jazz: Sonny-Rett kept playing throughout the final decade of his life, but his engagements, also because of his drug addiction, became less and less prestigious until he could barely find gigs playing dingy strip bars. Much like Charlie Parker, he was even eventually banned from the jazz club that still displays his portrait over its main entrance.

By linking the waning popularity of jazz music with the rise of social tensions in the city of Paris, prompted by the violent processes of decolonization, *The Fisher King* thus appears to imply that jazz is, or could be, the salve to heal the traumatic ruptures caused by the effects of transnational migration flows. Moreover, Edgar's script for the memorial concert honoring his late brother is true to the motto of the organization he heads: he hopes the concert will restore, reclaim, and resuscitate not only the legacy of the legendary pianist but also the community as a whole. His great-nephew picks up on Edgar's designs, too: finding himself thrust into the role of mediator between the still bitterly feuding Ulene and Florence, Sonny urges both of them to attend the memorial concert Edgar is staging. He even takes a peace offering, a branch from Florence's magnolia grandiflora—now "a piece of medieval weaponry"—to Ulene.[19] His efforts, however, are rudely rebuked, and his plans of reuniting the feuding great-grandmothers at the memorial concert are foiled. Edgar's plan of reclaiming, restoring, and rejuvenating his brother's music is successful, but the concert presents only a sanitized script, the folder of notes from which Hattie reads in between numbers recounting but "the public saga" of Sonny-Rett Payne.[20]

Moreover, the enactment of the public script comes at the heavy cost of deepening the private, divisive traumata of the past. Right after the concert, a triumphant celebration of improvisational Afro-kinesis over the stasis of musical script, Edgar reveals to Hattie that he intends not just to reclaim his brother's musical legacy but his brother's grandson as well. Hattie's personal script, the papers she had drawn up by a shady French lawyer to gain sole custody over Sonny, would not hold up in court, Edgar tells her, especially if accompanied by the extensive documentation he had his own lawyers dig up of her substance abuse, of her employment as wardrobe mistress at a lowly cabaret just a few skimpy garments removed from a strip club, and of their current living situation in a tiny apartment with virtually no amenities in a poverty-stricken neighborhood taken over by illegal immigrants and riddled by street crime. Lacking closure, the metascript of Marshall's own novel ultimately concedes that Afropolitan art can mediate traumatic "heartache" only in the *process* of its creation, appearing to champion the kinesis of sound over the stasis of script. But even then, even when improvisational artistry leads to reclaiming, restoring, and resuscitating the self as it does for Sonny-Rett at the Putnam Royal that night, what happens in the aftermath of that process may very well defy control, precisely *because* it is improvised. Hence, *The Fisher King* cannot help but release its characters into uncertainty and doubt.

To be sure, the character of little Sonny does embody the transnational triangle of the Black Atlantic. Upon learning that his biological father was Cameroonian, Florence tells her great-grandson, "You got some of all of us in you, dontcha? What you gonna do with all that Colored from all over creation you got in you? Better be something good."[21] What "good" Sonny might be able to do remains unanswered at the end. Sonny does not have an exceptional musical talent like his grandfather; in fact, he becomes bored rather quickly with Ulene's pianola. His graphic talents do inscribe a diasporic blackness onto the Arthurian legend—his sketches in this sense are a script within the script of *The Fisher King*—and thus draw a link between the human cost of pre- and postcolonial empire.[22] But Little Sonny's medieval fortresses also conceal a wound that cannot heal. Hence, he is about to experience yet another rupture, a new trauma: Hattie makes it unequivocally clear to Edgar that she does not intend to return to the United States under any circumstances; in fact, she has already purchased her burial plot in the Montmartre cemetery, as she proudly informs him. Sonny is therefore going to lose Hattie, whom he dearly loves, and whom he considers his "fathermothersisterbrother and the only 'kin' he'd ever known."[23] And so, Sonny, the personification of the Black Atlantic triangle of travel, trauma, and triumph, is going to find himself in the same ontological position as Billie Holiday:

> Good morning, heartache, here we go again.
> Good morning, heartache, you're the one who knew me when.
> Might as well get used to you hanging around:
> Good morning, heartache, sit down.[24]

Marshall's novel consistently privileges the flexible dynamic of improvised sound over the stabilizing codes of script, and as such it cannot help but deny us closure. What improvisational skills can Sonny-Rett's grandson develop? He will, without a doubt, ask heartache "what's new" when he wakes up in the morning. Even if he were to harness such skills, improvisation in and of itself is not guaranteed to heal trauma: the real life of Billie Holiday tells us this, as does the fictional life of Sonny-Rett Payne. For Tamil American jazz pianist Vijay Iyer, improvisation is a "primal" aspect of human consciousness: "It is something that structures who we are and how we move about in the world. This means," he is quick to add, "that there is improvisation that you could call 'bad' or 'evil.' That is, for every Roscoe Mitchell or Charlie Parker or John Coltrane or Alice Coltrane or Mary Lou Williams, you also have a Dick Cheney or a contractor with Halliburton with an itchy trigger finger. They're improvising too."[25]

Yes, the oppositional, liberatory *potential* of improvised jazz is intrinsic to the art form and, as Sonny-Rett's reinterpretation of "Sonny Boy Blue" demonstrates, becomes higher the further it distances itself from preconceived scripts, but whether improvisation, even "good" improvisation as per Iyer, can open up *sustainable* spaces of larger personal and communal freedom is anything but certain. Marshall's novel seeks to reenact such a distancing gesture, ironically in writing, by subverting the conventional, facile equation of jazz and self-determination. Just as Billie Holiday's life was a blues-tinged tale of both artistic triumph and personal trauma, just as "Good Morning Heartache" modulates from minor to major and back, so does *The Fisher King* orchestrate no swinging rainbow transnationalism, no groovy post-postcolonial harmonies: Sonny-Rett Payne's family name is, after all, a homonym of a symptom of trauma. If not tomorrow morning, then one morning soon when we wake up, all of us will find that "old gloomy sight" sitting in the recliner in the corner of our bedroom. The question Marshall and Holiday, Iyer and *The Fisher King* all pose in different ways, is what untapped improvisational resources will we manage to marshal in our next encounter, tomorrow morning, with the heartaches of history?

"Sonny Boy Blue," the tour de force at the heart of Marshall's novel, is ultimately an improvisation within an artistic *form*. To improvise *life* is a rather different proposition indeed, and a potentially much more hazardous one, because there *is* no "form" as such. After all, the etymology of *to improvise*, *im-provisius*, means dealing with the unforeseen. In the sociopolitical arena, the "script" is more often than not authored ex post facto, as Iyer's reference to Dick Cheney—one of the chief architects of the U.S. invasion of Iraq—suggests.[26] This, ultimately, is why *The Fisher King* lacks closure, and in this way the novel is like an alternate take of its famous predecessor, James Baldwin's "Sonny's Blues." Sonny-Rett's signature tune—a fictitious song—is Marshall's homage to the Baldwin short story: its protagonist is also a pianist, has also done a stint in the military, and also struggles with a debilitating heroin addiction. Baldwin's story, too, hears jazz improvisation as but a temporary easement of historical trauma: "Freedom lurked around us and I understood, at last, that he [Sonny] could help us to be free if we would listen, that he would never be free until we did. [. . .] And I was yet aware that this was only a moment, that the world awaited outside, as hungry as a tiger, and that trouble stretched above us, longer than the sky."[27] Cherisse does indeed listen to Sonny-Rett's jazz, and the improvised performance does set them free as they elope to Paris. But trouble, longer than the bluesy sky over the Black Atlantic, stretches above them as well. Much the same kind of trouble also informs Baldwin's *Another Country*, in which jazz possesses no healing powers either, collectively or individually. Yes, music does provide drummer Rufus Jones a cathartic outlet for both love and anger, but it cannot prevent him from taking his own life. It is not his music but his suicide that prompts the other characters in the novel to at least try and come to terms with their respective identities in a racist, heteronormative America.[28]

The dynamics of artistic script and social improvisation are therefore different, if overlapping, from the dynamics of artistic script and jazz improvisation, especially under conditions of oppression. Frederick Douglass, for one, clearly understood that musical improvisation was a humanizing response to the debasement of the peculiar institution. The slaves on Colonel Lloyd's plantation "would compose and sing as they went along, consulting neither time nor tune. The thought that came up, came out—if not in the word, in the sound;—and as frequently in the one as in the other." Without the ability to consult "time" or "tune"—without, in other words, access to a script or lead sheet—musical improvisation becomes a strategy of resistance in that "Every tone was a testimony against slavery." In *My Bondage and My Freedom*, Douglass actually replaces the verb *to compose* with the verb *to improvise* in his revised description of the slave songs, as he does in his final autobiography, *Life and Times of Frederick Douglass*.[29] Musical extemporization asserts the improviser's humanity, but it cannot itself effect freedom.

Later, when Douglass has availed himself of literacy and thus the ability to write a script, his very survival depends on nonmusical improvisation and the obviation of the script: when his first attempt to escape is betrayed and he and his coconspirators apprehended, they are forced to conceive instantly of a way to dispose of the incriminating slave passes Douglass had forged for them. In response to one comrade's frantic query, Douglass tells him to "eat it with his biscuit, and own nothing; and we passed the word around, '*Own nothing;*' and '*Own nothing!*' said we all."[30] If freedom is the ability to tell your own story in your own words—as it clearly is for Douglass the autobiographer as well as for Marshall's Sonny-Rett and Baldwin's Sonny the pianist—then to "own" another's voice, the very thing that makes us human, that makes us individuals, is a dangerous proposition, even if it is, in this case, his master's voice. Douglass's quick social improvisation calls for the destruction of the script. Just as in musical improvisation, the fugitives' desperate act of eating the forged script makes no sense without what might lie ahead of them—a trial of some sort, or maybe even summary execution—nor with what lies behind them—violation of the legal injunction against human chattel's literacy. But subsequent to an unscripted act tied to a specific instant in time, in the autobiographer's *artistic* script the improvisation becomes highly stylized as well as symbolic; it is, after all, extremely unlikely that Douglass reports his instructions verbatim, that his fellow captives would have immediately understood "*Own nothing*" as a synonym for *eat the script*. The escapees' scripts fail and must be destroyed in an act of social improvisation, and so the artist's subsequent script subsumes the improvised response to the artistic *form* of the slave narrative.

The crucial distinction between improvisation—sonic or social—and writing—that is, composing—is time, space, and reproducibility. Once the forged passes are ingested, this extemporization cannot be repeated in just the same way, not even in the same physical locale. Jürg Wickihalder limns both the continuum as well as the difference between playing and writing in his account of an aphorism from his former mentor, fellow soprano saxophonist and composer Steve Lacy. For one thing, says Wickihalder, the border between improvisation and composition is "fluid":

> Composing is nothing else than improvising and vice versa—for me. It's just that the conception of time is different. With composing, you have all the time in the world—a Lacy quote, by the way: with composing, you have all the time in the world to tell a story in ten seconds; with improvising, you have ten seconds to tell all the history of the world. The beautiful thing is [. . .] Lacy's answer took exactly ten seconds! Look, with composing, I enjoy it tremendously to end up with something on paper, something you can touch, something that is *there*. With improvisation, everything is always already gone, out there in the ether—and yes, it only happens once, you'll never be able to repeat it just like that. But the creative act is exactly the same at the beginning. [. . .] When I compose, I first start to improvise, like that.[31]

As a composer, Wickihalder has the opportunity to revisit, to revise, to rewrite the history of the world as he hears it; the script is the tangible end result of his creative engagement *with* time—but as an improviser, he also exists *in* time itself. On an aesthetic if not a social level, the distinction Wickihalder articulates is the same as that between Douglass the artist and Douglass the would-be fugitive slave, or that between little Sonny's drawings and his grandfather's music. Sonny's graphic translation of the Arthurian legend is akin to Sonny-Rett's improvised transposition of "Sonny Boy Blue" as both are based on an antecedent script, and both are responses to social pressures. Sonny's creativity results in "something on paper, something you can touch, something that is *there*," something that exists also in the stability of Marshall's printed words. Sonny-Rett's defining improvisation, however, is ethereal, "gone," since it is not recorded. Similarly, Hattie is no Madam Zajj with eyes and ears wide open to the many variegated impressions in the course of her sojourns; her travels do not constitute Afropolitan flânerie because she is committed only to guarding the past, in the form of Sonny-Rett's European legacy as embodied in his grandson.

Since it cannot help but be "something that is *there*," *The Fisher King* can only present the results of textual, discursive improvisation, but not its process. Improvisation, both musical as well as social, entails the instantaneization of a particular, (largely) unscripted space-time event.[32] Moreover, the musician's extemporized storytelling is performative as well as localized: without an audience present in the moment of its creation—even if it is but a microphone and recording device—it cannot transmit its meaning. Marshall's novel therefore is also *about* improvisation, but because it is preceded, presumably, by multiple antecedent scripts or drafts, Marshall the writer is creating art within a space and time negotiated very differently than that of Wickihalder the improviser. As an improvising jazz musician (as opposed to the composer), the saxophonist's embarkation on the passage of time is essentially and intimately bound up in the moment, as is Sonny-Rett's at the Putnam Royal.

❆ ❆ ❆

This highly complex interaction of temporality, locality, and creativity paralleling little Sonny and Hattie's pilgrimage from the Old World to the New is resituated in perhaps the most frequently traversed transnational space, the airport, in Steven Spielberg's romantic comedy *The Terminal*. While jazz music provides but an obliging crutch to the plotline, the motion picture dramatizes the fluidity of *social* improvisation and its intricate relationship to the stasis of script. Opening to mixed reviews in the summer of 2004—the *New York Times* called it "a light and pleasing soufflé," while the *Wall Street Journal* dismissed it as "terminally fraudulent and all-but-interminable"—*The Terminal* paints a jaunty, breezy picture of post-9/11 air travel.[33] With the exception of the closing sequence, the story is set entirely in the international transit lounge of New York City's John F. Kennedy International Airport. This is where Viktor Navorski, a carpenter from the (fictional) eastern European nation of Krakozhia, finds himself stranded: during his transatlantic flight, civil war erupted in his homeland after a military coup, and as a consequence he is denied entry into the United States because the State Department voided his visa and suspended all flights to Krakozhia, and because the new regime rescinded its citizens' international travel privileges. As Frank Dixon, director of Customs and Border Protection (CBP) and Viktor's nemesis, explains, "The thing is, you don't really have a home, you don't: technically, it doesn't exist."[34]

As far as the cold, ruthlessly efficient, by-the-book bureaucrat Dixon is concerned, "In my line of work, there are only three things that matter: the person, the document, and the story." Nationalizing scripts, however, are always written ex post facto. Because there is no script, no "document" to accompany the disintegration of the former Soviet empire and Warsaw Pact states, and because a Krakozhian passport's script is suddenly nugatory, Dixon has no choice but to let Viktor, "a citizen of nowhere," live for nine months in JFK's international transit lounge, a transnational space of perpetual transition, a space of stateless limbo.[35] But in Spielberg's aviatic fairy tale, the transit lounge is not at all Homeland Security's purgatory of post-9/11 air travel but a glitzy paradise of postmodern consumer capitalism reminiscent of Benjamin's Parisian arcades. The glass-encased, steel-reinforced, gleaming transit lounge sports a Starbucks, of course, and other corporations maintaining a franchise lining the liminal passages of international travelers include Burger King, Swatch, Panda Express, Borders, Baja Fresh, Hugo Boss, Sbarro, Verizon, La Perla, and Yoshinoya. This twenty-first-century arcade is bedecked with dozens of national flags, symbolically turning the international transit lounge into a nonnation and "a world in miniature" of sorts.[36] In the eye of Spielberg's camera, the transit lounge functions as a gateway to a harmoniously multiethnic America disinfected and sanitized by capitalist enterprise, a global village of product placement. When the befuddled persona non grata with the voided passport asks Dixon's right-hand man, Officer Thurman, for advice upon being released into the transit lounge with but a visitor badge and a handful of food vouchers, the response is, "There's only one thing you *can* do here, Mr. Navorski: shop!" In this oasis, where the outside world, including the civil war raging in Krakozhia, is safely contained on TV screens, Viktor soon makes alliances and friendships with those who keep the terminal humming.

Of course, stateless Viktor is relegated to the very margins of consumer capitalism, at least initially, as he learns to improvise life in the transit lounge. Played with Chaplinesque amiableness by (ironically) all-American actor Tom Hanks, Viktor makes himself a home at gate 67, which is slated for renovation, forages for food and money, and his exceptional carpentry skills even land him a job on a construction crew renovating a different gate, where he is being paid under the table. The very nature of the transit lounge as a space of perpetual change, as well as Dixon's relentless scheming, force Viktor to tap deeply into his reservoir of social improvisation—good morning, international transit lounge, what's new. In the process, he manages to teach himself English and assembles a veritable rainbow coalition of new friends and allies: Enrique, the Hispanic food service worker for Aero Gourmet; Enrique's love interest, pretty United States Citizenship and Immigration Services (USCIS) officer Dolores Torres; Joe, the African American baggage handler; Gupta, the surly Indian janitor in the employ of City Shine, who initially suspects Viktor of spying for the FBI or CIA; and Amelia, Viktor's flame, the beautiful flight attendant with an unlucky penchant for "poisonous men."

Viktor spends nine months extemporizing an existence in the international transit lounge, but not until almost the end does the film disclose the reason for his dogged determination to set foot in New York City. The most precious item among his initially meager but rapidly growing possessions is an old Planters peanuts can that contains a clipping from a Hungarian newspaper of Art Kane's famous photograph "A Great Day in Harlem." As Viktor finally reveals to Amelia, his father, a rabid jazz fan, saw the picture in the paper in 1958 and was mesmerized by it.[37] He started to write letters to all the jazz greats depicted and asked them to send him their autographs, carefully collecting them all in the can. Over the next four decades, they all replied—Dizzy Gillespie, Coleman Hawkins, Count Basie, Thelonious Monk, Jo Jones, and all the others—but he passed away before securing the final one, that of tenor saxophonist and composer Benny Golson. And so Viktor is on a mission to attend Golson's gig at the Ramada Inn in Manhattan and complete his late father's lifelong project with the tenorist's signature.

From the very beginning, the film pits the fluidity of social and musical improvisation against the rigidity of legal, diplomatic script. The sequence that introduces us to Viktor shows the Planters peanuts can resting atop his passport and neatly stacked travel documents in front of the CBP officer. Symbolically, the movie heralds jazz as the border-crossing catalyst for the entire plot. Dixon's explanation that his voided visa—that is, the legal script granting the privilege of crossing international borders—makes him "unacceptable" begins the newly stateless person's social improvisations in the transit lounge, where he navigates the ramifications of the Kafkaesque labyrinth that is U.S. immigration law and the alphabet soup stirred by USCIS, CBP, DHS, and the rest. Dixon, too, feels constrained by the legal script, as the highly complex and ever-shifting diplomatic situation only authorizes him to sign a "release form" that allows Viktor to wait in the transit hall. Viktor's ensuing social improvisations are structured by the daily ritual of visits to USCIS Officer Torres, who is officiating over the script of legal entry (Viktor's Godot, as it were) and the confusingly dense forest of documents—"green form" or "light green form"—that still cannot account for the patient transient's status and incur each day anew her red "denied" stamp. Even here, though, social improvisation subverts the legal scripts of USCIS: egged on by the smitten Enrique, Viktor uses his daily visits to play Cupid with Officer Torres, and in exchange he is paid handsomely with leftover trays of airline food.

Viktor is not the only one engaging in improvisation. As Iyer pointed out, improvisation can be "good" or "bad," and so the film's villain is improvising too. For example, when Dixon discovers that Viktor feeds himself by collecting quarters from abandoned baggage carts, he immediately creates the new position of "transportation liaison for passenger assistance," designed to deprive the unwelcome "problem" of his meager income, which in turn might entice the undocumentable foreigner to violate "section 2-14" by attempting to leave the lounge and enter New York City illegally. Whereas Viktor's improvisations are aimed at subverting a preexisting script, Dixon's improvisations are designed to reinforce it. When a Russian-speaking passenger creates a critical, dangerous situation after getting caught with expensive medicine for his gravely ill father in his luggage, Dixon grudgingly decides to tap Viktor to translate, but Dixon does so only to reinforce the legal script: he insists that the bereaved son cannot bring half a dozen pill bottles into the country without a "medicinal purchase license" and sundry other documents from the hospital and doctors. Once again, Viktor's quick improvisation is simply more successful than Dixon's: after his daily dealings with Officer Torres, he has amassed an expert's knowledge of the rules and regulations of immigration and customs; he knows that a simple "blue form" suffices for medication prescribed to pets and other animals. Therefore, he argues that he misunderstood the desperate passenger, who is actually carrying medication for pet goats—the Russian word for *goat*, he maintains, sounds very close to *father* in the Krakozhian dialect. Viktor, in other words, improvises on the script of the blue form.

Yet for all the film's valorization of social improvisation, in the end the stabilizing scripts of nationhood as well as the inexorable teleology of Hollywood scriptwriting supersede the fluid, transnational dynamics of social and musical improvisation. Of course, Viktor does succeed in completing his late father's dream and collects Benny Golson's autograph, but Viktor's peanut can becomes the cinematographic counterpoint to little Sonny's drawings. Spielberg has insisted that "*The Terminal* celebrates the great American melting pot"—the silver screen version of Dexter Gordon's "The Rainbow People," if you will—yet the price the script for the director's fairy-tale ode to social improvisation demands is that the Planters peanuts can becomes a synecdoche for the entire film, a receptacle inside which the transgressive, transnational energies of Afropolitanism are safely contained, no longer capable of undermining the borders drawn by geopolitical script.[38] Viktor is not just a gifted improviser but also a proud patriot. On various monitors in the terminal, watching in bits and pieces the civil war ravage his country brings tears to the stranded tourist's eyes, even though there is no indication that he is worried about any family members or friends. One of the schemes Dixon concocts to rid his domain of the pesky eastern European is to get Viktor a hearing for political asylum, which in turn would grant him temporary status until his case is resolved. The only condition the legal script demands is for Viktor to concede that he is afraid to return to his war-torn homeland. Despite Dixon's persistent nudging, the otherwise improvisationally savvy Viktor remains firm: Krakozhia, he says simply, "is home—I'm not afraid from my home."

Nine months after his arrival at the JFK airport, the civil war ends, and diplomatic relations between the Republic of Krakozhia and the United States are restored. As Viktor celebrates in the terminal's Daily Grill Restaurant and Bar, Amelia appears with the news that he has been granted a "one-day travel emergency visa": her married lover works in the capital and has friends in high places, so she asked him to work his connections at USCIS. In exchange, however, he demanded that Amelia, who had broken off the affair after meeting Viktor, renew their relationship. An added complication is that Dixon needs to sign the visa, which he refuses to do, and instead threatens to have Enrique, Joe, and Gupta arrested for various violations of the legal script. In order to protect them, Viktor finally relents, and he is then escorted to the gate where one of the first flights from Krakozhia is about to dock. Gupta, who is in fact wanted back in India for the killing of a corrupt police officer in 1979, taps his own reservoir of social improvisation and, armed with only a mop, stops the 747 on the tarmac in order to allow his friend to complete his jazzy mission. As Gupta is taken into custody, he voices the final destination of his own long journey: "I'm going home!" The ensuing delay allows

CBP, under sympathetic Officer Thurman, to engage in an act of improvised insubordination themselves as they decide to permit Viktor, clad in Thurman's coat, to exit the airport with the unsigned visa. However, the logic of the movie demands that CBP resort to social improvisation only *after* they are assured of the existence of a legal script—signed or not—that finally codifies Viktor's unresolved, unscripted status.

Uncharacteristically, Dixon decides not to pursue the Krakozhian any longer, and so Viktor is off to the Ramada Inn, where Benny Golson holds court. Having secured the tenorist's autograph, he hails a cab; once inside, the camera shot—echoing the scene that begins with the can placed atop the passport—shows him carefully placing the final piece of the puzzle in the peanut can. Asked about his destination, Viktor repeats verbatim his friend Gupta's final words, "I am going home," seals the can shut, kisses it, and is whisked away into the brightly lit streets of the Big Apple in the movie's concluding shot. And so, *The Terminal* repatriates every one of its characters whence they came. White Viktor returns to what is presumably his racially homogeneous, beloved homeland of Krakozhia, brown Gupta Rajan is deported back to his native India, and while pale Enrique Cruz does indeed marry dark Dolores Torres in the airport chapel, the visual allusion to miscegenation is mitigated by their Hispanic names, which signal at least a shared ethnic heritage. White Frank Dixon, newly promoted to CBP field commissioner, is back to doing what he knows best: channeling the bewildering, multicolored flow of persons, documents, and stories into the airport's complicated scripts of law and order. Played by Welsh actress Catherine Zeta-Jones, white but somehow mysteriously exotic Amelia—Gupta, paranoid as he is, at first ventures that "She look like a Russian, KGB!"—returns to flying the friendly skies punctuated by the occasional loveless tryst with her married beau. Again, the names signal that the film's script is simply unable, or unwilling, to tolerate anything but a fleeting transnational dynamic as it rules out a long-term relationship between Amelia Warren and Viktor Navorski: a tender nod of recognition of their love for each other as their paths cross for one last time, outside the terminal, as Viktor is about to climb into one cab and Amelia exits another, is all that the movie grants. As Amelia tries to explain to the love-struck Viktor earlier, "destiny" prevents their love for each other from becoming reality. Only the character of black Joe Mulroy, the baggage handler, is somehow too ancillary to be awarded with a destiny of his own, but with Dixon promoted and no longer consumed with foiling Viktor's social improvisations, it can be presumed that Joe, too, returns to where he belongs, performing the manual labor of handling other people's possessions in the catacombs of JFK.

Instead of fingering the Ellisonian jagged grain, let alone singing an Ellingtonian "Immigration Blues"—or, for that matter, at least Charlie Parker's "Visa" and "Passport," the former in particular showcasing Bird in full stratospheric flight—Spielberg's warmly glowing aerial yarn clinically disinfects the effects of historical trauma and the subtext of war in particular.[39] There is no indication that Viktor's bereavement over the violent upheaval in his homeland is caused by anything other than love of country; he is single and never mentions friends or family. The festive celebration of the cessation of hostilities at the Daily Grill, led by Viktor standing on a table, culminates in the singing of the national anthem by a whole gaggle of Krakozhians, who are apparently all apolitical and amiable, just like the protagonist. Moreover, the subtext of the budding romance between Viktor and Amelia is the ill-fated relationship of Napoleon and Josephine. Amelia picks up a biography of Napoleon Bonaparte at the Borders bookstore in the transit lounge because, she explains, history books "are long and cheap and usually all about men killing each other. Like, twelve-hundred pages for $9.99, you can't beat that." After Amelia explains to Viktor in the Daily Grill the price she had to pay for his visa and turns to walk into the waiting arms of her married lover, he still wants to know, "Why you go?" In response, she reminds him of Napoleon's wedding gift to Josephine, a gold locket with the word "Destiny" inscribed inside. In Spielberg's post-9/11 fairy tale, terror simply must not exist, and war is safely consigned to either TV screens or the bargain bin of Borders: the blurry, shaky footage from the Krakozhian front lines also shows the use of technicals (even if there are no Toyotas discernible), but their psychological range does not penetrate beyond the monitors in the transit lounge. Yet even if sublimating history is what fairy tales do, Spielberg's fails to exorcise historical trauma altogether: when an exasperated Dixon is unable to find any agency to which he can hand off the pesky Viktor, he fumes, "The country's detaining so many people, there's no damn room anywhere." The war on terror infiltrates even the hermetic script of *The Terminal*.

Just as *The Terminal* strives to suppress historical trauma, it equally mutes the Afro-kinesis of jazz almost completely. Once its transgressive, transnational energies are bundled in Viktor's Planters peanuts can and the top firmly sealed one last time, once his late father's script is complete, the narrow vector of the unswervingly linear flight plan of Hollywood screenplay repatriates even jazz where it "belongs," at the very margins of capitalist consumer culture. The only times we hear any jazz music in the film is when Viktor listens to "Something in B flat" while he puts his carpentry skills to work. Fittingly, the song is, as Golson explains in terms reminiscent of Wickihalder's, "a type of melody an instrumentalist might devise while ad-libbing. In other words, the written line is almost like an improvised solo."[40] But, neither is it a Golson composition—the tune is penned by pianist Ray Bryant—nor does the snippet used in the movie feature Golson's tenor saxophone—instead, it's Art Farmer's trumpet. Golson does have a brief appearance as himself at the very close of the movie when Viktor finally arrives at the Ramada Inn, but *The Terminal* terminates "Killer Joe," Golson's signature composition, after only four measures of improvisation past the head.[41]

Not even the rolling credits are accompanied by jazz; instead, they are engilded by the saccharinely orchestral score from the pen of Hollywood veteran John Williams, which prominently features a folksy clarinet but no saxophone. The commercial release of the soundtrack album consists entirely of Williams's compositions, including the national anthem of fictional Krakozhia, and appeared on the Decca label—the very same label for which Billie Holiday recorded "Good Morning Heartache" more than half a century earlier. Golson's Afro-kinetic music does not fit into this scripted, orchestral soundscape, and so the tenorist was essentially left to his own initiative to capitalize on the Spielberg vehicle, recording a sort of companion album entitled *Terminal 1* released on Concord, a subsidiary of Decca.[42] The album features "Killer Joe" of course, and the title track's arrangement in tandem with Carl Allen's busy drum-work mimic the hustle and bustle of an airport terminal, but none of the other selections has even an indirect connection to the film. The ex post facto scripts of capitalism and nationhood supersede both love and jazz. Thus, jazz great Benny Golson is relegated back to the virtual obscurity from which Spielberg's script ever so briefly granted him asylum: in the real world of American mass consumerism, *The Terminal* in effect issues a one-day visa for Golson.

Yes, Spielberg's fairy tale confirms that jazz is America's gift to the world, but as Berndt Ostendorf and Wolfgang Rathert point out, "If you think of nation as container, you need musical boundary maintenance as to who belongs."[43] Since *The Terminal* remains invested in the primacy of script, it patrols its own sonic borders vigilantly, confining the unruly transnationalism of Afro-kinesis in a literal "container," Viktor's Planters peanuts can. With its Afro-kinesis stunted, jazz's Afropolitanism, too, is rendered mute: jazz may speak *to* Krakozhians and Hungarians—and to the small audience of mostly Americans in the Ramada Inn lounge—but it is in and of itself not polyglot, according to the film. Moreover, the can contains not sounds but more scripts: autographs on coasters, playbills, promotional headshots, and cocktail napkins. Viktor does not travel with Hughes's Harlem Victrola or Rob's epistemologizing record collection, but with a photographic script around which the autographs coalesce.

That script, "A Great Day in Harlem," the most iconic photograph of jazz history, was the brainchild of Art Kane, then a graphic designer, and Robert Benton, in 1958 *Esquire*'s new art director—who went on to become an acclaimed Hollywood filmmaker in his own right, directing among other movies the Oscar-winning *Kramer vs. Kramer*. Kane at that point did not consider himself a professional photographer at all, and Benton was only beginning to learn the ropes of the business. When the former insisted on doing the photo shoot in Harlem, "that was the moment where I began to get very nervous," confesses Benton, "'cause we will *never* be able to control this up there."[44] In a way, Benton was correct, because there was no "script" for the realization of the picture beyond their request to all the New York musicians they knew to assemble in front of a brownstone at 17 East 126th Street. When fifty-eight of the world's greatest improvisers showed up, a number that far exceeded Benton's and Kane's expectations, the two were forced to tap into their own reservoirs of social improvisation. Remarks the latter, "There were a lot of mini-dramas going on in that group. All I could do was stand and watch it happen [. . .] and just watch it flow."[45] Many of the musicians hadn't seen each other in years, some of them had never met at all, and the "flow" of social interaction engulfing the stoop of the brownstone included a group of black children, some of whom had been playing just down the street but were now magnetically drawn to the assemblage of jazz nobility, and some more peering from the windows. What occurred, in other words, was an Afro-kinetic gathering that seemed to defy all the orderly processes of a photo shoot. But, Benton says in hindsight, "One of the things I learned about movie directing, from Art in this shot, is that finally, you don't tell everyone what to do, you let them do what they're going to do naturally, 'cause that's what's going to work."[46] And what they do "naturally," of course, is improvise. Kane in turn realized that what he would have to shoot was less of a group portrait and more of a record of Afro-kinetic social improvisation in the making. As a result, "A Great Day in Harlem" shows Dizzy Gillespie sticking out his tongue while joking with Roy Eldridge, and the neighborhood kids sitting on the curb suddenly finding themselves flanked by true jazz nobility when the Count simply got tired of standing and sat down next to them. Golson happened to stand shoulder-to-shoulder with Art Farmer at the very top of the stairs, and the two of them would soon thereafter form the famous Jazztet that recorded the tenorist's signature composition, "Killer Joe," for its debut album two years later.[47] Like Long Tall Dexter, Trane, and the Duke, Madam Zajj was occupied elsewhere that day—but she did send as her emissaries not only Mary Lou Williams, Marian McPartland, and Maxine Sullivan but also Sonny Greer, the man whose trap set had been such an integral part of Ellington's "jungle style."

Thus, "A Great Day in Harlem" is a document of Afro-kinetic social improvisation. As Kane puts it, "The picture became a movie; I mean it was a still but it was really a living thing."[48] Perhaps it became such an iconic shot precisely because it works like the photographic equivalent of a live recording, capturing a moment in time that is the result of extemporized and therefore unreproducible social interaction. And as such, it is a throwback to early photography as Walter Benjamin saw it, whose peculiar dialectic of the near and the distant, the fleeting and the permanent, lends portraits and group photographs in particular a depth and delicacy—a "breathy halo" or "aura"—that is erased completely from later photography, "which is able to install a can of food in the universe, but cannot grasp the human interconnections in which it exists, and which in even its dreamiest subject is more a precursor of its salability than of its understanding."[49] In *The Fisher King*, for instance, the photographs that adorn the office walls of Edgar with "any number of important-looking people, nearly all of them white"—most prominently Robert Kennedy, on whose staff Edgar once worked—are exhibited to promote the salability of the Three R Group's economic program.[50] Early photography is something different altogether: "Despite all of the photographer's skill and careful planning in posing his model, the observer feels irresistibly the compulsion to seek in such a picture the tiny spark of chance, Here and Now, with which reality has, as it were, seared the pictorial character."[51] "A Great Day in Harlem" ignites Benjamin's "tiny spark" Afro-kinetically, and the newspaper clipping carefully deposited in the can in which Viktor's late father collected his jazz heroes' autographs symbolizes "the cult of remembrance of the faraway or deceased loved ones" emanating from auratic portraiture—like, for example, the portrait of young Sonny before he became Sonny-Rett that is resting on Ulene's pianola, whose "sepia cast" fascinates his grandson.[52]

But what Viktor carries around in his Planters peanuts can is not a copy from the first, original print of Kane's photograph but a technologically reproduced copy of a copy from a Hungarian newspaper. Benjamin concludes his treatise on photography by predicting that technological progress will cause cameras to shrink to ever smaller sizes, "ever readier to capture fleeting and secret images," which in turn virtually arrest the observer's "associative mechanism." This is the point where "the caption"—writing, script—will have to supplement some kind of epistemological value, a process "which draws photography into the literarization of all relationships of life."[53] In the case of Viktor's newspaper clipping, it cannot tell a story in and of itself. Only the movie's script—Viktor's explanation to Amelia—and the collection of autographs accompanying the clipping can give the contents of the can an auratic authenticity that limns "A strange web of space and time: a unique appearance of a distance, however close it may be."[54] Viktor's newspaper clipping and the scripts that authenticate its historical meaning, however, all reside in a Benjaminian can of food, one that can travel halfway around the world and back but which contributes exactly nothing to an understanding of jazz's transnational Afropolitanism, nor anything about human interconnectedness when subjected to the traumas of history, precisely because its Afro-kinesis is arrested, stabilized, and confined.

To be sure, the can's contents tell the story of the connection between Viktor and his father, but it is a connection after all between two citizens of Krakozhia: all the other relationships Viktor forges in the course of his nine-month sojourn in the international transit lounge are severed at the end of the film. Because the Spielberg flick confines the Afro-kinesis of jazz to the photographic script of "A Great Day in Harlem," folded and deposited in a sealed peanut can, Viktor is no flâneur, despite his improvisational skills, and despite the Benjaminian architecture of the international transit lounge. Benjamin's Parisian arcades are "the classical corso of flânerie," but the transit lounge is not a destination in and of itself—except, of course, for those who work there, and for those whose government is overthrown while en route to the United States.[55] For Viktor, "Life Is Waiting," as the double entendre of *The Terminal*'s movie posters proclaims. The state of waiting may be framed by acts of (Afro-)kinesis, but it is the very opposite of flânerie. "The man who waits," writes Benjamin, is "the countertype of the flâneur. The flâneur's apperception of historical time [is] posited against the time of the one who waits. Not to look at the watch. Case of superposition in waiting: the image of the awaited woman slides in front of a random woman. We are a dam where time backs up, which at the appearance of the awaited woman plunges down in a mighty torrent into ourselves."[56] The transit lounge is no "double ground" in Benjamin's sense, and Viktor no flâneur. Amelia, "the awaited woman," finally prompts him to open the Planters peanuts can, its open lid now no longer "a dam where time backs up," and explain himself and his reason for waiting. But it is the personal self into which time plunges him, not a historical self. Or, as the officious Dixon puts it, Viktor is "in a crack—who the hell waits in a crack?" Benjamin's flâneur is certainly drawn to the "cracks" of the metropolis, but he does not wait in them. Lorenzo Thomas posits that "diasporic time—a vortex of intercultural contradictions—is troubling."[57] If we think of jazz as diasporic time made sound, and if improvisational creativity in jazz is fueled by Afro-kinesis, then it is no wonder that *The Terminal* mutes "trouble" as much as it can. Spielberg's aviatic arcade of globalization has no room for an "Afrovision," the name of the worldwide chain of record stores Manu Dibango dreams of—an Afropolitan Championship Vinyl—whose original franchise would be for the international terminal of the Douala airport.[58]

Viktor's destiny and destination both show that social improvisation is not some kind of transnational cure-all that miraculously soothes historical trauma. Neither is musical improvisation, as Marshall's *The Fisher King* shows. At a discussion hosted at New York City's New School in late September 2001, only weeks after the terrorist attacks of 9/11, panelists heard in improvised jazz, somewhat predictably perhaps, the kind of "radical freedom" and "a radical openness to global influence and dissent" that was now needed more than ever. Iyer was on that panel, and while he was not necessarily disagreeing, he confessed that, as an improviser who has always "been concerned with the aboutness of my music," he couldn't play his piano for nearly a week: "I like to see my music as a sort of thing that at least endeavors to push you into another world or tries to maybe challenge your sense of reality or normalcy. And now it's like, well, do we even need that anymore? I mean do we need to—does anyone need to be challenged?"[59] In the intimation of futility that resonates in Iyer's words, there is the recognition that music, improvised or not, cannot heal all trauma as if by magic. After all, Benjamin scribbled in the notes for his arcades project, "A Strasbourg piano manufacturer Schmidt made the first guillotine."[60] And not even at its most transcendent is improvisation exempt from his sobering insight that "There is no document of culture which is not simultaneously one of barbarity."[61]

Says drummer Lucas Niggli, Wickihalder's occasional partner in jazz: "The fascinating thing about improvisation is that the knowledge of possible failure is part of it. To make music in real time doesn't *have* to work. But when it does, you can penetrate regions you can't access through practice and through composition."[62] Neither *The Fisher King* nor *The Terminal* manages to penetrate to regions where improvisation heals transnational disruption precisely because both are ultimately scripts not made in "real time." Perhaps the much more pessimistic ramifications in these two stories of improvised jazz as a border-crossing catalyst also stem from the fact that African world citizen Madam Zajj appears not to have visited Sonny-Rett's Brooklyn since that momentous performance at the Putnam Royal back in 1947. The novel casts Hattie as "the materfamilias" of Sonny-Rett's improvisational *legacy*, but she is not a musical improviser herself, having given up her own singing career for the pianist and his art.[63] Madam Zajj, on the other hand, does not need an emergency visa to enter the United States of America or any other nation: piloting her own spaceship allows her to bypass the transnational limbo of airport immigration procedures altogether—but not without dropping off a batch of new discs at the Afrovision store on the international concourse.

CONCLUSION

Jürg Wickihalder Gets Around

Steven Spielberg's *The Terminal* celebrates improvisation, but its own teleology blunts improvisation's sociopolitical edge. When Viktor at long last walks through the doors of JFK's international transit terminal and sets foot on U.S. soil, he hails a cab in order to complete his mission. True to the director's warm, fuzzy, feel-good multiculturalism, the driver turns out to be from Albania, and when Viktor asks him when he came to America, the laconic response is, "Ooph—Thursday." On his way back from the Ramada Inn after Golson's gig, seated in another yellow cab with his mission complete, the driver this time is no recent immigrant but asks Viktor in a typically gruff New York accent, "Where you wanna go?" With a visible sense of satisfaction, the Krakozhian passenger responds by repeating the very words of Gupta when taken into custody: "I am going home."[1]

To be sure, Viktor's social improvisations create a community of individuals from various national and ethnic backgrounds, however temporary. But in jazz music, improvisation at its best comes with an "ethical valence," says Daniel Martin Feige: "successful jazz performances exemplify in ethical terms what it means to recognize and bear responsibility for each other." The mutual recognition and responsibility the jazz context demands is something pianist Iyer also highlights: "As a musician, I personally believe that the improviser is concerned more with making individual improvisations relate *to each other*, and to his or her conception of personal sound, than he or she might be with obeying some standard of coherence on the scale of the single improvisation."[2]

This interpersonal accountability is much more pronounced in a jazz context than in most other genres: each member of the collective bears a responsibility that the individual voice of the other can be heard. In European classical concert music, for example, the individual is accountable first to the script of the musical score as well as to the director's abstract sound ideal to which the ensemble aspires. For a bass player in an orchestra to perform, say, Rachmaninoff's Piano Concerto no. 2 in C minor doesn't require much adjustment whether the piano bench is occupied by Vladimir Ashkenazy or Rachmaninoff himself. The bass player in a jazz big band, on the other hand, will accompany the reading of a chart of Ellington's "The Village of the Virgins," even in the same key and in the exact same tempo, perhaps very differently if the piano bench is occupied by Iyer as opposed to the Duke himself. In this sense, then, the script of *The Terminal*, including Viktor's social improvisations, turns out to be much more accountable to John Williams's orchestral score than to anything Benny Golson has ever played. In fact, Golson could be replaced with any of the musicians depicted in Art Kane's photograph without requiring even the slightest alteration in the storyline.[3] By failing to listen, to recognize the sonorities of Madam Zajj's Afropolitan flânerie, *The Terminal*'s script fails to bear responsibility for its characters. What this failure indicates, then, is that transnationalism—as social dynamic, economic process, or indeed as a critical practice—must first and foremost *listen* if it wants to aspire to more than a cursorily multicultural shout-out to the *Ausland*—the "outland"—if it wants to strive for a multinational, multiethnic togetherness, a *Miteinander*, instead of a mere adjacency, a *Nebeneinander*. Hans Janowitz certainly listened to, and heard in jazz music, the sonic sign of a transnational *Miteinander*.

The Terminal may send all its characters back to their designated homes, but it does get at least one thing right: tireless Afropolitan flâneuse that she is, Madam Zajj has a knack for showing up in out-of-the-way places, not just New York or Paris, and not just behind the Iron Curtain. That Switzerland was on her itinerary early on shouldn't come as a surprise. Shortly after World War I, classical conductor Ernst-Alexandre Ansermet saw Will Marion Cook's Southern Syncopated Orchestra in London and was particularly taken with its star soloist, the young Sidney Bechet. The Swiss conductor was so impressed by what he heard that in 1919, he published in the *Revue Romande* what is still considered to be the first serious, musicological analysis of jazz by a representative of the classical European tradition. Because of his keen musical ears, Ansermet also understood how Bechet's improvisations oscillate between sound and script: "The work may be written, but it is not fixed and it finds complete expression only in actual performance." The result was so infectious that he believed to have heard the sound to which "the whole world will swing along tomorrow."[4] Ansermet was a native of the Romandy, Switzerland's French-speaking region, home not only to a venerable tradition of precision watchmaking but also to the International Olympic Committee, headquartered in Lausanne; to the second-largest office of the United Nations, housed in Geneva's Palais des Nations; as well as to the International Red Cross and Red Crescent, also in Geneva. Of course, there is an international airport with an international transit area, Genève-Cointrin, which also has the unusual feature of the so-called French Sector, where, before Switzerland joined the Schengen Treaty, passengers on French domestic flights could change planes without having to pass through Swiss customs. No wonder, then, that this cosmopolitan region was so attractive to Madam Zajj. Other parts of the mountainous country, however, seem most unlikely locales for her to tarry.

The canton of Glarus is such a place. Not quite central, not quite east, not quite north—Glaronians like to joke that they live in "the free, independent Alpine Republic of Glarus"—it consists of two narrow valleys carved by the rivers of the Linth and the smaller Sernf, its rugged appearances belying the fact that it is the most densely industrialized canton in the Swiss Confederation. Glarus, writes novelist Tim Krohn with insider knowledge, "lies in the mountains, like an ax cleaves a log. The valley floor is rarely wider than a stone's throw or two, sometimes only just a slit without any bottom really, rocky cliffs rising on the sides and in the back, steep and overhanging even, to the sky and beyond. A slit is therefore what the locals call the valley, which isn't really one but two, or more rather still one but forking in the middle just like a weathered fir branch forks."[5] The canton's topography would therefore not appear to be inviting to globetrotting Madam Zajj, given the sense of entrapment with which Krohn's characters struggle. Yet even there, Krohn became exposed early on to Madam Zajj's rhythms. In fact, before he turned to writing, he was a semiprofessional musician himself, playing tenor saxophone and bass clarinet in the free-jazz collective Shasimosa Tütü. Vreneli, the titular heroine of one of Krohn's novels, in some ways even recalls the protagonist of *A Drum Is a Woman*, albeit without the soundtrack to go with it: Vreneli is a so-called *Quatemberkind*, a child of uncertain parentage but with supernatural powers; she is able to morph, mythlike, into different creatures and is driven not by Afro-kinesis, to be sure, but by the flâneuse's innate curiosity, an openness to others' experiences and points of view.

Krohn's frequent musical collaborator is the saxophonist and composer Jürg Wickihalder. A few years younger than the novelist, Wickihalder attended the same high school in Glarus, the cantonal capital by the same name, but he stuck with music. Still, he sees himself as a storyteller, too, just in a different medium: "If I hadn't become a jazz musician," he muses, "I would've liked to be a songwriter or movie score composer."[6] Intriguingly, when he works with Krohn on projects, the music often comes before the text: he'll email the writer a few musical ideas or a fully developed melody, and sometimes within the same day the response arrives with the accompanying text. Wickihalder guesses that this was the case 95 percent of the time in their reimagining of two well-known stories, the Grimm brothers' Snow White and Ovid's Echo and Narcissus.[7]

As a young lad growing up in Glarus, Wickihalder picked up the saxophone after he saw the Glenn Miller Orchestra's saxophone section brandish their gleaming, golden instruments on TV—echoing Manu Dibango's first exposure to jazz music almost half a century earlier and half a world away. As it happened, Krohn not only attended the same school but lived on the same block and actually became his first saxophone instructor. Implausibly perhaps, Glarus back in the 1980s was "a rather interesting mecca for jazz," Wickihalder remembers.[8] The old textile factories dotting the valley floor, almost all now vacant, provided perfect concert and rehearsal spaces. In addition to young, local talent like Shasimosa Tütü or the fusion project Schildpatt featuring Roland Schiltknecht's *Hackbrett* (Swiss zither), international jazz stars would find their way to Glarus, too. Wickihalder vividly remembers hearing Abdullah Ibrahim at age twelve, or fishing in the nearby Klöntalersee with trumpeter Benny Bailey, another "expat" who frequently shared the stage with Dexter Gordon during the tenorist's European years. In fact, one of the first solos the budding horn player transcribed was Gordon's contribution to Herbie Hancock's classic "Watermelon Man." From the start, though, Wickihalder was interested in progressive jazz, and he also made the unusual decision to concentrate on the difficult soprano saxophone.[9]

Still, "the Slit" proved to be too narrow for Wickihalder's talents. Retracing Gordon's journey in reverse, as it were, he landed a full scholarship at the prestigious Berklee College of Music in Boston, where he studied with George Garzone and the legendary Joe Viola. But "it was a difficult arrival all right" in the homeland of jazz—"in every aspect," not just musically, he admits. Struggling also with the language barrier, Wickihalder lived in Roxbury, in a gang-infested black neighborhood: "To have the experience, for the first time, that you're a minority yourself—well, you're on the bus, and you somehow sense, something is just weird, but you don't know what, and then you realize: you're the only white person on the bus. To have this experience—it was a precious one, but difficult too." At the beginning of his sojourn, he was mugged twice at gunpoint, but they never took his horn. The instrument he was playing, the music he was studying, signaled something "connective" to the people on his street: "Now, I don't want to be mean, but it wasn't like I was a law student at Harvard," he laughs, and after a while, he felt both accepted and safe.[10] Four blocks over, though, he would still have to take a cab.

After his return to Europe, he took lessons from Steve Lacy in Paris, where he also became one of the "test subjects" for the soprano saxophonist's influential method book, *Findings*.[11] Settling in Zurich, Wickihalder developed into a remarkably versatile improviser. These days, he can be found playing the complex, graphic avant-garde charts in the Barry Guy New Orchestra just as easily as carving out free funk with Marco Käppeli and the Even Odds, recasting sixteenth-century Gregorian chants with percussion maverick Pierre Favre just as soon as grooving to the conventional soul jazz and standards of guitarist Werner Tian Fischer's Travelogue. "Jazz," he says decisively, "can't get around globalization," and music is to him as much a "universal passport" as it has been to Manu Dibango. His own groups and projects consequently also draw on a wide variety of styles and genres; he actually wrote most of the music for his debut album in Cuba—just a few islands over from where Madam Zajj first set foot in the New World. Wickihalder's career path as a professional musician as well as his discography show that he is not really interested in recreating the "mainstream" post-bop of, say, a Dexter Gordon. BEYOND, the name of his adventurous, free-wheeling trio with Guy and Lucas Niggli, is a "subconscious" if fitting echo of Ellington's favorite phrase, "beyond category."[12] He readily admits that while he admires the musicianship and artistry of a Wynton Marsalis, he has no personal relationship to the kind of ideological historicization of jazz the trumpeter stages at Lincoln Center. The sole aspect of this brand of jazz that interests him is "the play with fissures." Still, when asked who inspires him today as an improviser, he immediately cites Don Cherry, Ornette Coleman, Charlie Parker, and John Coltrane—all four Afropolitan masters of Afro-kinesis.[13]

The transnational resonances of Wickihalder as an improviser and composer are exemplified by his piece "Last Jump." First written for the 2011 concept album *Jump!*, recorded with his European Quartet, the haunting ballad—*beautiful* is a favorite adjective of Wickihalder's, just as it was of Ellington—is part and parcel of the saxophonist's general approach to the give-and-take between composition and improvisation, script and sound. As he explains apropos of *Jump!*, invoking metaphors of flight,

> The compositional material should function as a "rich musical spring-board" for the quartet's playing. Once the composition puts everybody in the air, we are drawn by a shared energy, going in one direction, creating movements influenced by unpredictable and chaotic circumstances (like the wind or hitting partners), but still from time to time managing some perfectly synchronized figures. But nobody knows exactly where and how we will land. We just know we will land for sure and so we better prepare that landing well. This is about responsibility—life and death are very close.[14]

The call-and-response and the responsibility that come with improvised music-making is intensified in a duo setting, where individual movements are much more exposed and therefore much more dependent on the partner's response, where there is no such thing as "simply" accompanying the other. Wickihalder revisited "Last Jump" for his live album *Spring* with Irène Schweizer. As uncanny coincidence would have it, the saxophonist first met Schweizer when he played a solo program of Thelonious Monk tunes at an information session by the Verkehrsbetriebe Zürich VBZ, the municipal organization in charge of Zurich's public transportation system; perhaps city officials had looked to reroute Dibango's Toyota Corolla and in the process inadvertently introduced Wickihalder to the First Lady of European jazz piano.[15]

Recorded at the Loft in Cologne, Germany, in February 2014, "Last Jump" is flanked mostly by the pair's own compositions, by two Monk tunes—and, at the close of the program, a tongue-in-cheek cover of Leonello Casucci's "Just a Gigolo."[16] For this particular version of "Last Jump," Wickihalder switches from his customary soprano to the more sonorous tenor saxophone, appropriately capable of descending to cavernous depths. The song begins with Schweizer repeating a simple, ascending three-note motif in rubato before Wickihalder states the mournful melody over a series of mostly diminished and minor chords. As he begins to embellish the theme, he inserts a few fast, ascending runs that appear to run counter to the story the song's title suggests. His solo, too, travels in an *upward* trajectory; at the end, he lands on the theme's concluding three-note motif, first ascending, then descending, shaped like an upside-down U. Schweizer picks up where her partner just left off, toying with the inverse U shape still in rubato, but before long, the little motif morphs into a strong, rhythmic, rousingly hymnal incantation of South African township jazz that showcases the pianist's trademark percussive attack over a simple C dominant seventh / D major vamp—this is swing by any definition.[17] When the saxophone reenters once again in rubato time, it restates the theme with a prolonged crescendo, and again the flight path is generally ascending, with Wickihalder taking the three-note motif to the upper register of his horn before softly paraphrasing it, embellished by a trill, in the middle register at the song's end.

The artists are both Swiss, the audience mostly central European, presumably, the location the birthplace of Nobel-winning novelist Heinrich Böll and late Romantic composer Max Bruch—and yet "Last Jump" is a decidedly Afropolitan affair propelled by Afro-kinesis even in the rubato sections. The duo's sonic flânerie in Cape Town, on the other side of the world, is neither a geographic nor an aesthetic coincidence: Schweizer was born within a stone's throw of French and German soil in the border town of Schaffhausen and taught herself Dixieland jazz piano before she began imitating Junior Mance and Paul Bley records, but she became "musically socialized," as she says, in Zurich in the early 1960s, where she met, and frequently played with, the cream of South Africa's jazz crop.[18] Zurich became the unlikely epicenter of township jazz in early 1962, when a well-connected Swiss concert promoter managed to secure exit visas for Abdullah Ibrahim, then still going by Dollar Brand, and his future wife, singer Sathima Bea Benjamin. Brand's trio, with Johnny Gertze on bass and Makaya Ntshoko on drums, landed a steady gig in the legendary Café Africana, located in the Niederdorf, Zurich's red-light district. A club without a liquor license but with a garish décor reminiscent of Ellington's Cotton Club, the Africana's main musical attraction heretofore had been the blues piano of Champion Jack Dupree. But the Dollar Brand Trio was soon followed by others from the Cape, notably the rough-and-tumble Blue Notes around Johnny Dyani, Louis Moholo, Dudu Pukwana, and white pianist Chris McGregor.

For the young Schweizer—who was often the only woman on the premises, too—the music these South Africans had brought to the city of Huldrych Zwingli was a transformative experience: "The piano was very percussive," she remembers; "the sound seemed raw and archaic overall, it looked wild and unclean. The sound pattern was rather monotonous, it sounded foreign to European ears. But it was just this monotony, the courage for radical reduction that the South Africans had that gave their music a trippy character. For me, those nights were like being in a spiritual witch's cauldron, their jazz exploded all the norms we knew from the Americans. It swept me up, and I literally soaked up and internalized this style of playing."[19] Others took note, too: after a concert by the Duke Ellington Orchestra in the venerable Kongresshaus, Sathima Benjamin piloted the Duke to the dingy Africana, and Ellington was so impressed by what he heard that he secured Brand a record deal with the Reprise label.[20]

The legendary nights in the Africana came to an end in 1966, and the South Africans eventually moved on; the only one who still makes Zurich his home is Ntshoko, who back in the day would occasionally accompany Dexter Gordon when Alex Riel wasn't available. But township jazz has left a lasting legacy in the city's progressive jazz circles—not just for Schweizer, whose subsequent discovery of keyboard iconoclast Cecil Taylor was equally transformative yet never drowned out the echoes from the Africana. Today, a handful of ensembles draw on the music that used to fill the Niederdorf dive night after night half a century before, and Wickihalder has played regularly with two of those. One is the Tommy Meyer Root Down organization: not a traditional big band by any means, the sixteen-piece orchestra features a turntablist in addition to two bass players and three percussionists, creating a swirling mélange of sounds where Chris McGregor and Fela Kuti meet Albert Ayler and Yannis Xenakis. The other is Omri Ziegele's Where's Africa? project, whose core consists of the Israeli-born leader, Schweizer, and Ntshoko, and which merrily mixes Ornette Coleman and George Gershwin with Abdullah Ibrahim and Johnny Dyani.[21] Neither of these groups is casting a nostalgic look back at the golden age of kwela jazz by the Limmat, but both propel the musical heritage forward by extending it into new sonic territories, by resituating, à la Manu Dibango, "Africa" as an Afro-kinetic signifier not bound to geographical place. Where's Africa, indeed.

Regardless of whether it is played by the Blue Notes or by Root Down, the political subtext of Cape Town jazz is quite evident, but Wickihalder, unlike Schweizer, has rarely been explicitly political in his art. Even so, "Last Jump" also tells a transnational story about the world in which we live and the price exacted by globalization. The song was inspired by a tragic accident that occurred while he was in the studio recording the material for *Jump!*, when a base jumper fell to his death from the Sunrise Tower in Zurich in the course of a PR event for Red Bull. The energy drink giant manufactures a product based on a Thai formula, is headquartered in Austria, owns a Formula 1 racing team and several soccer clubs, and is one of the most highly visible players in the global economy.[22] "Last Jump," however, tells of a different kind of transnationalism, offering up a counternarrative to the leveling effects of corporate capitalism and globalization. Its solemn theme does pay tribute to the human cost of globalization, but the way in which Wickihalder and Schweizer develop it merges loss with resurgence, recalling Langston Hughes's trumpet player, in whose improvisations

> Trouble
> Mellows to a golden note.[23]

The Afro-kinetic dynamics of the performance's overall trajectory, the recurring motif of the inverse U, the Afropolitan integration of rousing township jazz, all this is a celebration of the flights the human imagination is capable of, connecting flights across racial and national borders. Afro-kinesis gives you wings—of a different kind. Commenting on the international reception of Hughes's literary voice, R. Baxter Miller observes that "However diverse such readers may be, they are ultimately accountable as world citizens. Those who listen sincerely to African American stories claim the right to transmit them internationally, for they understand that every nation shapes part of the greater globe even as they are shaped by it."[24] Wickihalder and Schweizer are two such "readers"—or, rather, dislocated players, to draw on Rashida Braggs's terminology again. The Afro-kinesis of "Last Jump" points backward not to the Middle Passage and the American South but to the costs of globalization and the "trouble" of apartheid. It simultaneously points forward by remaining accountable to an alternate narrative about an ever more densely interconnected world: clearly, what happens in the course of "Last Jump" is neither musical tourism nor aleatory bricolage but what Christian Moraru would call a "worlding" that stems from close and responsible *listening*. The duo turns "with-ness" into sound, a sound that flows from "a necessarily conjunctive ontology." Moreover, the ontology informing "Last Jump" is that of two transnational, planetary flâneurs for whom "those 'other' tracks, flows, and ways do not stand in our way; they provide the way. The route *is* the root; the longer way home is the safest." Or as Walter Benjamin might add here, amidst the chaos of modern life, "Strength lies in improvisation. All decisive jabs are led with the left hand."[25]

Moraru elaborates that "the ethos planetarism affirms is world-making and world-remaking in that the mental maps the planetary sanctions connect the planet's dots in ways that make visible new configurations, allotments, and hierarchies of space, discourse, community, and power."[26] Another of Wickihalder's works that amplifies this kind of planetarism by taking the long way home is the music he composed for the multimedia spectacle *Brandruf*, commissioned to commemorate the 150th anniversary of the catastrophe that befell his birthplace of Glarus: during the night of May 10, 1861, a fire broke out—its cause never conclusively determined, though arson is most likely—in a shed near the Landsgemeindeplatz that quickly grew into a conflagration destroying two-thirds of the canton's capital.[27] Once again collaborating with Krohn as well as with arranger Manuel Perovic, Wickihalder conceived the music for *Brandruf* (a call-of-distress warning in a fire) to be played by the Harmoniemusik Glarus and its counterpart in neighboring Netstal.[28] Given that these community bands are composed of hobbyists, Wickihalder's score isn't as harmonically or rhythmically complex as "Last Jump," but in deliberately drawing on the European tradition of the military march, it also points to one of the constitutive elements in the amalgam of early New Orleans jazz. The transnationalism of the music for *Brandruf* doesn't end there. The concept calls for the two community bands to be divided into four "troops" that respond to the call of fire from the four cardinal points of the compass. Each troop's musical response is inspired by the folk music from a region of the world more recently victimized by a natural disaster. The north troop's response draws on Icelandic rimur and comes from the direction of the Eyjafjallajöküll eruption in the summer of 2010; the south troop's response harkens back to the music of the Aborigines and the floods in Australia that same year; the east troop's response is influenced by traditional Russian and Pakistani folk songs and the fires around Moscow as well as the flooding of the Indus River basin, also in 2010. The west troop, finally, arrives from the Crescent City, the mythical birthplace of jazz, and the devastation wrought by Hurricane Katrina in 2005: obviously and fittingly, its musical response is inspired by New Orleans brass band music, particularly the funeral marches. But, as in a "real" jazz funeral, the west troop doesn't just play a dirge—Wickihalder makes sure it cuts the body loose, too.

The four troops ultimately meet and intermingle beneath the burning church in the city center. From the church's north tower, a demon hurls fireballs, while from the south tower, a figure that looks suspiciously like Helvetia, the female allegory of Switzerland, squirts water from her breasts on the crowd below. From the roof of the nave, a mad mountain peasant (played by Krohn himself) upbraids the townspeople, hurling their faults and foibles at them, shouting in the Glaronese dialect, "*Furt mit Schadä, jetzt hät sich's uusgiiget!*" (away with harm, no more fiddlin' around!). *Brandruf* thus stages the destruction of the old, the price exacted by history, together with a rise from the literal ashes. Musicians, writes Daniel Fueter, "want counterworlds to be illuminated, not as holiday destinations, but as challenging alternatives," and the script of *Brandruf* is clearly penned by artists with a different vision of "home" than that of the cantonal tourism bureau.[29] Significantly, it is Wickihalder's musical script, not Krohn's textual script, that calls on Glaronians to *listen* to what happens in their contemporary world, not just to their own story and history. The music of *Brandruf* resituates this provincial capital on a sonic world map, connecting it to human tragedy and human triumph around the planet, and calling on the townsfolk to think of themselves also as *world* citizens, as true planetaristi. And so, Wickihalder's aesthetics in *Brandruf* as much as in "Last Jump" echo James Baldwin's: "My own effort is to try to bear witness to something which will have to be there when the storm is over. To help us get through the next storm; storms are always coming."[30]

To be sure, Amazon.com or Amazon.de for that matter would both be hard pressed to categorize the music of *Brandruf* as "jazz." What is more, Wickihalder's "difficult" awakening to the realities of white privilege on the bus in Boston, the fact that the radius of his conjunctive with-ness is much wider than that of the gangbangers in Roxbury, signals that his world, too, is racially and historically conditioned and hence necessarily different in that it offers more avenues of connectivity than the worlds of many others. But the point is that, as an improvising musician attuned to the Afro-kinesis of jazz, the saxophonist not only recognizes these transnational avenues but travels on and with them for a stretch with the flâneur's attentiveness, always listening.

As the twentieth century, sometimes also called the American century, was coming to a close, Gary Giddins viewed the "authenticating" institutionalization of jazz in its homeland with great alarm: "Unlike Ellington, who reveled in diversity and abhorred restrictions, the guardians of musical morality are appalled by such latitude [. . .] and mean to cleanse jazz of impurities transmitted through contact with European classics, American pop, new music, and other mongrel breeds. But this is merely what Walter Benjamin called 'processing of data in the Fascist sense.' If jazz ceases to interact with the musical world around it, will inbreeding bring it down? What's to become of a music that once epitomized play and is now flaunted as culture with a capital

K?"³¹ Whether Giddins's jeremiad is accurate or not, jazz in the twenty-first century remains a niche music; Wickihalder himself readily concedes that it probably had its artistic heyday in the 1950s.³² But the Swiss saxophonist's playful approach to and with jazz, his planetary "with-ness" both musical and social, his boundless curiosity, his firm conviction of improvisation as an *ethical* enterprise, should assure Giddins that Madam Zajj is not planning to park her spaceship and retire anytime soon.

In a post-9/11 age that now seems so far removed from the end of history announced just a few years prior to the attacks, an age where the vistas of transnationalism seem to be retrenching dramatically as we witness the resurgence of nationalism as well as sectarianism around the world; where many Western and Western-style democracies, once widely believed to be the victors of the Cold War, are paralyzed by ideological polarization or systematically, sometimes violently, dismantled by leaders with autocratic ambitions; where political cooperation between nation-states is increasingly seen as weakness rather than opportunity, even within institutions like the European Union; where the global economy has tended to intensify human suffering rather than ameliorate, let alone eradicate it—in such a world, perhaps the transnational resonances of jazz can serve as a reminder how important it is that we listen, really *listen*. To the stories we are told by others, and to the stories we tell ourselves in turn. Even, and perhaps especially, in the third millennium, we are well advised to pay attention wherever it may be that Madam Zajj lands next. After all, as fellow space traveler Sun Ra seconded from the flight deck of his Intergalactic Arkestra,

> It's all what the music says of you
> It's not what the music you say of it
> IT'S ALL WHAT THE MUSIC SAYS OF YOU . . .³³

Notes

PRELUDE

1. Schlegel, "Bloss nicht."
2. Bühler, "European Jazz Legends," 72; Broecking, *Dieses Unbändige Gefühl der Freiheit*, 72–73.
3. Wickihalder and Schweizer, "Monk and More . . ."
4. Jürg Wickihalder, interview with the author, June 22, 2013.
5. Hughes, "Jazz Band in a Parisian Cabaret."
6. Dimock, "Literature for the Planet," 175, 180.
7. Wiegman, *Object Lessons*, 213.
8. Moraru, *Cosmodernism*, 22, 81, 206, 304–305, 22–23.
9. Fisher Fishkin, "Crossroads of Culture," 43. See also Dvinge, "Keeping Time, Performing Place." The spring 2016 issue also reprints the introduction of Rashida Braggs's monograph: see Braggs, "Excerpt from *Jazz Diasporas*."
10. Lewis and Piekut, *Oxford Handbook*, 1:xi, 2:46, 2:144, 2:361, 2:365. Surely there is a way to hear, say, Johann Nepomuk Hummel's improvised piano fantasies as transnational, but neither this nor any of the other contributions avails itself of transnationalism as a critical lens. See Gooley, "Saving Improvisation," 192.
11. Sterne, *Audible Past*, 3.
12. Sterne, "Sonic Imaginations," 2, 4.
13. Born, Introduction, 24. See also Bohlman, "Music Inside Out," 218–223.
14. See E. Lewis, "What Is 'Great Black Music'?"; Barg, "Strayhorn's Queer Arrangements."
15. Stoever, *Sonic Color Line*, 18, 78–131.
16. Goyal, "Introduction," 1. See also Vertovec, *Transnationalism*, 161.
17. Bechet, *Treat It Gentle*, 3.
18. Ellington, *Music Is My Mistress*, 452.
19. See Reimer, "Yusef Lateef," 65; Nicholson, *Jazz and Culture*, 21–24.
20. Goyal, "Introduction," 5. The almost complete absence of jazz in interdisciplinary transnational humanities is all the more astounding since the music has contributed significantly to

studies with a transnational bent in architecture, economics, and even astrophysics: see David P. Brown, *Noise Orders*; Phillips, *Shaping Jazz*; S. Alexander, *Jazz of Physics*.

21. Braggs, *Jazz Diasporas*, 132–134.

22. Jones, *Theatrical Jazz*, 8. See also Turner, *Jazz Religion*, 92–108; S. Coleman and the Mystic Rhythm Society, *Sign and the Seal*.

23. See Doctor, "*Jazz is where you find it*," 103–143.

24. Appel, *Jazz Modernism*, 16.

25. Ellison, "Golden Age, Time Past," 237.

26. Ellison, *Invisible Man*, 581.

27. See Sabatini, "Fred Ho's Operatic Journey"; Atkins, *Blue Nippon*, 179–184, 207–219, 241–248. See also van Nuis and Brown, "Far Away Places."

INTRODUCTION. DEXTER GORDON GETS AROUND

1. Quoted in Schermer, "Maxine Gordon"; Britt, *Dexter Gordon*, 84. See also Pavlić, *Who Can Afford to Improvise?*, 152–161.

2. Gordon, *Our Man in Paris*.

3. Quoted in Reimer, "Larry Ridley," 85. See also Gordon, *Gettin' Around*; *Blue Note: A Story*.

4. Quoted in Berendt and Huesmann, *Jazz Book*, 390. On Montoliu's solo album *Catalonian Folksongs* from 1976, most of the tunes aren't folk songs at all but popular compositions by contemporary singer-songwriter Joan Manuel Serrat. While the album as a whole has a distinctly hymnal character—the closing bookend is the Catalan national anthem, "Els Segadors"—Montoliu's positively Ellingtonian voicings and unerring sense of swing (his left hand occasionally even plays a walking bass line) are squarely rooted in the African American jazz tradition.

5. Quoted in Gitler, *Swing to Bop*, 47.

6. Gordon, "Three O'Clock in the Morning," on *After Midnight*; Gordon, "Three O'Clock in the Morning," on *Go*; Schermer, "Maxine Gordon." See also Mortensen, "Dexter Gordon and His Style," 33; Dewey, "Swinging Up North," 26–28.

7. Quoted in Britt, *Dexter Gordon*, 93.

8. Ibid., 97, 90–94. See also Büchmann-Møller, *Someone to Watch over Me*, 270–271; Mortensen, "Dexter Gordon and His Style," 63–65. Gordon, who had dabbled in acting early in his career, starring in Jack Gelber's play *The Connection*, played an expatriate jazz musician in Paris in the 1986 French feature film *Autour de Minuit* (*Round Midnight*). Directed by Bertrand Tavernier, the movie is loosely based on the friendship of critic Francis Paudras with pianist Bud Powell. Gordon plays Dale Turner, a composite character with elements from the biographies of Powell, Lester Young, and Gordon himself; Gordon's portrayal of Turner even earned him an Academy Award nomination for best actor. For an in-depth discussion of *Autour de Minuit*, see Grandt, "No Cold Eyes in Paris."

9. Quoted in Mortensen, "Dexter Gordon and His Style," 15.

10. Holiday, "I Wished on the Moon," on *All or Nothing at All*.

11. Quoted in Berendt, *Das grosse Jazzbuch*, 203–204, 206–207. See also Schuller, *Swing Era*, 223–225, 855–859; Thompson, "African Art and Motion," 319–322; Butterfield, "Race and Rhythm," 301–305.

12. Quoted in Mortensen, "Dexter Gordon and His Style," 16.

13. Ellison, *Invisible Man*, 8, 9.

14. See also Gilroy, *Black Atlantic*, 7, 19; Weheliye, *Phonographies*, 20, 50, 63; Heffley, *Northern Sun, Southern Moon*, 242, 337.

15. Berendt, *Das grosse Jazzbuch*, 439. See also Schuller, *Early Jazz*, 7, 383–384.

16. Quoted in Berliner, *Thinking in Jazz*, 192.

17. Butterfield, "Race and Rhythm," 320.

18. Ellison, "Going to the Territory," 600–601. See also A. Davis, *Blues Legacies and Black Feminism*, 66–71; Levine, *Black Culture and Black Consciousness*, 261–267; Moten, *In the Break*, 33–36.

19. A. Davis, *Blues Legacies and Black Feminism*, 81.

20. Selasi, "Bye-Bye Babar."

21. Mbembe, "Afropolitanisme." See also Nuttall and Mbembe, "Afropolis"; Skinner, *Bamako Sounds*, 9–12; Gehrmann, "Cosmopolitanism with African Roots," 61–66; Gikandi, "Foreword," 9–12; Ledent and Tunca, "What Is Africa?" 6–7; Ray, "Oxford Street, Accra," 511.

22. Kubik, "African Matrix," 190–192.

23. Quoted in Santoro, *Stir It Up*, 173. See also Dibango and Rouard, *Three Kilos of Coffee*, 5–6; Nyamnjoh and Fokwang, "Entertaining Repression," 254–260.

24. Quoted in liner notes to *O Boso*, by Dibango.

25. Dibango, "Négropolitaines"; Dibango, *Négropolitaines Vol. II*. See also Dibango and Kelman, *Balade en saxo*, 63–71; Stewart, *Rumba on the River*, 94–100.

26. Dibango, "Ce sont les gens"; Dibango, "Interview with Manu Dibango," 5.

27. See also Miller, *On the Ruins of Modernity*, 24.

28. Quoted in Sir Ali, "La face B de Dibango Manu."

29. Braggs, *Jazz Diasporas*, 133.

30. Mortensen, "Dexter Gordon and His Style," 58. See also Gordon, *The Panther!*

31. Benjamin, *Ursprung des deutschen Trauerspiels*, 187. See also Daub, "Sonic Dreamworlds," 273–276; Fuld, *Walter Benjamin*, 133–134; Boutin, *City of Noise*, 10–15.

32. Mackey, *Discrepant Engagement*, 252–253.

33. Benjamin, "Kurze Schatten I," 300. See also Weheliye, *Phonographies*, 78–79; Garber, "Fabulating Jazz," 71–79; Perchard, "Hugues Panassié contra Walter Benjamin"; Eiland and Jennings, *Walter Benjamin*, 4, 205–206; Hanssen, *Walter Benjamin's Other History*, 110–113.

34. Benjamin developed many of the ideas in his famous artwork essay in correspondence with his close friend Theodor Adorno, whose writings on jazz are grossly misinformed at best, racist at worst. It is quite telling, however, that Benjamin was aware of his own limitations and never engaged in an analysis of music or sound, nor did he expound on Adorno's thoughts on music in his letters. See Miklitsch, *Roll over Adorno*, 43–56; Patke, "Benjamin on Art and Reproducibility," 187–191; Harding, "Adorno, Ellison, and the Critique," 139–158; Feige, *Philosophie des Jazz*, 28–32. Though Benjamin wasn't concerned with what we today would call "critical race studies" or "postcolonial theory," he was—again unlike his friend—quite aware of the consequences of colonialism. In his arcades manuscript, he writes that "In approaching the consumptive negress in the capital, Baudelaire captured a much truer aspect of France's colonial empire than Dumas, who boarded a ship to Tunis at the behest of Salvandy" (Benjamin, *Passagen-Werk*, 412). In this particular convolute, convolute J, Benjamin refers to the second section of "Le Cygne"—dedicated

to Hugo—where the speaker is confronted with an ever-changing metropolis, in which "tout pour moi devient allégorie" (Baudelaire, "Le Cygne," line 31). As he ponders the nature of Time, the speaker is also reminded of "la négresse, amaigre et phtisique" he recently encountered, who pines for her long-lost "superbe Afrique" irretrievably lost behind walls of Parisian fog (41, 43). She becomes representative for all those displaced and dispossessed, "quiconque a perdu ce qui ne se retrouve / Jamais, jamais!" (45–46).

35. Dibango and Kelman, *Balade en saxo*, 9.

36. Quoted in Lock, *Blutopia*, 130. See also Monson, *Saying Something*, 199–215; Ho, "What Makes 'Jazz'?"

37. Benjamin, "Ankündigung der Zeitschrift," 186.

38. Ellison, "Charlie Christian Story," 4–5, 38–39; Hanssen, *Walter Benjamin's Other History*, 66–68, 79–81.

39. Benjamin, *Passagen-Werk*, 164, 666, 556.

40. Ellison, "Going to the Territory," 596.

41. Baraka, *Blues People*, 17.

42. Marsalis and O'Meally, "Duke Ellington," 143. See also Lawrence, *Duke Ellington and His World*, 302.

43. Ellington, *Music Is My Mistress*, xi, 130. For Ellington's lifelong and somewhat puzzling reverence for Whiteman, who premiered George Gershwin's "Rhapsody in Blue" and infamously sought to "make a lady out of jazz," see Lawrence, *Duke Ellington and His World*, 90–91; Cohen, *Duke Ellington's America*, 76–79.

44. Quoted in Cohen, *Duke Ellington's America*, 430. See also Lawrence, *Duke Ellington and His World*, 344–346; Von Eschen, *Satchmo Blows Up the World*, 144–147, 136.

45. Benjamin, *Passagen-Werk*, 83, 530.

46. Moraru, *Cosmodernism*, 25.

47. Ellington, *Drum Is a Woman*, recorded 1956; Benjamin, *Passagen-Werk*, 55.

48. Ellington and Dance, *Duke Ellington*, 86.

49. Quoted in Gioia, *History of Jazz*, 95. See also Huggins, *Harlem Renaissance*, 9–10; Ogren, *Jazz Revolution*, 139–146; Lock, *Blutopia*, 105–107.

50. Goll, "Die Neger erobern Europa," 256.

51. Quoted in Rippey, "Rationalization, Race," 76, 81. See also Phillips, *Shaping Jazz*, 53–54, 62.

52. Janowitz, *Jazz*, 12, 7.

53. Spellman, liner notes to *John Coltrane and Johnny Hartman*.

54. Benjamin, *Passagen-Werk*, 498.

55. Rasula, *History of a Shiver*, 206, 253.

56. See also Bailey, *Improvisation*, 39–43.

57. Barzel, "Subsidy, Advocacy, Theory," 161.

58. Ewart et al., "Ancient to the Future," 256. See also Berkowitz, *Improvising Mind*, xix.

59. Moten, *In the Break*, 131.

60. Golson and Merod, "Forward Motion," 81. See also Gordon, "Stablemates."

61. Interview with the author, June 22, 2013.

62. Moraru, *Reading for the Planet*, 51, emphasis in original.

63. Fueter, *Das Lächeln am Fusse*, 7.

CHAPTER I. THE AFRO-KINETIC PASSAGES OF MADAM ZAJJ

1. See Azevedo, *Roots of Violence*, 120–121; Pollack, *Arabs at War*, 387–388; Burr and Collins, *Africa's Thirty Years' War*, 257–263.

2. Dibango, "Toyota Makossa"; Makeba, "Toyota Fantaisie." See also Dibango and Rouard, *Three Kilos of Coffee*, 81–83, 107. The technicals that saw such widespread deployment in the Toyota War were mostly Land Cruisers and Hi-Luxes; the Corolla is available in subcompact or compact versions and was never offered as a pickup truck, though it was available as a van, which could easily be converted into a pickup. While Dibango praises only the Corolla in the lyrics, promotional material accompanying the single also included pictures of the Hi-Lux and the Land Cruiser, the iconic vehicles of the Toyota War. The flexibility and durability of the Land Cruiser in particular continues to make it the favorite technical of armed insurgencies around the world. In the fall of 2015, for example, the U.S. Department of the Treasury led a joint counterterrorism investigation to determine how hundreds of seemingly brand-new Toyota pickups could have been delivered to ISIL, which likes to showcase whole fleets of Land Cruisers in its gruesome propaganda videos. Spokespersons for the Japanese carmaker claimed not to know how such "product placement" was possible. See Stapleton, "U.S. Treasury"; Mosk, Ross, and Hosenball, "U.S. Officials"; Burns, "Trucks of the Taliban."

3. Nester, "Japanese Neomercantilism," 44–45; Kohl, "Modern Nomads, Vagabonds, or Cosmopolitans?" 450–54; Stewart, *Rumba on the River*, 134. See also Von Eschen, *Satchmo Blows Up the World*, 66–70, 253–254.

4. Quoted in Santoro, "Manu Dibango," 471; Dibango, "Interview with Manu Dibango," 7.

5. Savary, liner notes to *Drum Is a Woman*. In his pseudo-autobiography, *Three Kilos of Coffee*, Dibango cites "Concerto for Cootie," later retitled "Do Nothing till You Hear from Me," as the very first jazz record he purchased. *Three Kilos of Coffee* is a curious and deeply troubling affair: French journalist Danielle Rouard is listed as a collaborator, but in her foreword she discloses that "Not a single line reproduce[s] the raw words of the interview" she conducted with the musician, but that she instead replaced Dibango's own voice with "a Romanesque 'I,'" a "hybrid creature," as Rouard "saw with the eyes of an African, heard with his long ears, laughed and suffered with his heart of a black man." Her blatant negrophilia is accentuated even more when she quotes, as if a point of pride, her subject as saying "When we worked on that book, it was like Danielle raped me" (Dibango and Rouard, *Three Kilos of Coffee*, 15, x, ix, xi). *Three Kilos of Coffee* reflects disconcertingly the uneven power dynamic between the former colonizer and the postcolonial subject; whenever Dibango is quoted here, it is therefore from other, more reliable sources. See also Pacini Hernandez, "New Perspectives on Music."

6. Quoted in Santoro, "Manu Dibango," 471. In Dibango's prolific but artistically uneven output, his tribute album to Sidney Bechet is easily his jazziest one. Wisely sticking to alto saxophone, a horn sopranoist Bechet hardly ever used, Dibango contributes only one original composition, "Cousin Bechet Blues," harmonically a standard twelve-bar blues, with its only unusual feature Danny Doritz's lengthy solo on vibraphone, the marimba's electrified descendant. See Dibango, *Manu Dibango Plays Sidney Bechet*.

7. Dibango and Kelman, *Balade en saxo*, 132–134; Dibango, *Surtension*. See also its successor released the following year, *Electric Africa*. This preoccupation culminated in the 2011 *Ballad*

Emotion album marketed as "20 ballades electro-jazzy." The rather awful covers of well-known jazz standards sound as if Dibango "phoned in" his contributions—and maybe he did, if digitally so, since the whole affair appears to have been cobbled together on the laptop of producer Gérard Tempesti. Then again, Ellington himself, who relished the role of entertainer greatly, was not above recording utter kitsch either if it meant a financial boost: his 1954 recording of "Tyrolean Tango" sounds transnationalism at its arguably worst, so embarrassingly bad, in fact, that most Ellington discographies politely decline to list it, or only under its alternate title, "Echo Tango." See also Cohen, *Duke Ellington's America*, 283–288, 310–312; Hasse, *Beyond Category*, 313.

8. Bolling, *Drum Is a Woman*; Bolling and Daubresse, *Bolling Story*, 235–237; Savary, liner notes; Sklar, "Claude Bolling," 35; Lawrence, *Duke Ellington and His World*, 355–356; Ellington, *Music Is My Mistress*, 143–145.

9. Duke Ellington, *Drum Is a Woman*, recorded 1956.

10. Ellington, *Music Is My Mistress*, 156.

11. Quoted in Rampersad, *Life of Langston Hughes*, 2:254. See also Ellington, *Ellington Complete at Newport*; Cohen, *Duke Ellington's America*, 319–325; Hajdu, *Lush Life*, 150–155; Morton, *Backstory in Blue*, 145–190.

12. Quoted in Lawrence, *Duke Ellington and His World*, 222.

13. Cohen, *Duke Ellington's America*, 187–194, 203–242; Howland, *Ellington Uptown*, 143–156; Schiff, *Ellington Century*, 165–187; Ellington, *Music Is My Mistress*, 239–241; Hajdu, *Lush Life*, 90–94, 111–112.

14. Quoted in Hajdu, *Lush Life*, 157–158. See also Vogel, "Madam Zajj and U.S. Steel," 1–3.

15. Quoted in Hajdu, *Lush Life*, 157.

16. Ellington, *Drum Is a Woman*, recorded 1956.

17. Quoted in Weinstein, *Night in Tunisia*, 44.

18. Not all the music for the TV broadcast was played live in the studio: for example, on "What Else Can You Do with a Drum," it sounds as if Harry Carney's baritone saxophone begins to state the theme early by mistake, but a tape splice is clearly audible, and Jimmy Hamilton's fingerings don't match the sound coming from his clarinet when Madam Zajj makes her entrance into New Orleans, nor do Hodges's in the Chicago nightclub scene. The credits at the end spell their names "Madame Zajj" and "Caribee Joe"; I shall herein adhere to Ellington's own spellings, however. *A Drum Is a Woman* aired May 8, 1957. A black-and-white copy was viewed at the Paley Center for Media in New York City on June 22, 2017. According to Jane Klain, the Paley Center's manager of research services, no color copies survive of any CBS kinescopes. Neither CBS nor SFM Entertainment, the company holding the distribution rights for the network's shows, are aware of any color copies either. Personal communication with Jane Klain, Paley Center for Media, New York City, June 22, 2017; telephone conversation with Peter Murray, CBS Entertainment Division, Los Angeles, February 13, 2017; telephone conversation with Stanley Moger, president of SFM Entertainment, February 15, 2017. See also Hajdu, *Lush Life*, 162.

19. Ellington, *Drum Is a Woman*, May 8, 1957.

20. Ibid.

21. Quoted in Lock, *Blutopia*, 139, 138. See also Cohen, *Duke Ellington's America*, 329–334; Ellington, *Music Is My Mistress*, 191, 239–241; Hajdu, *Lush Life*, 156–164; Townsend, liner notes to *Drum Is a Woman*.

22. Quoted in Edwards, "The Literary Ellington," 3.
23. Ellington, "Pomegranate"; MacHare, *Duke Ellington Panorama*.
24. Quoted in Hajdu, *Lush Life*, 161.
25. Ellington, *Drum Is a Woman*, May 8, 1957.
26. Quoted in Edwards, "Literary Ellington," 3. See also Hajdu, *Lush Life*, 158–160; Celenza, "Duke Ellington, Billy Strayhorn," 14; Lawrence, *Duke Ellington and His World*, 344–345; Townsend, liner notes; Willard, "Dance," 409–410; van de Leur, *Something to Live For*, 133–134, 304.
27. Ellington, *Drum Is a Woman*, recorded 1956.
28. Cortez and the Firespitters, "If the Drum." Cortez, formerly married to free-jazz pioneer Ornette Coleman, did not dismiss Ellington's oeuvre in its entirety. "Rose Solitude," for example, is an exquisitely jazzy paean to the bandleader. Moreover, she often performed her poetry with an experimental jazz group that usually included Denardo, her son with Coleman, on drums. See Bolden, "All the Birds Sing Bass," 65–67; Nielsen, *Black Chant*, 225–227.
29. Quoted in Cohen, *Duke Ellington's America*, 331.
30. Ellington's worship of his mother, Daisy, was legendary, but his relationships with other women were ambivalent at best. Mercer, his son and right-hand man, averred that "other than his mother and sister, he had a basic contempt for women. He spent so much time praising and charming them, but basically he hated them. It was kind of a love-hate thing, and more hate than love" (M. Ellington and Dance, *Duke Ellington*, 124). Ellington biographer A. H. Lawrence, who played trombone in Luis Russell's orchestra before transforming himself into a professor of psychiatry, diagnoses in his "patient" "an inherent psychological tragedy" that caused him to venerate Daisy "almost to the point of saintliness" while regarding "all other women (with the exception of those in religious work[s]) essentially as whores": "Following the breakup of his marriage, Ellington recreated the family closer to his heart's desire. Playing out his Oedipal wishes, he removed his father from his mother's bed. With such success at realizing infantile wishes, one should not be surprised, psychologically speaking, that Ellington was unable to tolerate his mother's loss when she died, nor was he able to commit himself fully to another woman. There are some wishes better unattained as their accomplishment leads to unrealistic expectations and, more tragically, profound narcissism. At his death, Ellington further validated this conjecture. He left no will. Later, while clearing up his father's papers, Mercer came upon the following note: 'I'm easy to please, I just want everybody in the palm of my hand'" (Lawrence, *Duke Ellington and His World*, 14, 401). Ellington apparently wanted Madam Zajj in the palm of his hand too; he told Irving Townsend that he fancied himself her Carribee Joe. But the narrative arc of Madam Zajj's travels contravene even the Duke: while she cannot forget Carribee Joe—and how could any history of jazz music forget Duke Ellington?—the trajectories of her flânerie are not curtailed by Joe or her abiding love for him, not even on *The United States Steel Hour*. See Townsend, "Ellington in Private."
31. Morrison, *Song of Solomon*, 129, 127.
32. Ellington, *Music Is My Mistress*, 447, 4.
33. Ellington, *Drum Is a Woman*, recorded 1956.
34. Ibid.
35. Ellington, *Drum Is a Woman*, May 8, 1957.
36. Ibid.

37. Ibid.
38. See also Vogel, "Madam Zajj and U.S. Steel," 10, 17.
39. Ellington, *Drum Is a Woman*, recorded 1956.
40. Ellington, *Music Is My Mistress*, 227.
41. Ellington, *Drum Is a Woman*, recorded 1956.
42. Ibid.
43. Cortez and the Firespitters, "If the Drum." See also Lim, "Complications," 118–119.
44. Benjamin, "Die Wiederkehr des Flaneurs," 417. While intriguing, the allusion to Joseph Kosma and Jacques Prévert's standard "Les feuilles mortes"—anglicized as "Autumn Leaves"—is entirely coincidental, seeing as the chanson was copyrighted in 1947. See Goeman and Schaal, "Autumn Leaves," 46–48. There are only two other mentions of jazz that I have been able to unearth in Benjamin's critical writings. One occurs in a lengthy quoted fragment in convolute M of the arcades project, dated 1936. There, "the last flâneur" is "deafened by car horns, stupefied by big talkers . . . , demoralized by snatches of conversation, of political references and of jazz which escape slyly from windows" (quoted in Benjamin, *Passagen-Werk*, 547). Again, it is telling that jazz is linked explicitly to flânerie. The other occurs in the preliminary notes: "Noise emancipates itself in jazz. Jazz appears at a moment when noise is increasingly eliminated from the process of production, of traffic, and of trade. Likewise radio" (*Passagen-Werk*, 1032). Generally, music seems to have been of some, albeit very minor, interest to Benjamin in the preliminary notes. An early and uncharacteristically short sketch on the significance of the passages themselves mentions at the outset "a monster orchestra in uniform" accompanying the opening of a new passage in Paris (*Passagen-Werk*, 1041). Still, almost all these references to music are eventually abandoned and no longer figure in the materials Benjamin continued to assemble, dismissing instead the whole subject matter with the observation that "Music seems to have settled into these spaces only with their demise, only when music orchestras themselves began to become old-fashioned, so to speak, because mechanical music was on the rise" (*Passagen-Werk*, 270).
45. Benjamin, "Die Wiederkehr des Flâneurs," 417. Much like his more famous critical concept of "aura," Benjamin's flâneur appears in ambiguous and occasionally contradictory forms—sometimes as dandified fop who likes to parade up and down the Parisian arcades with a turtle on a leash, sometimes as archaeologist of memory, as poet-philosopher, as amateur detective, sometimes as heroic protester against industrial capitalism, and sometimes as its product, whose female counterpart is the figure of the prostitute. The indeterminacy of the figure of the flâneur is also, in part, due to the fact that the unwieldy, labyrinthine, and enigmatic arcades project remained unfinished at Benjamin's death. In the manuscript, the flâneur vanishes with the demise of the Parisian arcades: "The sandwich man is the last incarnation of the flâneur," finally co-opted for good by the forces of consumer capitalism, remarks Benjamin repeatedly. Even so, many of the fragments in convolute M come from twentieth-century sources, and Benjamin himself saw the figure of the flâneur reincarnated after his ostensible disappearance in the late 1800s, as for example in Hessel's Berlin, of all places. Thus, the aim here is not to proffer a new, exhaustive reading of Benjaminian flânerie (or aura, for that matter)—which would have to read against Benjamin's own critical practice anyway—but to use certain aspects of the figure of the flâneur to help illuminate Madam Zajj's transnational jazz. See Benjamin, *Passagen-Werk*, 567, 562, 967. See also Eiland and Jennings, *Walter Benjamin*, 285–293; Parsons, *Streetwalking the Metropolis*,

222–225; Witte, *Walter Benjamin*, 195–197; Bolz and van Reijen, *Walter Benjamin*, 65–66; Missac, *Walter Benjamin's Passages*, 190–197.

46. Benjamin, "Die Wiederkehr des Flaneurs," 418; Benjamin, "Das Paris des Second Empire," 525, 530.

47. Benjamin, *Passagen-Werk*, 524–525.

48. Ibid., 679. See also Eiland and Jennings, *Walter Benjamin*, 288; Gilloch, *Walter Benjamin*, 221–223; Brodersen, *Walter Benjamin*, 236–240, 174–177.

49. Benjamin, "Das Paris des Second Empire," 537–545. See also Butler, *Undoing Gender*, 198–199.

50. Ellington, *Drum Is a Woman*, May 8, 1957.

51. Butler, *Undoing Gender*, 1. See also Scheper, "New Negro *Flâneuse*," 687–691; A. Davis, *Blues Legacies and Black Feminism*, 71–80; McMullen, "The Improvisative," 115–118.

52. Benjamin, *Passagen-Werk*, 1053.

53. Hughes, "Negro Artist," 901, 902. See also Graham, Introduction, 4–5; Bernard, "Langston Hughes, the Tom-Tom," 40–43; Parsons, *Streetwalking the Metropolis*, 5–6, 41–42, 208–209; Gilloch, *Walter Benjamin*, 243–244.

54. Quoted in Lawrence, *Duke Ellington and His World*, 87.

55. Ellington, *Music Is My Mistress*, 108–109, 47. See also M. Ellington and Dance, *Duke Ellington*, 61–62; Schuller, *Early Jazz*, 323, 327–333, 344–345.

56. Ellington, *Drum Is a Woman*, recorded 1956.

57. Ellington, *Music Is My Mistress*, 87–88.

58. Bernard, *Carl Van Vechten*, 71.

59. Ellington, *Music Is My Mistress*, 180.

60. Stearns, *Story of Jazz*, 184. See also Cohen, *Duke Ellington's America*, 146–149, 380–386; Gioia, *History of Jazz*, 126–129.

61. As did Toni Morrison: the disembodied narrator's description of "the City" at the outset of *Jazz*, set in 1926, includes a "colored man" who "floats down out of the sky blowing a saxophone." See Morrison, *Jazz*, 8. See also Gennari, *Blowin' Hot and Cool*, 101–103; Douglas, "Skyscrapers, Airplanes, and Airmindedness," 215–219; Shaftel, "Black Eagle of Harlem."

62. Quoted in Cohen, *Duke Ellington's America*, 55.

63. Ulanov, "Ellington Programme," 169. See also Schiff, *Ellington Century*, 24; Lawrence, *Duke Ellington and His World*, 113–119; Wald, *How the Beatles Destroyed Rock*, 103–108.

64. Wheatley, "On Being Brought from Africa," 98. See also Vogel, "Madam Zajj and U.S. Steel," 17.

65. Benjamin, *Ursprung des deutschen Trauerspiels*, 28. See also Benjamin, "Über einige Motive bei Baudelaire," 189–193; Friedlander, "On the Musical Gathering," 631–632; Hanssen, *Walter Benjamin's Other History*, 40–43.

66. Ellison, "Homage to Duke Ellington," 679. See also Lock, *Blutopia*, 138–141.

67. Quoted in Gabbard, *Jammin' at the Margins*, 177–178.

68. Ellington, *Togo Brava Suite*, recorded October 22, 1971.

69. Ellington, *Afro-Eurasian Eclipse*. By a strange if fitting coincidence, one of the sections in Walter Benjamin's *One Way Street*, the critic's first sustained foray into the semiotics of urban modernity, is also entitled "Chinoiserie." See Benjamin, *Einbahnstrasse*, 79–80.

70. Ellington, *Togo Brava Suite*, recorded June 28 and 29, 1971; Ellington, *Togo Brava Suite*, recorded October 22, 1971; Ellington, "Limbo Jazz." See also Ellington, *Music Is My Mistress*, 204; Kubik, "African Matrix," 190; Lawrence, *Duke Ellington and His World*, 315, 377; Dance, liner notes to *Togo Brava Suite*; Hasse, *Beyond Category*, 262; Zenni, "Aesthetics of Duke Ellington's Suites," 11; Jaji, *Africa in Stereo*, 89–91.

71. Ellington, *Togo Brava Suite*, recorded October 22, 1971.

72. Quoted in Hasse, *Beyond Category*, 283.

73. Ellington, *Togo Brava Suite*, recorded October 22, 1971. Ellington was in the habit of temporarily assigning new compositions four-letter titles before deciding on a final title. For a more thoroughly musicological analysis of the *Togo Brava* suite and its evolution, as well as its intimate connection with *The Afro-Eurasian Eclipse*, see Stefano Zenni's detailed account. Given the enormous output of Ellingtonia over decades, it is no wonder that discographies and liner notes often provide erroneous data. For example, the CD sleeve of the first commercial release on the Storyville label of the June 1972 rehearsal tapes of the *Togo Brava* suite misspells some titles and misrepresents others entirely. The Internet-based *Duke Ellington Panorama*, often a very useful resource indeed, is also not above suspicion at all times. See Zenni, "Aesthetics of Duke Ellington's Suites," 11–22. See also MacHare, *Duke Ellington Panorama*.

74. Ellington, *Music Is My Mistress*, 457, 459, 334.

75. Benjamin, *Passagen-Werk*, 528.

76. Ra, liner notes to *Sun Song*. See also Szwed, *Space Is the Place*, 154–162; Parliament, *Mothership Connection*; Bowie, *Space Oddity*. For a few months in early 1951, the Ellington organization included young dancer and singer Nichelle Nichols, who also choreographed "Pretty and the Wolf," a light, short piece of Ellingtonia whose protagonist shares some character traits with Madam Zajj. Nichols, of course, would herself go on to intergalactic fame as Lieutenant Uhura, the USS *Enterprise*'s communications officer on *Star Trek*. See Nichols, *Beyond Uhura*, 51–56; Ellington, "Monologue."

77. Quoted in Le Gros, "Manu Dibango." See also Dibango and Kelman, *Balade en saxo*, 58–59, 161–169; Dibango, "Soul Makossa"; Dibango, "Makossa '87"; Dibango, "Soul Makossa 2.0."

78. See Gennari, *Blowin' Hot and Cool*, 43–44; Cohen, *Duke Ellington's America*, 384; Lawrence, *Duke Ellington and His World*, 159–160.

79. Dibango, "Interview with Manu Dibango," 7; Weheliye, *Phonographies*, 102. See also R. Kelley, *Africa Speaks, America Answers*, 6–10.

80. M. Davis and Troupe, *Miles*, 285.

81. Quoted in Broecking, "Don't Call My Music J***?" 24.

82. Ellington, *Drum Is a Woman*, May 8, 1957. On the album, Ellington's narration is almost identical.

83. Benjamin, *Passagen-Werk*, 93.

CHAPTER 2. SHEETS OF JAZZ

1. Quoted in Cohen, *Duke Ellington's America*, 657.

2. See Badger, *Life in Ragtime*, 161–163, 177–199; Nicholson, *Jazz and Culture*, 75–77.

3. Rasula, "Jazzbandism," 81.

4. Hesse, *Steppenwolf*, 37–38.

5. Partsch, "Hannibal ante Portas," 107, 105–106.

6. Quoted in Robinson, "Jazz Reception in Weimar Germany," 113. See also Nagl, *Die unheimliche Maschine*, 669–672; Rasula, "Jazzbandism," 72–73.

7. Quoted in Sharpley-Whiting, *Bricktop's Paris*, 68. See also Danzi, *American Musician in Germany*, 17; Petrescu, "Social Dancing and Rugged Masculinity," 604.

8. Weiner, "*Urwaldmusik* and the Borders," 478. See also Wipplinger, *Jazz Republic*, 98–114.

9. Coincidentally, just one year earlier, in 1926, Violet Trace mutilates the face of a dead girl at a Harlem funeral in Toni Morrison's novel *Jazz*. The two novels are radically different in many ways—Janowitz's light comedy of errors contrasts sharply with Morrison's sweeping epic. But they also share stunning similarities in narrative strategy. For a comparative reading of the two novels, see Grandt, *Kinds of Blue*, 77–104.

10. Janowitz remains something of an enigma today, partly because he had to leave behind his papers when he fled Europe in 1939. The most comprehensive biographical sketch is Rolf Riess's entry in the third volume of *Deutsche Exilliteratur seit 1933*; for a firsthand account of the making of *Das Cabinet des Dr. Caligari*, see Janowitz's own reminiscences as well as Siegfried Kracauer's memoirs: Riess, "Hans Janowitz," 258–282; Janowitz, "Caligari," 221–239; Kracauer, *From Caligari to Hitler*, 62–66. See also Otto, "*Schaulust*," 143–144.

11. Janowitz, *Jazz*, 112.

12. Hesse, *Steppenwolf*, 38.

13. See Janowitz, *Jazz*, 14.

14. Morrison, *Playing in the Dark*, 6–7.

15. Janowitz, *Jazz*, 10, 6–7.

16. Ibid., 19.

17. See (and hear), for instance, Gordon's solo on "Catalonian Nights," a composition he dedicated to his favorite pianist during his European sojourn, Tete Montoliu.

18. Benjamin, *Passagen-Werk*, 678–679.

19. For detailed discussions of the technical aspects of Janowitz's literary transposition of jazz music, see Avenel-Cohen, "*Jazz* de Hans Janowitz," 131–138; Baumann, "Die Literatur war Jazz geworden," 362–373; Brady, "Saxophon—guter Ton!" 465–468; Grandt, *Kinds of Blue*, 77–104.

20. Janowitz, *Jazz*, 47.

21. Ibid., 87–88.

22. Ibid., 46, 86. See also Shakespeare, *Second Part of King Henry the Fourth*, 2.6.

23. Janowitz, *Jazz*, 46.

24. Benjamin, "Das Paris des Second Empire," 529, 530.

25. Janowitz, *Jazz*, 67.

26. Benjamin, "Das Paris des Second Empire," 532. See also Eiland and Jennings, *Walter Benjamin*, 614–615; Salzani, "City as Crime Scene," 168–177; Werner, "Detective Gaze," 5–10.

27. Janowitz alludes to the box-office hit when *Jazz*'s narrator proclaims, "The time had found its Offenbach. It was called: Jazz! Thus was called the expression of the time, which had taken to heart, in its fashion, the dictum of our mad psychiatrist: 'You shall become Caligari.' The world hadn't exactly become Caligari, but jazz it had become, thoroughly jazz" (Janowitz, *Jazz*, 8). An influential precursor of the film noir and horror genres, *Das Cabinet des Dr. Caligari* is set in the

remote village of Holstenwall and begins with the arrival of a traveling carnival. Coincidentally, in 1994 jazz bassist Mark Dresser performed music he had written for the silent film classic at New York City's Knitting Factory, together with trumpeter Dave Douglas and Denman Maroney on piano. See *Cabinet des Dr. Caligari;* Dresser, *Cabinet of Dr. Caligari.*

28. Janowitz, *Jazz,* 19.

29. Ibid., 117; Steve Lacy, liner notes to *Straight Horn of Steve Lacy.*

30. In one of the many ironic twists and turns in the history of the music, the Original Dixieland Jass Band, ODJB for short, became in 1917 the first jazz group to make a recording. Billing themselves as "The Originators of Jazz," the music of the five white New Orleanians was actually largely derivative. The ODJB's influence on German musicians was probably negligible: Frank Tirro estimates that the ODJB's recordings did not become available in Germany until around 1923, while J. Bradford Robinson claims that none of their recordings were issued there at all. Pianist Georg Haentzschel, on the other hand, remembers that "in 1925 the first records by the Wolverines, by Redman and Armstrong, arrived; you could order them in America, and fourteen days later you got them. I ordered these records and wrote all these 'hot' arrangements for a small combo with a gramophone, and it was a joy when they [his band members] heard their own band and it sounded like on record" (quoted in Hoffmann, "Albtraum der Freiheit," 77). See also Robinson, "Jazz Reception in Weimar Germany," 115; Tirro, "Jazz Leaves Home," 77; Schuller, *Early Jazz,* 175–187.

31. Janowitz, *Jazz,* 75–76.

32. See Baumann, "Die Literatur war Jazz geworden," 371–373; Hoffmann, "Albtraum der Freiheit," 70–72; Kater, "Jazz Experience in Weimar Germany," 152. Given the description of Lord Punch's Jazz-Band-Boys and their music, it is likely that Janowitz himself had little exposure to "authentic" African American jazz. At the same time, his collaborator at Trude Hesterberg's cabaret, the famous Wilde Bühne, was Friedrich Hollaender, pianist of the Weintraub Syncopators, considered to be Berlin's best "hot" jazz band. Hollaender—who would later strike gold with his composition "Falling in Love with Love," Marlene Dietrich's signature song from *The Blue Angel*—was a jazz aficionado who disliked Paul Whiteman's symphonic jazz with a passion and who championed the hard-to-get jazz of the genre's originators. As Hollaender would later remember about the 1920s, echoing his colleague Haentzschel, "Yass! Yass! everybody shouts, as if someone had forgotten to turn off the faucet. It's 'Jazz' they mean, and everyone wants it and no one can play it. You run and buy yourself the new discs from America, schlep them home, bang them onto the turntable as if to fry eggs and then let them spin, ten times, twenty times, until they get so hot that the needle gets stuck in the melting wax" (Hollaender, *Von Kopf bis Fuss,* 98–99). Coincidentally, John Coltrane's 1957 album *Traneing In* features one of Hollaender's lesser-known compositions, the ballad "You Leave Me Breathless." Janowitz's own initial exposure to jazz (or what passed as jazz) actually seemed to have resulted in anything but enthusiastic interest: an early, if passing, reference in his Berlin journal complains of the city's "entertainment venues with a little jazz-band torture" (quoted in Brady, "Saxophon—guter Ton!" 465). In the satirical lyrics and poetry he wrote for the Wilde Bühne and other cabarets, jazz figures as but one among myriad features of the modern metropolis Berlin: the texts do not yet portend "the translation of the world into jazz music" that was to follow. He never returned to jazz music after his 1927 novel: during his years in American exile, he concentrated his artistic energies, in vain, on a remake of *Das Cabinet des Dr. Caligari.* See also Appignanesi, *Cabaret,* 178–181; Geuen,

"Das hat die Welt," 54–55; Jelavich, *Berlin Cabaret*, 150–151, 190–191. Lareau, *Wild Stage*, 106–112; Riess, "Hans Janowitz," 275–278; Coltrane, *Traneing In*.

33. In a nod to Janowitz's place of origin, the narrator transposes the locale of Adolphe Sax's invention to "Kraslice, in Bohemia, the home of Mr. August Wilhelm Sachs, inventor of the saxophone" (Janowitz, *Jazz*, 31). Saxophone production in the Sudetenland began in 1900 with the Kohlert company, followed over the next four decades by a confusing array of brands and stencils like Adler, Hüller, Keilwerth, Köhler, Monning, or Schuster, all manufactured whole or in part by various instrument makers in the Kraslice (formerly Graslitz) area. Today, wind instruments continue to be built in Kraslice under the Amati-Denak trademark. See Gazarek, "Amati Instrument Manufacturer"; Hales, "Kohlert History"; "Amati History"; Segell, *Devil's Horn*, 12–28.

34. Janowitz, *Jazz*, 6, 8, emphasis in original.

35. See also Chaney, "Traveling Harlem's Europe," 60–61.

36. Schuller, *Early Jazz*, 8.

37. See Kater, "Jazz Experience in Weimar Germany," 145–147, 150–51; Robinson, "Jazz Reception in Weimar Germany," 123–125; Phillips, *Shaping Jazz*, 63–65; Partsch, "That Weimar Jazz," 184–185; Wipplinger, *Jazz Republic*, 141–164. It is likely, however, that Janowitz maintained his connections in Berlin after 1924. Moreover, jazz was popular among Czechs as well: the Prague-based journal *Auftakt* covered jazz music regularly throughout the 1920s, and Janowitz, self-described "musician by inner necessity" and a piano prodigy who had played the "Moonshine Sonata" by rote at the age of eight, surely kept tabs on the musical avant-garde. See Cook, "Jazz as Deliverance," 30, 37–40; Riess, "Hans Janowitz," 258.

38. See Tirro, "Jazz Leaves Home," 63–67; Robinson, "Jazz Reception in Weimar Germany," 114–115.

39. Quoted in Baumann, "Die Literatur war Jazz geworden," 364. See also Cook, "Jazz as Deliverance," 39–40; Heffley, *Northern Sun, Southern Moon*, 119–123; Robinson, "Jazz Reception in Weimar Germany," 124–134; Avenel-Cohen, "*Jazz* de Hans Janowitz," 130–131; Dümling, "Musikalische Verfahrensweise," 119–122.

40. Quoted in Ward, *Dark Midnight When I Rise*, 355.

41. See Chilton, *Sidney Bechet*, 85–86; Lotz, *Black People*, 21, 65–88, 283–296; Tirro, "Jazz Leaves Home," 71–77; Schmidt, "Visual Music," 212–213.

42. See Lotz, *Black People*, 22; Tirro, "Jazz Leaves Home," 70–71.

43. See Partsch, *Schräge Töne*, 80–86; Weiner, "*Urwaldmusik* and the Borders," 477–478; Phillips, *Shaping Jazz*, 52–62.

44. Bechet, *Treat It Gentle*, 157; Chilton, *Sidney Bechet*, 85–87; Nagl, *Die unheimliche Maschine*, 648.

45. Roth, "Jazzband," 543–546. See also Nagl, *Die unheimliche Maschine*, 650–651; Otte, *Jewish Identities*, 251–252.

46. Roth, "Jazzband," 544. See also Partsch, *Schräge Töne*, 84–85.

47. See Hollaender, *Von Kopf bis Fuss*, 117; Nagl, *Die unheimliche Maschine*, 706–708, 714–715. See also Schmidt, "Visual Music," 216–218.

48. Butterfield, "Race and Rhythm," 315.

49. Janowitz, *Jazz*, 102.

50. Ibid., 111.

51. Morrison, *Playing in the Dark*, 52, 57.

152 NOTES TO CHAPTERS TWO AND THREE

52. Partsch, "Hannibal ante Portas," 115. Paul Whiteman, self-proclaimed "King of Jazz," acquired instant fame when he premiered George Gershwin's *Rhapsody in Blue* at New York's Aeolian Hall in 1924, regarded by contemporaries as the first performance of jazz as "serious" concert music. Two years later, Whiteman brought his orchestra to Berlin, where its *Kunstjazz* ("art jazz") was also a smashing success. Whiteman's desire "to make a lady out of jazz" entailed his repeated proclamation that jazz music had nothing at all to do with black people. See Gennari, *Blowin' Hot and Cool*, 44–46; Hoffmann, "Albtraum der Freiheit," 72–76; Partsch, "That Weimar Jazz," 185–186; Wipplinger, *Jazz Republic*, 86–98; Welburn, "Jazz Criticism," 748.

53. Atkinson, "Maurice Chevalier, Minstrel," 26.

54. Janowitz, *Jazz*, 20.

55. See Cook, "Jazz as Deliverance," 40–42; Otte, *Jewish Identities*, 3–5, 172–175; Partsch, "Hannibal ante Portas," 111–112.

56. Gitler, liner notes to *Traneing In*.

57. Gitler, "'Trane on the Track," 17; Gitler, liner notes to *Soultrane*.

58. Janowitz, *Jazz*, 6–7.

59. See Porter, *John Coltrane*, 132–136.

60. Coltrane, "Coltrane on Coltrane," 27.

61. Given the narrative voice's sometimes frantic attempts to maintain control over its own storyline, perhaps the better analogue than Coltrane—who, though always overly critical of his playing, certainly could not be said ever to lose control over his instrument—is pianist Red Garland. The fleet-fingered Garland had clearly studied his Art Tatum, but the blistering pace of "Russian Lullaby" obviously taxes the limits of his skills (although, to these ears, he acquits himself much better on the similarly fast-paced "Soft Lights and Sweet Music"); it's his misfortune, too, that his solo follows Coltrane's. Another intriguing parallel between Janowitz's *Jazz* and the Coltrane of the "sheets of sound" period and beyond are the respective endings of their "solos." When he rejoined Miles Davis's band after kicking his heroin habit, the tenorist became notorious for solos that had no closure either, as he would often simply walk away from the microphone, horn in mouth, and continue to solo backstage. "I get involved in this thing and just don't know when to stop," he defended himself to his boss, and an exasperated Davis shot back, "Try taking the saxophone out of your mouth!" (quoted in Crow, *Jazz Anecdotes*, 325). Janowitz's novel, too, is decidedly anticlimactic and lacks closure, with the narrator heeding Davis's advice to Trane as he does just that—simply lay the pen down.

62. The jazz poetry of giovanni singleton experiments with freeing written language from its monophonic moorings in several of the poems in *Ascension*, a collection inspired by the music of pianist Alice Coltrane, John's wife. See giovanni singleton, "Day 45" or "exodus," in *Ascension*, 54, 61–62.

63. Coltrane, "Coltrane on Coltrane," 27.

64. Janowitz, *Jazz*, 24. See also Dibango and Kelman, *Balade en saxo*, 55–57.

CHAPTER 3. HIGH FIDELITY ON THE BLACK ATLANTIC

1. Baraka, liner notes to *Coltrane Live at Birdland*. See also Woideck, "John Coltrane," 200–208; Porter, *John Coltrane*, 93–94.

2. Hughes, *Big Sea*, 3–4.
3. Hughes, *I Wonder as I Wander*, 69, 150.
4. Ibid., 401.
5. Miller, "Café de la Paix," 81–83. The Café de la Paix was also the location where a decade or so later Billy Strayhorn would occasionally meet with Orson Welles to work on another short-lived project, the revue *The Blessed and the Damned*. See Hajdu, *Lush Life*, 111–114.
6. Hughes, *I Wonder as I Wander*, 405.
7. Benjamin, "Über den Begriff der Geschichte," 255.
8. Walker, preface to *I Wonder as I Wander*, xi. See also Barton, *Old Plantation Hymns*, 9; Levine, *Black Culture and Black Consciousness*, 32.
9. Jackson, "I Wonder as I Wander."
10. Niles, "Folk Inspiration."
11. See Pen, *I Wonder as I Wander*, 149–158, 252–257; Rozema, Introduction, 22–23. See also Lott, *Love and Theft*, 4–7.
12. Benjamin, "Über den Begriff der Geschichte," 253.
13. Benjamin, *Passagen-Werk*, 473, 531, 533, 582.
14. Miller, "Café de la paix," 92.
15. Quoted in Kahn, *House That Trane Built*, 52, 50. See also Rampersad, *Langston Hughes*, 2:347; Kahn, *Love Supreme*, 39–42; Porter, *John Coltrane*, 8–13, 180–181; Ho, "Damned Don't Cry," 129–133, 136–137; Wild, liner notes to *Complete Africa/Brass Sessions*; R. Williams, *Blue Moment*, 138–140. As with "I Wonder as I Wander," the origins of "Follow the Drinking Gourd" are in dispute. The song was not "collected" (ostensibly transcribed) until the twentieth century by two white folklorists: H. B. Parks claimed to have heard it on several occasions in the 1910s, and Lee Hays in 1947 published an arrangement of it based on a song he avowed to remember from attending black church services in his childhood. See J. Kelley, "Song, Story, or History," 266–270.
16. Porter, *John Coltrane*, 212–213; Wild, liner notes, 5–6.
17. Quoted in Porter, *John Coltrane*, 211. See also Coltrane, *Ballads*; Coltrane, *Complete 1961 Village Vanguard Recordings*; R. Williams, *Blue Moment*, 138–140.
18. Miller, "Reinvention and Globalization," 73–74.
19. Moraru, *Cosmodernism*, 22–23. See also Koshy, "Minority Cosmopolitanism," 596–598.
20. Hughes, *I Wonder as I Wander*, 114, 122, emphasis added.
21. Quoted in Kahn, *House That Trane Built*, 47.
22. Ellison, "Going to the Territory," 300.
23. Hughes, *Big Sea*, 225.
24. Hughes, "Jazz as Communication," 493.
25. Ibid., 494.
26. Benjamin, *Passagen-Werk*, 1036, 1027.
27. Hornby, *High Fidelity*, 147, 3.
28. Ibid., 54, 55.
29. Benjamin, *Passagen-Werk*, 271, 272.
30. Ibid., 274.
31. Hornby, *High Fidelity*, 3.
32. Guillory, "Canon," 234, 238.

33. See "Box Office Mojo"; Knowles, *Nick Hornby's* High Fidelity, 20–29, 81–82. Rob Gordon, as he is called in the movie, is a much more likable character than Hornby's Rob Fleming. In part, this is also a result of the translation of the literary bildungsroman into the cinematic genre of the romantic comedy. Rob Fleming's interior monologue is directed at no one in particular, whereas Rob Gordon repeatedly breaches the fourth wall, sometimes in a conspiratorial manner (in bed with Marie, for example, or at the service for Laura's father), and speaking directly to the camera provides a level of intimacy with the moviegoer that the novel does not for its reader.

34. Except where otherwise noted, all quotations from the film and its makers come from the expanded DVD release. See also Khoury, "Behind the Music," 40–46.

35. Quoted in Husband, "Tracks of My Frears." See also Higson, *Film England*, 114; Ostwald, "Sein wunderbarer Filmsalon," 84.

36. Hornby, *High Fidelity*, 62, 60.

37. Keskinen, "Single, Long-Playing, and Compilation," 3–4.

38. Hornby, *High Fidelity*, 96.

39. Casting Hjejle in the role of Laura was apparently Frears's idea, too. He met the actress, who as a child had spent a year Stateside, at a film festival in Berlin and observed that "She never learned to speak English; she learned to speak American, and so it was quite unique."

40. Broonzy, "White, Brown, and Black."

41. See Grazian, *Blue Chicago*, 25–28.

42. Kenney, *Chicago Jazz*, xiv; Jacquet, "Robbin's Nest."

43. Hornby, *High Fidelity*, 75.

44. See Hamilton, *Just Around Midnight*, 89–91.

45. Hornby, *High Fidelity*, 36; See also O'Neal, "I Once Was Lost," 369–370.

46. Hughes, *I Wonder as I Wander*, 340, 341.

47. Hornby, *High Fidelity*, 323.

48. Ibid., 89, 264.

49. See also Borshuk, "Noisy Modernism," 19; Tracy, *Langston Hughes and the Blues*, 225.

50. See Kahn, *House That Trane Built*, 174–179. See also E. Lewis, "What Is 'Great Black Music?'" 139.

51. Gov't Mule, *Tel-Star Sessions*; Gov't Mule, "Trane"; Gov't Mule, *By a Thread*; E. Alexander, *Full Range*; E. Alexander, *Chim Chim Cheree*.

52. Hornby, *High Fidelity*, 117.

53. Feige, *Philosophie des Jazz*, 113. See also Jagoda, *Network Aesthetics*, 194–216; Sparti, "On the Edge," 189.

54. Simon, *Graceland*; Living Colour, *Time's Up*. See also *Under African Skies*; Bennighof, "Fluidity in Paul Simon's 'Graceland,'" 231–236; Mentjes, "Paul Simon's *Graceland*," 38–40.

55. Asheru and Kweli, "Mood Swing"; Ellington and Coltrane, *Duke Ellington and John Coltrane*. See also H.E.L.P.

56. Die Fantastischen Vier, "Die da!?!"; Washington "Mr. Magic"; Puthli, "Right Down Here"; Cale, "Right Down Here." See also O. Coleman, *Science Fiction*; Schumacher, "Rainer Trüby über Samples."

57. Smudo, "Als der Hip-Hop Deutsch lernte." See also Pennay, "Rap in Germany," 119–123; Brown, "Keeping it Real," 140–142; Gruber, *Performative Lyrik*, 53–57.

58. Die Fantastischen Vier, *Heimspiel.*
59. Born, "After Relational Aesthetics," 41.
60. Hornby, *High Fidelity*, 221, 291.
61. See Kahn, *House That Trane Built*, 53.
62. Braggs, "Evoking Baldwin's Blues," 155.
63. Hughes, *I Wonder as I Wander*, 399.

CHAPTER 4. "GOOD MORNING, HEARTACHE"

1. Janowitz, *Jazz*, 6; Micucci, "Nice Jazz Festival Canceled"; Braggs, *Jazz Diasporas*, 76–79.
2. *High Fidelity*, DVD.
3. Quoted in McKaie, liner notes to *Billie Holiday*, 7. Gabler sometimes claimed to have written "Good Morning Heartache" himself in order to help shape his client's new image. In truth, the tune was composed by Teddy Wilson's ex-wife and Holiday's close friend, Irene Higginbotham. See Lasker, "Lady Day," 20; McKaie, liner notes, 8; Clarke, *Wishing on the Moon*, 185–186; Nicholson, *Billie Holiday*, 140–150.
4. Holiday, "Good Morning Heartache."
5. F. Davis, "Our Lady of Sorrows," 105.
6. Quoted in Gourse, *Billie Holiday*, 77.
7. Marshall, *Fisher King*, 165.
8. Ibid., 25.
9. Brodie, "Sound of Postmemory"; Pollard, "Writing Bridges of Sound," 34–36; Muyumba, *Shadow and the Act*, 28. See also Rogers, "Embodying Cultural Memory," 91–93; Lowney, "New Kind of Music," 105.
10. Marshall, *Fisher King*, 80. Certain aspects of Sonny-Rett's life echo faintly the biography of Bud Powell, legendary bebop pianist and cohort of Charlie Parker, like Holiday a tragic, haunted figure, whom Marshall remembers hearing often in the New York clubs when she was young. Her jazz novel is dedicated to her cousin Sonny Clement, a baritone saxophonist ostracized by his family for his dogged pursuit of music, who was drafted into the army in the early 1940s and suffered a premature death that remains unsolved. The only tangible memory Marshall has of her cousin is a photograph propped on the piano in her parental living room. See Lowney, "New Kind of Music," 103; Stander, "Conversation with Paule Marshall."
11. Marshall, *Fisher King*, 136–137.
12. Feige, *Philosophie des Jazz*, 76–78.
13. Marshall, *Fisher King*, 140–141.
14. Ibid., 96, 20, 173, 21. See also Saint-Amour, "*Ulysses* Pianola," 18–20.
15. Marshall, *Fisher King*, 139, 38–39, 112–117, 160.
16. Ibid., 75, 154–155.
17. Ibid., 185, 186, 201.
18. Ibid., 105–107.
19. Ibid., 176.
20. Ibid., 185.
21. Ibid., 34.

22. See also Miller, *On the Ruins of Modernity*, 55–70
23. Marshall, *Fisher King*, 16.
24. Holiday, "Good Morning Heartache."
25. DJ Spooky and Vijay Iyer, "Improvising Digital Culture," 227.
26. I am indebted to DoVeanna S. Fulton and especially R. Baxter Miller for pointing out to me the socio-aesthetic dynamics between artistic form and social improvisation.
27. Baldwin, "Sonny's Blues," 1316.
28. Baldwin, *Another Country*, 8–9. See also Hogue, "Blues, Individuated Subjectivity," 6–7; Lordi, *Black Resonance*, 121–123.
29. Douglass, *Autobiographies*, 23, 24, 184, 502. See also Stoever, *Sonic Color Line*, 47–51; Messmer, "If Not in the Word," 11–14.
30. Douglass, *Autobiographies*, 78.
31. Interview with the author, June 22, 2013. Lacy was apparently more generous with Frederic Rzewski, whom he lent exactly fifteen seconds; see Bailey, *Improvisation*, 141.
32. Feige, *Philosophie des Jazz*, 73. See also Heile, "Play It Again, Duke," 241–245.
33. Scott, "Émigré's Paradise"; Morgenstern, "Case of 'Terminal' Boredom."
34. *Terminal*, DVD. All subsequent quotations from the film come from this source.
35. The script for *The Terminal* was in part inspired by the story of Merhan Karimi Nasseri, an Iranian national who lived in terminal 1 of Paris's Charles de Gaulle International Airport for an incredible eighteen years. Much of his story remains murky to this day, despite several documentaries and an autobiography, but Nasseri, in addition to lacking the proper travel and immigration documents, seems to have suffered from some kind of mental disorder as well. See Rose, "Waiting for Spielberg"; Berczeller, "Man Who Lost His Past"; McBride, *Stephen Spielberg*, 500.
36. Benjamin, *Passagen-Werk*, 83; Virilio, *Negative Horizon*, 104. See also Ferguson, "Aviation Cinema," 312; Hall, *Transparent Traveler*, 28–34, 55–56; Schaberg, *Textual Life of Airports*, 71–79.
37. *Esquire* magazine published Kane's famous photograph only in its January 1959 issue, so Viktor's father could not possibly have seen it in a Hungarian newspaper a year prior, even if it had slipped past the censors in the wake of the bloody oppression of the 1956 revolution by Soviet troops. This is but one of a whole host of impossibilities and contradictions that push *The Terminal* into the realm of the fairy tale. See *Great Day in Harlem*.
38. "Total Film Interview—Steven Spielberg"; Gordon, "Rainbow People."
39. Ellison, "Richard Wright's Blues," 129; Ellington, "Immigration Blues"; Parker, "Visa"; Parker, "Passport." Ellington's "Immigration Blues" features trumpeter Bubber Miley, so integral to Ellington's "jungle style," whose trademark plunger-work paired with a persistent growl creates a speechlike effect on his solo chorus.
40. Quoted in Hentoff, liner notes to *Benny Golson's New York Scene*.
41. According to Golson, both Spielberg and leading actor Tom Hanks cite the haunting ballad "I Remember Clifford" as one of their favorite songs, which is how they settled on Golson to provide the MacGuffin for the motion picture. Golson wrote "I Remember Clifford" as an antidote to trauma, the premature death of trumpeter Clifford Brown, who perished in an automobile accident at age twenty-five along with pianist Richie Powell and his wife, Nancy. Given its somber context and melody, it is certainly no coincidence that the filmmaker decided on the

bouncy "Killer Joe" instead. See Ratliff, "Saxophone Hero's Big Break"; Heckman, "Talent for Landing"; Catalano, *Clifford Brown*, 184–186; Farmer and Golson, "I Remember Clifford," on *Meet the Jazztet*.

42. See Ratliff, "Saxophone Hero's Big Break"; J. Williams, *The Terminal*; Golson, *Terminal 1*.

43. Ostendorf and Rathert, "America's 'Musical Unconscious.'" See also Von Eschen, *Satchmo Blows Up the World*, 249.

44. Quoted in *Great Day in Harlem*.

45. Ibid.

46. Ibid.

47. Farmer and Golson, "Killer Joe," on *Meet the Jazztet*.

48. Quoted in *Great Day in Harlem*.

49. Benjamin, "Kleine Geschichte der Photographie," 295, 302.

50. Marshall, *Fisher King*, 52.

51. Benjamin, "Kleine Geschichte der Photographie," 290.

52. Benjamin, "Das Kunstwerk im Zeitalter," 148; Marshall, *Fisher King*, 19.

53. Benjamin, "Kleine Geschichte der Photographie," 312. See also Eiland and Jennings, *Walter Benjamin*, 363–366; Powers, "Wolkenwandelbarkeit," 279–287.

54. Benjamin, "Kleine Geschichte der Photographie," 297.

55. Benjamin, *Passagen-Werk*, 481.

56. Ibid., 855. See also Schaberg, *End of Airports*, 97–101.

57. L. Thomas, *Extraordinary Measures*, 170.

58. Dibango and Kelman, *Balade en Saxo*, 256.

59. Quoted in "Jazz Matters How and Why." Four days after the attacks, Sonny Rollins, one of the most uncompromising improvisers in jazz—Viktor mentions him by name when he explains to Amelia the significance of "A Great Day in Harlem"—gave a concert in Boston's Berklee Performance Center. Following the band introductions, Rollins echoes Iyer's remarks, with a sense of doubt and futility even: "We must remember that music is the—one of the beautiful things of life, so we have to try to keep the music alive some kind of way. And, uhm, maybe music can help, I don't know but we have to try *something* these days." He then launches into a wistful rendition of "A Nightingale Sang in Berkeley Square," a standard whose lyrics have the titular bird sing its tune in a topsy-turvy world. See Rollins, *Without a Song*.

60. Benjamin, *Passagen-Werk*, 1004.

61. Benjamin, "Über den Begriff der Geschichte," 254.

62. Quoted in R. Thomas, "Lucas Niggli," 34.

63. Marshall, *Fisher King*, 195.

CONCLUSION. JÜRG WICKIHALDER GETS AROUND

1. *The Terminal*, DVD.

2. Feige, *Philosophie des Jazz*, 118; Iyer, "Exploding the Narrative," 400, emphasis in original.

3. I draw here on Feige's argument that jazz makes explicit what remains implicit in the classical European concert tradition, that the difference in question is a difference of degree, in other words, not a difference in kind necessarily. See Feige, *Philosophie des Jazz*, 56–89. See also

Iyer, "Village of the Virgins"; Ellington, "Village of the Virgins"; Rachmaninoff, *Rachmaninoff Plays Rachmaninoff*; Ashkenazy, *Rachmaninov*.

4. Ansermet, "Bechet and Jazz Visit Europe," 117, 118. See also Braggs, *Jazz Diasporas*, 12–13; Gennari, *Blowin' Hot and Cool*, 20–21; Polillo, *Jazz*, 89–90, 288–290.

5. Krohn, *Vrenelis Gärtli*, 9.

6. Interview with the author, July 20, 2016.

7. Krohn and Wickihalder, *Schneewittchen*; Wickihalder and Jürg Wickihalder Orchestra, *Narziss und Echo*.

8. Interview with the author, June 22, 2013. See also Fischer-Tian, "Vom Jazzkeller zur Bohemia," 227–232.

9. Interview with the author, June 22, 2013. See also Shasimosa Tütü, *Lugano*; Schildpatt, *Bunju*; Gordon and Bailey, *Round Midnight*; Hancock, "Watermelon Man"; Davatz, "Industriearchitektur," 93–95.

10. Interview with the author, June 22, 2013.

11. Interview with the author, July 20, 2016. See also Lacy, *Findings*.

12. Jürg Wickihalder, email message to author, May 4, 2017; Wickihalder and BEYOND, *Beyond*.

13. Interview with the author, June 22, 2013; Dibango and Kelman, *Balade en saxo*, 21; Pfeifer, "Heute hier, morgen dort," 9. See also Guy and Barry Guy New Orchestra, *Amphi/Radio Rondo*; Käppeli and the Even Odds, *Prisoner of Time*; Wickihalder, Favre, Klusman, and Glarner Kammerchor; Travelogue, *The Light Is On*; Wickihalder, *Jürg Wickihalder Directing*; Meyer, "Bird Gong Game."

14. Quoted in Lange, liner notes to *Jump!*

15. Interview with the author, June 22, 2013.

16. Schweizer and Wickihalder, *Spring*. The album title sounds a transnationally polyglot as well as aerial pun: in German, *spring* is the imperative of *to jump*.

17. Wickihalder refers to Schweizer as "my favorite 'drummer' on the piano" (quoted in Lange, liner notes to *Jump!*). In fact, Schweizer has occupied the trap set in a variety of ensembles, the Feminist Improvising Group FIG or the also all-female combo Canaille, for example. Once again, Madam Zajj is tapping her foot approvingly. See Broecking, *Dieses Unbändige Gefühl*, 145–160; Born, "After Relational Aesthetics," 53–57.

18. Quoted in Wyss, "Das archaische Herz der Finsternis."

19. Quoted in ibid.

20. See *Irène Schweizer*, DVD; Broecking, *Dieses Unbändige Gefühl*, 48–58, R. Kelley, *Africa Speaks*, 136–153; Liebman, "Free Jazz," 117–122.

21. Gordon, *Stella by Starlight*; Gordon, *Those Were the Days*; Meyer and Root Down, *Root Down*; Ziegele and Where's Africa?, *Can Walk on Sand*.

22. Wickihalder and Schweizer, "Monk and More . . ." See also Aeschimann, "Das Spiel mit dem Tod"; McCarthy, "Reading the Red Bull Sublime," 543–545, 547–549, 552–555.

23. Hughes, "Trumpet Player," 115.

24. Miller, "Langston Hughes," 283.

25. Moraru, *Cosmodernism*, 53, 122; Benjamin, *Einbahnstrasse*, 79.

26. Moraru, *Reading for the Planet*, 69.

27. Brunner, *Glarner Geschichte*, 142–143; Hauser, *Stadt in Flammen*, 63–79; Wickihalder et al., *Brandruf*. See also Wickihalder, *Brandruf, Jürg Wickihalder*; "Brandruf."

28. In Switzerland, a Harmoniemusik is essentially a community band consisting of woodwind and brass instruments and some percussion that developed out of the tradition of the marching bands. Today, marches still make up an important segment of a Harmoniemusik's repertoire, but they will be complemented by rearranged light classics and pop.

29. Fueter, *Das Lächeln am Fusse*, 118

30. Quoted in Pavlić, *Who Can Afford to Improvise?*, 70.

31. Giddins, *Visions of Jazz*, 8.

32. Interview with the author, June 22, 2013.

33. Ra, "Sound Image," 351. See also Fukuyama, *End of History*, xii.

Bibliography

Aeschimann, Walter. "Das Spiel mit dem Tod," *Neue Zürcher Zeitung*, July 3, 2015. www.nzz.ch/gesellschaft/lebensart/outdoor/das-spiel-mit-dem-tod-1.18573368.
Alexander, Eric. *Chim Chim Cheree*. Recorded October 3, 2009. Venus VHCD78175, 2010, CD.
———. *Full Range*. Recorded January 3, 1994. Criss Cross Jazz 1098, 1995, CD.
Alexander, Stephon. *The Jazz of Physics: The Secret Link between Music and the Structure of the Universe*. New York: Basic Books, 2016.
"Amati History." Amati, 2016. www.amati.cz/en/company/history.
Ansermet, Ernst-Alexandre. "Bechet and Jazz Visit Europe, 1919." Translated by Walter J. Schaap. In *Frontiers of Jazz*. 3rd rev. ed. Edited by Ralph de Toledano, 111–118. Gretna: Pelican, 1994.
Appel, Alfred, Jr. *Jazz Modernism: From Ellington and Armstrong to Matisse and Joyce*. New York: Knopf, 2002.
Appignanesi, Lisa. *The Cabaret*. New Haven: Yale University Press, 2004.
Asheru and Talib Kweli. "Mood Swing." Recorded 2003. YouTube, www.youtube.com/watch?v=7xkoeGIUoYs.
Ashkenazy, Vladimir. *Rachmaninov: Piano Concertos 2 and 3*. Decca 289 466 375-2, 1999, CD.
Atkins, E. Taylor. *Blue Nippon: Authenticating Jazz in Japan*. Durham: Duke University Press, 2001.
Atkinson, J. Brooks. "Maurice Chevalier, Minstrel." *New York Times*, March 31, 1930, 26. *ProQuest Historical Newspapers*.
Avenel-Cohen, Pascale. "*Jazz* de Hans Janowitz, ou l'ère de la syncope." *Cahiers d'Études Germaniques* 46 (2004): 129–141.
Azevedo, Mario J. *Roots of Violence: A History of War in Chad*. Amsterdam: Gordon and Breach, 1998.
Badger, Reid. *A Life in Ragtime: A Biography of James Reese Europe*. New York: Oxford University Press, 2007.
Bailey, Derek. *Improvisation: Its Nature and Practice in Music*. 2nd rev. ed. New York: Da Capo, 1993.
Baldwin, James. *Another Country*. New York: Vintage, 1992.
———. "Sonny's Blues." In *Call and Response: The Riverside Anthology of the African American Literary Tradition*, edited by Patricia Liggins Hill et al., 1298–1316. Boston: Houghton Mifflin, 1998.

Baraka, Amiri. *Blues People: The Negro Experience in America and the Music That Developed from It.* New York: Morrow Quill, 1963.

———. Liner notes to *Coltrane Live at Birdland*, by John Coltrane. Recorded 1963. Impulse! IMP-198, 1997, CD.

Barg, Lisa. "Strayhorn's Queer Arrangements." In *Improvisation and Social Aesthetics*, ed. Georgina Born, Eric Lewis, and Will Straw, 183–212. Durham: Duke University Press, 2017.

Barton, William E. *Old Plantation Hymns: A Collection of Hitherto Unpublished Melodies of the Slave and the Freedman, with Historical and Descriptive Notes.* Whitefish: Kessinger, 2006.

Barzel, Tamar. "Subsidy, Advocacy, Theory: Experimental Music in the Academy, in New York City, and Beyond." In *People Get Ready: The Future of Jazz Is Now!*, edited by Ajay Heble and Rob Wallace, 153–165. Durham: Duke University Press, 2013.

Baudelaire, Charles. "Le Cygne." In *Les Fleurs du Mal: Die Blumen des Bösen*, rev. ed., 176–179. Stuttgart: Reclam, 2002.

Baumann, Nathalie. "Die Literatur war Jazz geworden: Hans Janowitz' 'Jazz' Roman als polyphones Stimmungsbarometer der zwanziger Jahre." *Weimarer Beiträge* 52, no. 3 (2006): 354–377.

Bechet, Sidney. *Treat It Gentle: An Autobiography.* New York: Da Capo Press, 1978.

Benjamin, Walter. "Ankündigung der Zeitschrift: Angelus Novus." In *Walter Benjamin: Ein Lesebuch*, edited by Michael Opitz, 181–186. Frankfurt am Main: Suhrkamp, 1996.

———. Einbahnstrasse. In *Walter Benjamin: Ein Lesebuch*, edited by Michael Opitz, 75–138. Frankfurt am Main: Suhrkamp, 1996.

———. "Kleine Geschichte der Photographie." In *Walter Benjamin: Ein Lesebuch*, edited by Michael Opitz, 287–312. Frankfurt am Main: Suhrkamp, 1996.

———. "Das Kunstwerk im Zeitalter seiner technischen Reproduzierbarkeit." In *Illuminationen: Ausgewählte Schriften 1*, edited by Siegfried Unseld, 136–169. Frankfurt am Main: Suhrkamp, 1974.

———. "Kurze Schatten I." In *Illuminationen: Ausgewählte Schriften 1*, edited by Siegfried Unseld, 297–306. Frankfurt am Main: Suhrkamp, 1974.

———. "Das Paris des Second Empire bei Baudelaire." In *Walter Benjamin: Ein Lesebuch*, edited by Michael Opitz, 500–591. Frankfurt am Main: Suhrkamp, 1996.

———. *Das Passagen-Werk.* Edited by Rolf Tiedemann. Frankfurt am Main: Suhrkamp, 1983.

———. "Über den Begriff der Geschichte." In *Illuminationen: Ausgewählte Schriften 1*, edited by Siegfried Unseld, 251–261. Frankfurt am Main: Suhrkamp, 1974.

———. "Über einige Motive bei Baudelaire." In *Illuminationen: Ausgewählte Schriften 1*, edited by Siegfried Unseld, 185–229. Frankfurt am Main: Suhrkamp, 1974.

———. *Ursprung des deutschen Trauerspiels.* Edited by Rolf Tiedemann. Frankfurt am Main: Suhrkamp, 1996.

———. "Die Wiederkehr des Flaneurs: Zu Franz Hessels 'Spazieren in Berlin.'" In *Angelus Novus: Ausgewählte Schriften 2*, edited by Siegfried Unseld, 416–421. Frankfurt am Main: Suhrkamp, 1988.

Bennighof, James. "Fluidity in Paul Simon's 'Graceland': On Text and Music in a Popular Song." *College Music Symposium* 33/34 (1993–1994): 212–236.

Berczeller, Paul. "The Man Who Lost His Past," *Guardian*, September 6, 2004. www.theguardian.com/film/2004/sep/06/features.features11.

Berendt, Joachim Ernst. *Das grosse Jazzbuch: Von New Orleans bis Jazz Rock*. 5th rev. ed. Fischer: Frankfurt am Main, 1985.

Berendt, Joachim Ernst, and Günther Huesmann. *The Jazz Book: From Ragtime to the 21st Century*. 7th rev. ed. Translated by H. Bredigkeit et al. Chicago: Lawrence Hill, 2009.

Berkowitz, Aron L. *The Improvising Mind: Cognition and Creativity in the Musical Moment*. New York: Oxford University Press, 2010.

Berliner, Paul F. *Thinking in Jazz: The Infinite Art of Improvisation*. Chicago: University of Chicago Press, 1994.

Bernard, Emily. *Carl Van Vechten and the Harlem Renaissance: A Portrait in Black and White*. New Haven: Yale University Press, 2012.

Bernard, Patrick. "Langston Hughes, the Tom-Tom, and the Discursive Place of Memory in Culture." *Langston Hughes Review* 17 (2002): 35–48.

Blue Note: A Story of Modern Jazz. Directed by Julian Benedikt. Poing: Medici Arts, 2008, DVD.

Bohlman, Philip V. "Music Inside Out: Sounding Public Religion in a Post-Secular Europe." In *Music, Sound, and Space: Transformations of Public and Private Experience*, edited by Georgina Born, 205–223. Cambridge: Cambridge University Press, 2013.

Bolden, Tony. "All the Birds Sing Bass: The Revolutionary Blues of Jayne Cortez." *African American Review* 35, no. 1 (2001): 61–71.

Bolling, Claude. *A Drum Is a Woman*. Recorded in 1996. Frémaux & Associés FA 476, 2005, CD.

Bolling, Claude, and Jean-Paul Daubresse. *Bolling Story*. Paris: Alphée, 2008.

Bolz, Norbert, and Willem van Reijen. *Walter Benjamin*. Frankfurt am Main: Campus, 1991.

Born, Georgina. "After Relational Aesthetics: Improvised Music, the Social, and (Re)Theorizing the Aesthetic." In *Improvisation and Social Aesthetics*, edited by Georgina Born, Eric Lewis, and Will Straw, 33–57. Durham: Duke University Press, 2017.

———. Introduction to *Music, Sound, and Space: Transformations of Public and Private Experience*, edited by Georgina Born, 1–69. Cambridge: Cambridge University Press, 2013.

Borshuk, Michael. "'Noisy Modernism': The Cultural Politics of Langston Hughes's Early Jazz Poetry." *Langston Hughes Review* 17 (2002): 4–21.

Boutin, Aimée. *City of Noise: Sound and Nineteenth-Century Paris*. Urbana: University of Illinois Press, 2015.

Bowie, David. *Space Oddity*. RCA Victor LSP-4813, 1972, LP.

"Box Office Mojo: High Fidelity." *Box Office Mojo*. n.d. www.boxofficemojo.com/movies/?id=highfidelity.htm.

Brady, Philip. "'Saxophon—guter Ton!': On Hans Janowitz's Jazz-Novel of 1927." In *Expeditionen nach der Wahrheit: Poems, Essays, and Papers in Honour of Theo Stammler*. Edited by Stefan Horlacher and Marion Islinger, 461–470. Heidelberg: Carl Winter, 1996.

Braggs, Rashida K. "Evoking Baldwin's Blues: The Experience of Dislocated Listening." *James Baldwin Review* 1 (2015): 152–163.

———. "Excerpt from *Jazz Diasporas: Race, Music, and Migration in Post–World War II Paris*." *Journal of Transnational American Studies* 7, no. 1 (2016): 1–20.

———. *Jazz Diasporas: Race, Music, and Migration in Post–World War II Paris*. Oakland: University of California Press, 2016.

"Brandruf," SF Kultur, Kulturplatz Lokaltermin, May 7, 2011. www.srf.ch/play/tv/kulturplatz/video/lokaltermin?id=c2b4a892-b437-49c8-84eb-27cf04527183.

Britt, Stan. *Dexter Gordon: A Musical Biography*. New York: Da Capo, 1988.

Brodersen, Momme. *Walter Benjamin: A Biography*. Translated by Malcolm R. Green and Ingrida Ligers. Edited by Martina Dervis. London: Verso, 1997.

Brodie, Laura. "The Sound of Postmemory in Paule Marshall's *Praisesong for the Widow*." Presentation at the annual convention of the Modern Language Association of America, Vancouver, B.C., January 8, 2015.

Broecking, Christian. *Dieses Unbändige Gefühl der Freiheit: Irène Schweizer—Jazz, Avantgarde, Politik*. Berlin: Broecking, 2016.

———. "Don't Call My Music J***?" *Jazz Thing*, February–March 2014, 24.

Broonzy, Big Bill. "White, Brown, and Black." Recorded 1951. On *Trouble in Mind*, Smithsonian Folkways SFW 40131, 2000, CD.

Brown, David P. *Noise Orders: Jazz, Improvisation, and Architecture*. Minneapolis: University of Minnesota Press, 2006.

Brown, Timothy S. "'Keeping it Real' in a Different 'Hood: (African-)Americanization and Hip Hop in Germany." In *The Vinyl Ain't Final: Hip Hop and the Globalization of Black Popular Culture*, ed. Dipannita Basu and Sidney J. Lemelle, 137–150. London: Pluto, 2006.

Brunner, Christoph H. *Glarner Geschichte in Geschichten*. Glarus: Baeschlin, 2004.

Büchmann-Møller, Frank. *Someone to Watch over Me: The Life and Music of Ben Webster*. Translated by Paul Banks. Ann Arbor: University of Michigan Press, 2006.

Bühler, Götz. "European Jazz Legends: Begegnungen mit den Wegbereitern." *Jazz Thing*, January 2014, 66–75.

Burns, John F. "Trucks of the Taliban: Durable, not Discreet," *New York Times*, November 23, 2001. www.nytimes.com/2001/11/23/automobiles/autos-on-friday-international-trucks-of-the-taliban-durable-not-discreet.html.

Burr, J. Millard, and Robert O. Collins. *Africa's Thirty Years' War: Chad, Libya, and the Sudan, 1963–1993*. Boulder: Westview, 1999.

Butler, Judith. *Undoing Gender*. New York: Routledge, 2004.

Butterfield, Matthew W. "Race and Rhythm: The Social Component of the Swing Groove." *Jazz Perspectives* 4, no. 3 (2010): 301–355.

Das Cabinet des Dr. Caligari. Filmed 1920. Directed by Robert Wiene. Hollywood, Image Entertainment, 1996, DVD.

Cale, J. J. "Right Down Here." On *Really*. Philips 6369 112, 1973, LP.

Catalano, Nick. *Clifford Brown: The Life and Art of the Legendary Jazz Trumpeter*. New York: Oxford University Press, 2000.

Celenza, Anna. "Duke Ellington, Billy Strayhorn, and the Adventures of *Peer Gynt* in America." *Music and Politics* 5, no. 2 (2011): 1–22.

Chaney, Michael A. "Traveling Harlem's Europe: Vagabondage from Slave Narratives to Gwendolyn Bennett's *Wedding Day* and Claude McKay's *Banjo*." *Journal of Narrative Theory* 32, no. 1 (2002): 52–76.

Chilton, John. *Sidney Bechet: The Wizard of Jazz*. New York: Da Capo, 1996.

Clarke, Donald. *Wishing on the Moon: The Life and Times of Billie Holiday*. New York: Penguin, 1994.

Cohen, Harvey G. *Duke Ellington's America*. Chicago: University of Chicago Press, 2010.

Coleman, Ornette. *Science Fiction*. Recorded 1972. Columbia 64774, n.d., LP.
Coleman, Steve, and the Mystic Rhythm Society. *The Sign and the Seal*. BMG France 74321407272, 1996, CD.
Coltrane, John. *Ballads*. Recorded 1961 and 1962. Impulse! 314 589 548-2, 2002, 2 CDs.
———. *Coltrane Live at Birdland*. Recorded 1963. Impulse! IMP-198, 1997, CD.
———. "Coltrane on Coltrane." *Down Beat*, September 1960, 26–27.
———. *The Complete 1961 Village Vanguard Recordings*. GRP IMPD4-232, 1997, 4 CDs.
———. *The Complete Africa/Brass Sessions*. Recorded 1961. Impulse! IMPD-2-168, 1995, 2 CDs.
———. *Soultrane*. Recorded February 7, 1958. Prestige PRCD-30006-2, 2006, CD.
———. *Traneing In*. Recorded August 23, 1957. Prestige PRCD-30156-2, 2007, CD.
Cook, Susan C. "Jazz as Deliverance: The Reception and Institution of American Jazz during the Weimar Republic." *American Music* 7, no. 1 (1989): 30–47.
Cortez, Jayne, and the Firespitters. "If the Drum Is a Woman." On *There It Is*, Bola Press BP 8201, 1982, LP.
Crow, Bill. *Jazz Anecdotes*. New York: Oxford University Press, 1990.
Dance, Stanley. Liner notes to *Togo Brava Suite*, by Duke Ellington. Recorded October 22, 1971. Blue Note CDP 7243 8 30082 2 3, 1994, CD.
Danzi, Michael. *American Musician in Germany, 1924–1939: Memoirs of the Jazz, Entertainment, and Movie World of Berlin During the Weimar Republic and the Nazi Era, and in the United States*. Edited by Rainer E. Lotz. Schmitten: Ruecker, 1986.
Daub, Adrian. "Sonic Dreamworlds: Benjamin, Adorno, and the Phantasmagoria of the Opera House." In *A Companion to the Works of Walter Benjamin*, edited by Rolf Goebel, 273–294. New York: Camden House, 2009.
Davatz, Jürg. "Industriearchitektur im Kanton Glarus." In *Industriekultur im Kanton Glarus: Streifzüge durch 250 Jahre Geschichte und Architektur*, edited by Rolf von Arx, Jürg Davatz, and August Rohr, 43–98. Glarus: Südostschweiz Buchverlag, 2005.
Davis, Angela Y. *Blues Legacies and Black Feminism: Gertrude "Ma" Rainey, Bessie Smith, and Billie Holiday*. New York: Pantheon, 1998.
Davis, Francis. "Our Lady of Sorrows." *Atlantic Monthly*, November 2000, 105.
Davis, Miles, and Quincy Troupe. *Miles: The Autobiography*. London: Picador, 2012.
Dewey, Donald. "Swinging up North." *Scandinavian Review* 95, no. 3 (2008): 18–29.
Dibango, Manu. *Ballad Emotion*. Wagram 3244182, 2011, CD.
———. "Ce sont les gens qui font un tube, pas toi," *leJJD.fr*, November 22, 2011. www.lejdd.fr/Culture/Musique/Actualite/Manu-Dibango-sort-un-nouvel-opus-intitule-Past-Present-Futur-427655.
———. *Electric Africa*. Polydor 827 014-1, 1985, LP.
———. "Interview with Manu Dibango." UNESCO *Courier*, March 1991, 4–7.
———. "Makossa '87." On *Afrijazzy*. Polydor/GEMA 831 720-1, 1986, LP.
———. *Manu Dibango Plays Sidney Bechet: Homage to New Orleans*. Goya 442 027-2, 2007, CD.
———. "Négropolitaines." On *Négropolitaines*. Soul Paris/Mélodie 85904-2, 1989, CD.
———. *Négropolitaines Vol. II*. Soul Paris/Mélodie 85905-2, 1992, CD.
———. *O Boso*. Société Française du Son SH.8451, 1973, LP.
———. "Soul Makossa." On *Soul Makossa*. Teldec/Decca SLK 17025-P, 1973, LP.

———. "Soul Makossa 2.0." On *Past Present Future*. BorderBlaster/Sony Bbcd021, 2012, CD.
———. *Surtension*. Garima ZL 37829, 1984, LP.
———. "Toyota Makossa." Toshiba EMI 4 RS 962, n.d., single.
Dibango, Manu, and Gaston Kelman. *Balade en saxo: Dans les coulisses de ma vie*. Paris: L'Archipel, 2013.
Dibango, Manu, and Danielle Rouard. *Three Kilos of Coffee: An Autobiography*. Translated by Beth G. Raps. Chicago: University of Chicago Press, 1994.
Dimock, Wai Chee. "Literature for the Planet." *PMLA* 116, no. 1 (2001): 173–188.
DJ Spooky and Vijay Iyer. "Improvising Digital Culture." In *People Get Ready: The Future of Jazz Is Now!*, edited by Ajay Heble and Rob Wallace, 225–243. Durham: Duke University Press, 2013.
Doctor, Jenny. "*Jazz is where you find it:* Encountering Jazz on BBC Television, 1946–66." In *Watching Jazz: Encounters with Jazz Performance on Screen*, edited by Björn Heile, Peter Elsdon, and Jenny Doctor, 103–143. New York: Oxford University Press, 2016.
Douglas, Ann. "Skyscrapers, Airplanes, and Airmindedness: 'The Necessary Angel.'" In *The Jazz Cadence of American Culture*, edited by Robert G. O'Meally, 196–223. New York: Columbia University Press, 1998.
Douglass, Frederick. *Autobiographies*. Edited by Henry Louis Gates Jr. New York: Library of America, 1996.
Dresser, Mark. *The Cabinet of Dr. Caligari: Music for the Silent Film by Mark Dresser*. Knitting Factory Works KFW 155, 1996, CD.
Dümling, Albrecht. "Musikalische Verfahrensweise und gesellschaftliche Funktion: Hanns Eisler und der Jazz." In *"Es liegt in der Luft was idiotisches . . .": Populäre Musik zur Zeit der Weimarer Republik*, ed. Helmut Rösing, 118–138. Freudenberg: ASPM, 1995.
Dvinge, Anne. "Keeping Time, Performing Place: Jazz Heterotopia in Candace Allen's Valaida." *Journal of Transnational American Studies* 4, no. 2 (2012): 1–19.
Edwards, Brent Hayes. "The Literary Ellington." *Representations* 77 (2002): 1–29.
Eiland, Howard, and Michael W. Jennings. *Walter Benjamin: A Critical Life*. Cambridge: Belknap, 2014.
Ellington, Duke. *The Afro-Eurasian Eclipse*. Recorded 1971. Original Jazz Classics OJCCD-645-2, 1991, CD.
———. *A Drum Is a Woman*. Recorded 1956. Jazz Wax JWR 4527, 2010, LP.
———. *A Drum Is a Woman*. Aired May 8, 1957. CBS television. Paley Center for Media, New York City, catalog ID T79:0105. Viewed June 22, 2017.
———. "Echo Tango." Recorded September 1, 1954. On *Complete Capitol Recordings of Duke Ellington*. Mosaic MQ8-160, 1999, 5 CDs.
———. *Ellington Complete at Newport*. Recorded July 7, 1956. Columbia/Sony Legacy C2K 64932, 1999, 2 CDs.
———. "Immigration Blues." Recorded December 29, 1926. On *Early Ellington: The Complete Brunswick and Vocalion Recordings of Duke Ellington, 1926–1931*. Decca GRD-3-640, 1994, 3 CDs.
———. "Limbo Jazz." On *Duke Ellington Meets Coleman Hawkins*. Recorded 1962. Impulse! IMPD-162, 1995, CD.

———. "Monologue (Pretty and the Wolf)." On *The Duke: The Essential Collection, 1927–1962*. Columbia 65841, 1999, 3 CDs.

———. *Music Is My Mistress*. New York: Da Capo Press, 1973.

———. "Pomegranate." On *A Drum Is a Woman . . . Plus*. Recorded March 7, 1957. Musica Jazz MJCD 1269, 2013, CD.

———. *Togo Brava Suite*. Recorded June 28 and 29, 1971. Storyville STCD 8323, 2001, CD.

———. *Togo Brava Suite*. Recorded October 22, 1971. Blue Note CDP 7243 8 30082 2 3, 1994, CD.

———. "The Village of the Virgins." On *The Suites: New York 1968 and 1970*. Saja 91045-2, 1987, CD.

Ellington, Duke, and John Coltrane. *Duke Ellington and John Coltrane*. Recorded September 26, 1962. Impulse! IMP 11662, 1993, CD.

Ellington, Mercer, and Stanley Dance. *Duke Ellington*. Translated by Rudolf Fischer. Rüschlikon: Albert Müller, 1980.

Ellison, Ralph. "The Charlie Christian Story." In *The Collected Essays of Ralph Ellison*, edited by John F. Callahan, 266–272. New York: Modern Library, 1995.

———. "Going to the Territory." In *The Collected Essays of Ralph Ellison*, edited by John F. Callahan, 591–612. New York: Modern Library, 1995.

———. "The Golden Age, Time Past." In *The Collected Essays of Ralph Ellison*, edited by John F. Callahan, 237–249. New York: Modern Library, 1995.

———. "Homage to Duke Ellington on His Birthday." In *The Collected Essays of Ralph Ellison*, edited by John F. Callahan, 676–683. New York: Modern Library, 1995.

———. *Invisible Man*. New York: Vintage International, 1995.

———. "Richard Wright's Blues." In *The Collected Essays of Ralph Ellison*, edited by John F. Callahan, 128–144. New York: Modern Library, 1995.

Ewart, Douglas, and Nicole Mitchell, Roscoe Mitchell, Famoudou Don Moye, Matana Roberts, Jaribu Shahid, Wadada Leo Smith, and Corey Wilkes. "Ancient to the Future: Celebrating Forty Years of the AACM." In *People Get Ready: The Future of Jazz Is Now!*, edited by Ajay Heble and Rob Wallace, 244–264. Durham: Duke University Press, 2013.

Die Fantastischen Vier. "Die da!?!" On *4 gewinnt*. Columbia 472263 2, 1992, CD.

———. *Heimspiel*. Columbia 886975608225, 2009, 3 CDs.

Farmer, Art, and Benny Golson. *Meet the Jazztet*. Recorded 1960. Chess CHD-91550, 1990, CD.

Feige, Daniel Martin. *Philosophie des Jazz*. Berlin: Suhrkamp, 2014.

Ferguson, Kevin L. "Aviation Cinema." *Criticism* 57, no. 2 (2015): 309–331.

Fischer-Tian, Werner. "Vom Jazzkeller zur Bohemia: Die Pionierphase des Jazz in Glarus Ende der fünfziger Jahre." In *Jazz in der Schweiz: Geschichte und Geschichten*, edited by Bruno Spoerri, 227–232. Zurich: Chronos, 2006.

Fisher Fishkin, Shelley. "Crossroads of Culture: The Transnational Turn in American Studies—Presidential Address to the American Studies Association, November 12, 2004." *American Quarterly* 57, no. 1 (2005): 17–57.

Friedlander, Eli. "On the Musical Gathering of Echoes of the Voice: Walter Benjamin on Opera and the *Trauerspiel*." *Opera Quarterly* 21, no. 4 (2006): 631–646.

Fueter, Daniel. *Das Lächeln am Fusse der Tonleiter: Betrachtungen zu Musik und Gesellschaft*. Zurich: Rüffer und Rub, 2011.

Fukuyama, Francis. *The End of History and the Last Man*. Rev. ed. New York: Free Press, 2006.
Fuld, Werner. *Walter Benjamin: Eine Biographie*. Hamburg: Rowohlt, 1990.
Gabbard, Krin. *Jammin' at the Margins: Jazz and the American Cinema*. Chicago: University of Chicago Press, 1996.
Garber, Frederick. "Fabulating Jazz." In *Representing Jazz*, edited by Krin Gabbard, 70–103. Durham: Duke University Press, 1995.
Gazarek, Dennis. "Amati Instrument Manufacturer: The History." *Sax on the Web*. 2008. www.saxontheweb.net/Resources/Amati-History.html.
Gehrmann, Susanne. "Cosmopolitanism with African Roots: Afropolitanism's Ambivalent Mobilities." *Journal of African Cultural Studies* 28, no. 1 (2016): 61–72.
Gennari, John. *Blowin' Hot and Cool: Jazz and Its Critics*. Chicago: University of Chicago Press, 2006.
Geuen, Heinz. "'Das hat die Welt noch nicht gesehen': Kabarett, Operette und Revue als Embleme populärer Kultur der 20er Jahre." In *"Es liegt in der Luft was idiotisches . . .": Populäre Musik zur Zeit der Weimarer Republik*, ed. Helmut Rösing, 52–68. Freudenberg: ASPM, 1995.
Giddins, Gary. *Visions of Jazz: The First Century*. New York: Oxford University Press, 1998.
Gikandi, Simon. "Foreword: On Afropolitanism." In *Negotiating Afropolitanism: Essays on Borders and Spaces in Contemporary African Literature and Folklore*, edited by Jennifer Wawrzinek and J. K. S. Makokha, 9–12. Amsterdam: Rodopi, 2011.
Gilloch, Graeme. *Walter Benjamin: Critical Constellations*. Cambridge: Polity, 2002.
Gilroy, Paul. *The Black Atlantic: Modernity and Double Consciousness*. Cambridge: Harvard University Press, 1993.
Gioia, Ted. *The History of Jazz*. New York: Oxford University Press, 1998.
Gitler, Ira. Liner notes to *Soultrane*, by John Coltrane. Recorded February 7, 1958. Prestige PRCD-30006-2, 2006, CD.
———. Liner notes to *Traneing In*, by John Coltrane. Recorded August 23, 1957. Prestige PRCD-30156-2, 2007, CD.
———. *Swing to Bop: An Oral History of the Transition in Jazz in the 1940s*. New York: Oxford University Press, 1985.
———. "'Trane on the Track." *Down Beat*, October 1958, 16–17.
Goeman, Ulfert, and Hans-Jürgen Schaal. "Autumn Leaves (Les Feuilles Mortes)." In *Jazz-Standards: Das Lexikon*, edited by Hans-Jürgen Schaal, 46–48. Kassel: Bärenreiter, 2002.
Goll, Ivan. "Die Neger erobern Europa." In *Weimarer Republik: Manifeste und Dokumente zur deutschen Literatur*, edited by Anton Kaes, 256–259. Stuttgart: Metzler, 1983.
Golson, Benny. *Benny Golson's New York Scene*. Recorded 1957. Contemporary C-3552, 1988, CD.
———. *Terminal 1*. Concord CCD-2259-2, 2004, CD.
Golson, Benny, and Jim Merod. "Forward Motion: An Interview with Benny Golson." *Boundary 2* 22, no. 2 (1995): 53–93.
Gooley, Dana. "Saving Improvisation: Hummel and the Free Fantasia in the Early Nineteenth Century." In *The Oxford Handbook of Critical Improvisation Studies*, edited by George E. Lewis and Benjamin Piekut, 2:185–205. New York: Oxford University Press, 2016.
Gordon, Dexter. "Catalonian Nights." On *Bouncin' with Dex*. SteepleChase SCS-1060, 1976, LP.
———. *Gettin' Around*. Recorded May 28–29, 1965. Blue Note CDP 7 46681 2, 1987, CD.

———. *Our Man in Paris*. Recorded May 23, 1963. Blue Note BST 84146, 1986, LP.
———. *The Panther!* Recorded 1970. Original Jazz Classics OJCCD-770-2, CD.
———. "The Rainbow People." On *The Tower of Power*. Prestige P-7623, 1993, CD.
———. "Stablemates." On *Stable Mable*. Recorded 1975. SteepleChase SCS-1040, 1990, CD.
———. *Stella by Starlight*. Recorded January 6, 1966. SteepleChase SCCD 36036, 2005, CD.
———. *Those Were the Days*. Recorded 1969. Moon MCD 059-2, 1992, CD.
———. "Three O'Clock in the Morning." On *After Midnight*. Recorded ca. 1969. SteepleChase SCCD-31226, 1988, CD.
———. "Three O'Clock in the Morning." On *Go*. Recorded 1962. Blue Note BST 84112, 1983, LP.
Gordon, Dexter, and Benny Bailey. *Round Midnight*. Recorded 1974. SteepleChase SCCD 31290, 1987.
Gourse, Leslie. *Billie Holiday: The Tragedy and Triumph of Lady Day*. New York: Franklin Watts, 1995.
Gov't Mule. *By a Thread*. Evil Teen 68751-12052-2, 2009, CD.
———. *The Tel-Star Sessions*. Recorded June–September 1994. Evil Teen 65175I-1227-2, 2016, CD.
———. "Trane." On *Gov't Mule*. Relativity CRT 1515, 1995, CD.
Goyal, Yogita. "Introduction: The Transnational Turn." In *The Cambridge Companion to Transnational American Literature*, edited by Yogita Goyal, 1–5. Cambridge: Cambridge University Press, 2017.
Graham, Shane. Introduction to *Langston Hughes and the South African* Drum *Generation*, edited by Shane Graham and John Walters, 1–24. New York: Palgrave Macmillan, 2010.
Grandt, Jürgen E. *Kinds of Blue: The Jazz Aesthetic in African American Narrative*. Columbus: Ohio State University Press, 2004.
———. "'No Cold Eyes in Paris': Walter Benjamin, the Aura of Jazz, and the Politics of *Autour de Minuit*." In *Traveling Sounds: Music, Migration, and Identity in the U.S. and Beyond*, edited by Wilfried Raussert and John Miller Jones, 205–222. Berlin: LIT Verlag, 2008.
Grazian, David. *Blue Chicago: The Search for Authenticity in Urban Blues Clubs*. Chicago: University of Chicago Press, 2003.
A Great Day in Harlem. Directed by Jean Bach. New York: Homevision, 2006, DVD.
Gruber, Johannes. *Performative Lyrik und lyrische Performance: Profilbildung im deutschen Rap*. Bielefeld: transcript, 2017.
Guillory, John. "Canon." In *Critical Terms for Literary Study*, 2nd ed., edited by Frank Lentricchia and Thomas McLaughlin, 233–249. Chicago: University of Chicago Press, 1995.
Guy, Barry, and the Barry Guy New Orchestra. *Amphi/Radio Rondo*. Intakt 235, 2014, CD.
Hajdu, David. *Lush Life: A Biography of Billy Strayhorn*. New York: North Point, 1996.
Hales, Pete. "Kohlert History." *The Vintage Saxophone Gallery*, 2016. www.saxpics.com/?v=man&manID=11#history.
Hall, Rachel. *The Transparent Traveler: The Performance and Culture of Airport Security*. Durham: Duke University Press, 2015.
Hamilton, Jack. *Just Around Midnight: Rock and Roll and the Racial Imagination*. Cambridge: Harvard University Press, 2016.

Hancock, Herbie. "Watermelon Man." On *Takin' Off*, Blue Note BST 84109, LP.
Hanssen, Beatrice. *Walter Benjamin's Other History: Of Stones, Animals, Human Beings, and Angels*. Berkeley: University of California Press, 1998.
Harding, James M. "Adorno, Ellison, and the Critique of Jazz." *Cultural Critique* 31 (1995): 129–158.
Hasse, John Edward. *Beyond Category: The Life and Genius of Duke Ellington*. Cambridge: Da Capo, 1995.
Hauser, Walter. *Stadt in Flammen: Der Brand von Glarus im Jahr 1861*. Zurich: Limmat, 2011.
Heckman, Don. "A Talent for Landing in the Pictures," *Los Angeles Times*, July 4, 2004. http://articles.latimes.com/2004/jul/04/entertainment/ca-heckman4.
Heffley, Mike. *Northern Sun, Southern Moon: Europe's Reinvention of Jazz*. New Haven: Yale University Press, 2005.
Heile, Björn. "Play It Again, Duke: Jazz Performance, Improvisation, and the Construction of Spontaneity." In *Watching Jazz: Encounters with Jazz Performance on Screen*, edited by Björn Heile, Peter Elsdon, and Jenny Doctor, 239–266. New York: Oxford University Press, 2016.
H.E.L.P. Hip-Hop Education Literacy Program, 2017. https://edlyrics.com/about-us.
Hentoff, Nat. Liner notes to *Benny Golson's New York Scene*, by Benny Golson. Recorded 1957. Contemporary C-3552, 1988, CD.
Hesse, Herman. *Steppenwolf*. Translated by Basil Creighton. Edited by Joseph Milek and Horst Frenz. New York: Henry Holt, 1990.
High Fidelity. Directed by Stephen Frears. Burbank: Touchstone Home Entertainment, n.d., DVD.
Higson, Andrew. *Film England: Culturally English Filmmaking Since the 1990s*. New York: Palgrave Macmillan, 2011.
Ho, Fred. "The Damned Don't Cry: The Life and Music of Cal Massey." In *Wicked Theory, Naked Practice: A Fred Ho Reader*, edited by Diane C. Fujino, 129–150. Minneapolis: University of Minnesota Press, 2009.
———. "What Makes 'Jazz' the Revolutionary Music of the 20th Century, and Will It Be Revolutionary for the 21st Century?" *African American Review* 29, no. 2 (1998): 288–330.
Hodges, Johnny. "Castle Rock." On *Castle Rock*. Recorded 1951, Verve POCJ-2726, 1999, CD.
Hoffmann, Bernd. "Albtraum der Freiheit oder: Die Zeitfrage 'Jazz.'" In *"Es liegt in der Luft was idiotisches . . .": Populäre Musik zur Zeit der Weimarer Republik*, ed. Helmut Rösing, 69–81. Freudenberg: ASPM, 1995.
Hogue, W. Lawrence. "The Blues, Individuated Subjectivity, and James Baldwin's *Another Country*." *CLA Journal* 56, no. 1 (2012): 1–29.
Holiday, Billie. "Good Morning Heartache." Recorded January 22, 1946. On *Billie Holiday: The Complete Decca Recordings*, GRP, D217027, 1991, 2 CDs.
———. "I Wished on the Moon." Recorded January 1957. On *All or Nothing at All*. Verve/Analogue Productions CVRJ 8329 SA, 2012, CD.
Hollaender, Friedrich. *Von Kopf bis Fuss: Revue meines Lebens*. Edited by Volker Kühn. Berlin: Aufbau, 2001.
Hornby, Nick. *High Fidelity*. New York: Riverhead, 1995.
Howland, John. *Ellington Uptown: Duke Ellington, James P. Johnson, and the Birth of Concert Jazz*. Ann Arbor: University of Michigan Press, 2009.

Huggins, Nathan Irvin. *Harlem Renaissance*. New York: Oxford University Press, 1971.
Hughes, Langston. *The Big Sea*. New York: Hill & Wang, 1996.
———. *I Wonder as I Wander*. New York: Hill & Wang, 1993.
———. "Jazz as Communication." In *The Langston Hughes Reader*, 492–494. New York: George Braziller, 1958.
———. "Jazz Band in a Parisian Cabaret." In *The Poems: 1921–1940*, vol. 1 of *The Collected Works of Langston Hughes*, edited by Arnold Rampersad, 106. Columbia: University of Missouri Press, 2001.
———. "The Negro Artist and the Racial Mountain." In *Call and Response: The Riverside Anthology of the African American Literary Tradition*, edited by Patricia Liggins Hill et al., 899–902. Boston: Houghton Mifflin, 1998.
———. "Trumpet Player." In *Selected Poems*, 114–115. New York: Vintage Classics, 1990.
Husband, Stuart. "Tracks of My Frears," *Guardian*, April 21, 2000. www.theguardian.com/film/2000/apr/21/2.
Irène Schweizer. Directed by Gitta Gsell. Zurich: RECK Filmprodukton/Intakt, 2006, DVD.
Iyer, Vijay. "Exploding the Narrative in Jazz Improvisation." In *Uptown Conversation: The New Jazz Studies*, edited by Robert G. O'Meally, Brent Hayes Edwards, and Farah Jasmine Griffin, 393–403. New York: Columbia University Press, 2004.
———. "The Village of the Virgins." On *Accelerando*, ACT 9524, 2012, CD.
Jackson, Mahalia. "I Wonder as I Wander." On *Mahalia Sings Songs of Christmas!*, Columbia Legacy CK64675, 1995, CD.
Jacquet, Illinois. "Robbin's Nest." Recorded August 11, 1959. On *Illinois Jacquet Flies Again*, Roulette CDP 7972722, 1991, CD.
Jagoda, Patrick. *Network Aesthetics*. Chicago: University of Chicago Press, 2016.
Jaji, Tsitsi Ella. *Africa in Stereo: Modernism, Music, and Pan-African Solidarity*. New York: Oxford University Press, 2014.
Janowitz, Hans. "Caligari—The Story of a Famous Story (Excerpts)" In *The Cabinet of Dr. Caligari: Texts, Contexts, Histories*, edited by Mike Budd, 221–239. New Brunswick: Rutgers University Press, 1990.
———. *Jazz*. Edited by Rolf Riess. Bonn: Weidle, 1999.
"Jazz Matters How and Why, in Wake of Events of Sept. 11." *Jazz House*, Jazz Journalists Association, 2001. www.jazzhouse.org/library/?read=mandel14.
Jelavich, Peter. *Berlin Cabaret*. Cambridge: Harvard University Press, 1996.
Jones, Omi Osun Joni L. *Theatrical Jazz: Performance, Àse, and the Power of the Present Moment*. Columbus: Ohio State University Press, 2015.
Kahn, Ashley. *The House That Trane Built: The Story of Impulse Records*. New York: Norton, 2006.
———. *A Love Supreme: The Story of John Coltrane's Signature Album*. New York: Viking, 2002.
Käppeli, Marco, and the Even Odds. *Prisoner of Time*. Altrisuoni AS197, 2006, CD.
Kater, Michael H. "The Jazz Experience in Weimar Germany." *German History* 6, no. 2 (1988): 145–158.
Kelley, James B. "Song, Story, or History: Resisting Claims of a Coded Message in the African American Spiritual 'Follow the Drinking Gourd.'" *Journal of Popular Culture* 41, no. 2 (2008): 262–280.

Kelley, Robin D. G. *Africa Speaks, America Answers: Modern Jazz in Revolutionary Times.* Cambridge: Harvard University Press, 2012.

Kenney, William Howland. *Chicago Jazz: A Cultural History, 1904–1930.* New York: Oxford University Press, 1993.

Keskinen, Mikko. "Single, Long-Playing, and Compilation: The Formats of Audio and Amorousness in Nick Hornby's *High Fidelity.*" *Critique* 47, no. 1 (2005): 3–21.

Khoury, George. "Behind the Music of *High Fidelity:* George Khoury Talks with D. V. DeVincentis, Steve Pink, and John Cusack." *Creative Screenwriting* 8, no. 1 (2001): 40–46.

Knowles, Joanne. *Nick Hornby's* High Fidelity: *A Reader's Guide.* New York: Continuum, 2002.

Kohl, Ines. "Modern Nomads, Vagabonds, or Cosmopolitans? Reflections on Contemporary Tuareg Society." *Journal of Anthropological Research* 66, no. 4 (2010): 449–462.

Koshy, Susan. "Minority Cosmopolitanism." *PMLA* 126, no. 3 (2011): 596–598.

Kracauer, Siegfried. *From Caligari to Hitler: A Psychological History of German Film.* Princeton: Princeton University Press, 1970.

Krohn, Tim. *Vrenelis Gärtli.* Zurich: Diogenes, 2010.

Krohn, Tim, and Jürg Wickihalder. *Schneewittchen.* Christoph Merian [unnumbered], 2008, CD.

Kubik, Gerhard. "The African Matrix in Jazz Harmonic Practices." *Black Music Research Journal* 25, nos. 1/2 (2005): 167–222.

Lacy, Steve. *Findings: My Experience with the Soprano Saxophone.* Paris: Outre Mesure, 1994.

———. Liner notes to *The Straight Horn of Steve Lacy.* Recorded 1960. Candid CCD 79007, 1989, CD.

Lange, Art. Liner notes to *Jump!,* by the Jürg Wickihalder European Quartet. Intakt 194, 2011, CD.

Lareau, Alan. *The Wild Stage: Literary Cabarets of the Weimar Republic.* Columbia: Camden House, 1995.

Lasker, Steve. "Lady Day." In *Billie Holiday: The Complete Decca Recordings,* by Billie Holiday, 12–33. GRP, D217027, 1991, 2 CDs.

Lawrence, A. H. *Duke Ellington and His World: A Biography.* New York: Routledge, 2001.

Le Gros, Julien. "Manu Dibango: 'J'ai grandi entre Halléluia et le début de Soul Makossa,'" *Africultures,* November 14, 2011. www.africultures.com/php/?nav=article&no=10474.

Ledent, Bénédicte, and Daria Tunca. "What Is Africa to Me Now? The Continent and Its Literary Diasporas." *Transition* 113 (2014): 1–10.

Levine, Lawrence W. *Black Culture and Black Consciousness: Afro-American Folk Thought from Slavery to Freedom.* New York: Oxford University Press, 2007.

Lewis, Eric. "What Is 'Great Black Music'? The Social Aesthetics of the AACM in Paris." In *Improvisation and Social Aesthetics,* ed. Georgina Born, Eric Lewis, and Will Straw, 135–159. Durham: Duke University Press, 2017.

Lewis, George E., and Benjamin Piekut, eds. *The Oxford Handbook of Critical Improvisation Studies.* 2 vols. New York: Oxford University Press, 2016.

Liebman, Nick. "Free Jazz: Vom Abwerfen harmonischer und rhythmischer Fesseln." In *Jazz in der Schweiz: Geschichte und Geschichten,* edited by Bruno Spoerri, 116–135. Zurich: Chronos, 2006.

Lim, Shirley Geok-Lin. "Complications of Feminist and Ethnic Literary Theories: Asian American Literature." In *Challenging Boundaries: Gender and Periodization*, edited by Joyce W. Warren and Margaret Dickie, 107–133. Athens: University of Georgia Press, 2000.

Living Colour. *Time's Up*. Epic EK 46202, 1990, CD.

Lock, Graham. *Blutopia: Visions of the Future and Revisions of the Past in the Work of Sun Ra, Duke Ellington, and Anthony Braxton*. Durham: Duke University Press, 1999.

Lordi, Emily J. *Black Resonance: Iconic Women Singers and African American Literature*. New Brunswick: Rutgers University Press, 2013.

Lott, Eric. *Love and Theft: Blackface Minstrelsy and the American Working Class*. New York: Oxford University Press, 1993.

Lotz, Rainer E. *Black People: Entertainers of African Descent in Europe and Germany*. Bonn: Birgit Lotz, 1997.

Lowney, John. "'A New Kind of Music': Jazz Improvisation and the Diasporic Dissonance of Paule Marshall's *The Fisher King*." *MELUS* 40, no. 1 (2015): 99–123.

MacHare, Peter. *A Duke Ellington Panorama*. www.depanorama.net.

Mackey, Nathaniel. *Discrepant Engagement: Dissonance, Cross-Culturality, and Experimental Writing*. New York: Cambridge University Press, 1993.

Makeba, Miriam. "Toyota Fantaisie." Warner Pioneer WPS-3, n.d., single.

Marsalis, Wynton, and Robert G. O'Meally, "Duke Ellington: 'Music Like a Big Hot Pot of Good Gumbo.'" In *The Jazz Cadence of American Culture*, edited by Robert G. O'Meally, 143–153. New York: Columbia University Press, 1998.

Marshall, Paule. *The Fisher King*. New York: Scribner, 2000.

Mbembe, Achille. "Afropolitanisme," *Africultures*, December 25, 2005. http://africultures.com/afropolitanisme-4248.

McBride, Joseph. *Stephen Spielberg: A Biography*. 2nd ed. Jackson: University Press of Mississippi, 2010.

McCarthy, Anne C. "Reading the Red Bull Sublime." *PMLA* 132, no. 3 (2017): 543–557.

McKaie, Andy. Liner notes to *Billie Holiday: The Complete Decca Recordings*, by Billie Holiday, 4–11. GRP, D217027, 1991, 2 CDs.

McMullen, Tracy. "The Improvisative." In *The Oxford Handbook of Critical Improvisation Studies*, edited by George E. Lewis and Benjamin Piekut, 1:115–127. New York: Oxford University Press, 2016.

Mentjes, Louise. "Paul Simon's *Graceland*, South Africa, and the Mediation of Musical Meaning." *Ethnomusicology* 34, no. 1 (1990): 37–73.

Messmer, David. "'If Not in the Word, in the Sound': Frederick Douglass's Mediation of Literacy Through Song." *American Transcendental Quarterly* 21, no. 1 (2007): 5–21.

Meyer, Thomas. "Bird Gong Game: Barry Guys Grafische Partituren." *Jazz 'n' More*, August 2016, 56–58.

Meyer, Tommy, and Root Down. *Root Down*. Intakt 135, 2007, CD.

Micucci, Matt. "Nice Jazz Festival Canceled," *Jazziz*, July 17, 2016. www.jazziz.com/nice-jazz-festival-canceled.

Miklitsch, Robert. *Roll over Adorno: Critical Theory, Popular Culture, Audiovisual Media*. Albany: State University of New York Press, 2006.

Miller, R. Baxter. "Café de la paix: Mapping the Harlem Renaissance." *South Atlantic Review* 65, no. 2 (2000): 73–94.

———. "Chesnutt and the African American Arthur: Reshaping 'English' Identity." Presentation at the annual convention of the College Language Association, Dallas, Texas, April 10, 2015.

———. "Langston Hughes and the Reinvention of Global Memory." In *A Literary Criticism of Five Generations of African American Writing*, 273–287. Lewiston: Edwin Mellen, 2008.

———. *On the Ruins of Modernity: New Chicago Renaissance from Wright to Fair*. Champaign: Common Ground, 2012.

———. "The Performance of African-American Autobiography." *Style* 27, no. 2 (1993): 285–299.

———. "Reinvention and Globalization in Hughes's Stories." *MELUS* 30, no. 1 (2005): 69–83.

Missac, Pierre. *Walter Benjamin's Passages*. Translated by Shierry Weber Nicholsen. Cambridge: MIT Press, 1995.

Monson, Ingrid. *Saying Something: Jazz Improvisation and Interaction*. Chicago: University of Chicago Press, 1996.

Montoliu, Tete. *Catalonian Folksongs*. Timeless SJP 116, 1976, LP.

Moraru, Christian. *Cosmodernism: American Narrative, Late Globalization, and the New Cultural Imaginary*. Ann Arbor: University of Michigan Press, 2011.

———. *Reading for the Planet: Toward a Geomethodology*. Ann Arbor: University of Michigan Press, 2015.

Morgenstern, Joe. "Case of 'Terminal' Boredom: In Spielberg Airport Comedy, Feeble Story Strands Hanks," *Wall Street Journal*, June 18, 2004. www.wsj.com/articles/sb108751186830440905.

Morrison, Toni. *Jazz*. New York: Knopf, 1992.

———. *Playing in the Dark: Whiteness and the Literary Imagination*. Cambridge: Harvard University Press, 1992.

———. *Song of Solomon*. New York: Signet, 1978.

Mortensen, Tore. "Dexter Gordon and His Style." *Col Legno: musikalske studier fra Institut for Musik og Musikterapi og Nordjysk Musikkonservatorium* (2003): 1–98.

Morton, John Fass. *Backstory in Blue: Ellington at Newport '56*. New Brunswick: Rutgers University Press, 2008.

Mosk, Matthew, Brian Ross, and Alex Hosenball. "U.S. Officials Ask How ISIS Got So Many Toyota Trucks," *ABCNews.com*, October 6, 2015. abcnews.go.com/International/us-officials-isis-toyota-trucks/story?id=34266539.

Moten, Fred. *In the Break: The Aesthetics of the Black Radical Tradition*. Minneapolis: University of Minnesota Press, 2003.

Muyumba, Walter M. *The Shadow and the Act: Black Intellectual Practice, Jazz Improvisation, and Philosophical Pragmatism*. Chicago: University of Chicago Press, 2009.

Nagl, Tobias. *Die unheimliche Maschine: Rasse und Repräsentation im Weimarer Kino*. Munich: edition text + kritik, 2009.

Nester, William. "Japanese Neomercantilism toward Sub-Saharan Africa." *Africa Today* 38, no. 3 (1991): 31–51.

Nichols, Nichelle. *Beyond Uhura: Star Trek and Other Memories*. New York: G. P. Putnam's Sons, 1994.
Nicholson, Stuart. *Billie Holiday*. Boston: Northeastern University Press, 1995.
———. *Jazz and Culture in a Global Age*. Boston: Northeastern University Press, 2014.
Nielsen, Aldon Lynn. *Black Chant: Languages of African-American Postmodernism*. New York: Cambridge University Press, 1997.
Niles, John Jacob. "Folk Inspiration: John Jacob Niles on Collecting, Composing, and Performing His Classic Folk Songs." *John Jacob Niles: Dean of American Balladeers*, October 30, 2006. www.john-jacob-niles.com/music.htm.
Nuttall, Sarah, and Achille Mbembe. "Afropolis: From Johannesburg." *PMLA* 122, no. 1 (2007): 281–288.
Nyamnjoh, Francis B., and Jude Fokwang. "Entertaining Repression: Music and Politics in Postcolonial Cameroon." *African Affairs* 105, no. 415 (2005): 251–274.
Ogren, Kathy. *The Jazz Revolution: Twenties America and the Meaning of Jazz*. New York: Oxford University Press, 1989.
O'Neal, Jim. "I Once Was Lost, but Now I'm Found: The Blues Revival of the 1960s." In *Nothing but the Blues: The Music and the Musicians*, edited by Lawrence Cohn, 347–387. New York: Abbeville, 1993.
Ostendorf, Berndt, and Wolfgang Rathert. "America's 'Musical Unconscious,' or, The Hidden Choreography of American Music." Presentation at the "America and the Musical Unconscious" conference, Ludwig-Maximilians-Universität Munich, May 30, 2014.
Ostwald, Susanne. "Sein wunderbarer Filmsalon." *Neue Zürcher Zeitung*, June 20, 2011, 84.
Otte, Marline. *Jewish Identities in German Popular Entertainment, 1890–1933*. New York: Cambridge University Press, 2006.
Otto, Elizabeth. "*Schaulust:* Sexuality and Trauma in Conrad Veidt's Masculine Masquerades." In *The Many Faces of Weimar Cinema: Rediscovering Germany's Filmic Legacy*, edited by Christian Rogowski, 134–152. Rochester: Camden House, 2010.
Pacini Hernandez, Deborah. "New Perspectives on Music and Identity in the African Diaspora." *Reviews in Anthropology* 27, no. 3 (1998): 225–249.
Parker, Charlie. "Passport." On *Boss Bird: Studio Recordings, 1944–1951*. Proper Properbox 46, 2002, 4 CDs.
———. "Visa." On *Bird at St. Nick's*. Original Jazz Classics OJC-041, 1983, LP.
Parliament. *Mothership Connection*. Recorded 1975. Casablanca 25 102 I, 1977, LP.
Parsons, Deborah L. *Streetwalking the Metropolis: Women, the City, and Modernity*. New York: Oxford University Press, 2003.
Partsch, Cornelius. "Hannibal ante Portas: Jazz in Weimar." In *Dancing on the Volcano: Essays on the Culture of the Weimar Republic*, edited by Thomas W. Kniersche and Stephan Brockmann, 105–166. Columbia: Camden House, 1994.
———. *Schräge Töne: Jazz und Unterhaltungsmusik in der Kultur der Weimarer Republik*. Stuttgart: Metzler, 2000.
———. "That Weimar Jazz." *New England Review* 23, no. 4 (2002): 179–194.
Patke, Rajeev S. "Benjamin on Art and Reproducibility: The Case of Music." In *Walter Benjamin and Art*, edited by Andrew Benjamin, 185–208. London: Continuum, 2006.

Pavlić, Ed. *Who Can Afford to Improvise? James Baldwin and Black Music, the Lyric and the Listeners*. New York: Fordham University Press, 2016.

Pen, Ron. *I Wonder as I Wander: The Life of John Jacob Niles*. Lexington: University of Kentucky Press, 2010.

Pennay, Mark. "Rap in Germany," In *Global Noise: Rap and Hip-Hop outside the USA*, edited by Tony Mitchell, 111–132. Middletown: Wesleyan University Press, 2001.

Perchard, Tom. "Hugues Panassié contra Walter Benjamin: Bodies, Masses, and the Iconic Jazz Recording in Mid-century France." *Popular Music and Society* 35, no. 3 (2012): 375–398.

Petrescu, Mihaela. "Social Dancing and Rugged Masculinity: The Figure of the *Eintänzer* in Hans Janowitz's Novel *Jazz*." *Monatshefte* 105, no. 4 (2013): 593–608.

Pfeifer, Beate. "Heute hier, morgen dort." *Glarner Woche*, February 1, 2017, 9.

Phillips, Damon J. *Shaping Jazz: Cities, Labels, and the Global Emergence of an Art Form*. Princeton: Princeton University Press, 2013.

Polillo, Arrigo. *Jazz: Geschichte und Persönlichkeiten*. Translated by Egino Biagioni. Munich: Goldmann Schott, 1982.

Pollack, Kenneth M. *Arabs at War: Military Effectiveness, 1948–1991*. Lincoln: University of Nebraska Press, 2002.

Pollard, Velma. "Writing Bridges of Sound: *Praise Song for the Widow* and *Louisiana*." *Caribbean Quarterly* 55, no. 1 (2009): 33–41.

Porter, Lewis. *John Coltrane: His Life and Music*. Ann Arbor: University of Michigan Press, 1998.

Powers, Michael. "Wolkenwandelbarkeit: Benjamin, Stieglitz, and the Medium of Photography." *German Quarterly* 88, no. 3 (2015): 271–290.

Puthli, Asha. "Right Down Here." On *Asha Puthli*, CBS S 65804, 1973, LP.

Ra, Sun. Liner notes to *Sun Song*. Recorded 1957. Delmark DD-411, 1990, CD.

———. "The Sound Image." In *The Immeasurable Equation: The Collected Poetry and Prose*, edited by James L. Wolf and Hartmut Geerken, 350–351. Wartaweil: Waitawhile, 2005.

Rachmaninoff, Sergei. *Rachmaninoff Plays Rachmaninoff*. RCA Victor Gold Seal / BMG Classics 09026-61658-2, 1994, 2 CDs.

Rainey, Ma, and Her Georgia Band. "Ma Rainey's Black Bottom." Recorded Dec. 1927. On *Ma Rainey: Mother of the Blues*, JSP 7793, 2007, 5 CDs.

Rampersad, Arnold. *1941–1967: I Dream a World*. Vol. 2 of *The Life of Langston Hughes*. New York: Oxford University Press, 2002.

Rasula, Jed. *History of a Shiver: The Sublime Impudence of Modernism*. New York: Oxford University Press, 2016.

———. "Jazzbandism." *Georgia Review* 60, no. 1 (2006): 61–124.

Ratliff, Ben. "A Saxophone Hero's Big Break," *New York Times*, June 13, 2004. www.nytimes.com/2004/06/13/movies/film-a-saxophone-hero-s-big-break.html.

Ray, Carina. "*Oxford Street, Accra*: Rethinking the Roots of Cosmopolitanism from an Africanist Historian's Perspective." *PMLA* 131, no. 2 (2016): 505–514.

Reimer, Arne. "Larry Ridley." *Jazz Thing*, November 2012–January 2013, 84–85.

———. "Yusef Lateef." *Jazz Thing*, February–March 2013, 64–65.

Riess, Rolf. "Hans Janowitz." In *Deutsche Exilliteratur seit 1933*, edited by John M. Spalek und Joseph Strelka, 3:258–282. Bern: Francke, 2000.

Rippey, Theodore F. "Rationalization, Race, and the Weimar Response to Jazz." *German Life and Letters* 60, no. 1 (2007): 75–97.

Robinson, J. Bradford. "Jazz Reception in Weimar Germany: In Search of a Shimmy Figure." In *Music and Performance During the Weimar Republic*, edited by Bryan Gilliam, 107–134. New York: Cambridge University Press, 1994.

Rogers, Susan. "Embodying Cultural Memory in Paule Marshall's *Praisesong for the Widow*." *African American Review* 34, no. 1 (2000): 77–93.

Rollins, Sonny. "A Nightingale Sang on Berkeley Square." On *Without a Song: The 9/11 Concert*. Recorded 2001. Milestone MCD 9342-2, 2005, CD.

Rose, Matthew. "Waiting for Spielberg," *New York Times Magazine*, September 21, 2003. www.nytimes.com/2003/09/21/magazine/waiting-for-spielberg.html.

Roth, Joseph. "Jazzband." *Berliner Börsen-Courier*, May 1, 1921. Rpt. in *Joseph Roth Werke I: Das journalistische Werk, 1915–1923*, edited by Klaus Westermann, 543–547. Cologne: Kiepenheuer und Witsch, 1989.

Rozema, Vicki. Introduction to *Voices from the Trail of Tears*, edited by Vicki Rozema, 3–41. Winston-Salem: John F. Blair, 2007.

Sabatini, Arthur J. "Fred Ho's Operatic Journey." In *Yellow Power, Yellow Soul: The Radical Art of Fred Ho*, edited by Roger N. Buckley and Tamara Roberts, 65–91. Urbana: University of Illinois Press, 2013.

Saint-Amour, Paul K. "*Ulysses* Pianola." *PMLA* 130, no. 1 (2015): 15–36.

Salzani, Carlos. "The City as Crime Scene: Walter Benjamin and the Traces of the Detective." *New German Critique* 100 (2007): 165–187.

Santoro, Gene. "Manu Dibango." *The Nation*, October 24, 1994, 469–472.

———. *Stir It Up: Musical Mixes from Roots to Jazz*. New York: Oxford University Press, 1997.

Savary, Jérôme. Liner notes to *A Drum Is a Woman*, by Claude Bolling. Recorded in 1996. Frémaux & Associés FA 476, 2005, CD.

Schaberg, Christopher. *The End of Airports*. New York: Bloomsbury, 2016.

———. *The Textual Life of Airports: Reading the Culture of Flight*. New York: Continuum, 2012.

Scheper, Jeanne. "The New Negro *Flâneuse* in Nella Larsen's *Quicksand*." *African American Review* 42, nos. 3–4 (2008): 679–695.

Schermer, Victor L. "Maxine Gordon: The Legacy of Dexter Gordon," *All About Jazz*, March 19, 2012. www.allaboutjazz.com/maxine-gordon-the-legacy-of-dexter-gordon-dexter-gordon-by-victor-l-schermer.php.

Schiff, David. *The Ellington Century*. Berkeley: University of California Press, 2012.

Schildpatt. *Bunju*. Schildrecords/Suisa 84242-SI, 1989, CD.

Schlegel, Stefan. "Bloss nicht zu viel der Ehre," *Tages-Anzeiger*, August 24, 2008. www.tagesanzeiger.ch/zuerich/stadt/Bloss-nicht-zu-viel-der-Ehre/story/18928608.

Schmidt, Michael J. "Visual Music: Jazz, Synaesthesia and the History of the Senses in the Weimar Republic." *German History* 32, no. 2 (2014): 201–223.

Schuller, Gunther. *Early Jazz: Its Roots and Musical Development*. New York: Oxford University Press, 1986.

———. *The Swing Era: The Development of Jazz, 1930–1945*. New York: Oxford University Press, 1991.

Schumacher, Alexander. "Rainer Trüby über Samples, Edits und 'Die da,'" *Badische Zeitung*, June 1, 2016. www.badische-zeitung.de/rock-pop/rainer-trueby-ueber-samples-edits-und-die-da--122641462.html.

Schweizer, Irène, and Jürg Wickihalder. *Spring*. Intakt 234, 2014, CD.

Scott, A. O. "An Émigré's Paradise Lost and Found," *New York Times*, June 18, 2004. www.nytimes.com/2004/06/18/movies/film-review-an-emigre-s-paradise-lost-and-found.html.

Segell, Michael. *The Devil's Horn: The Story of the Saxophone, from Noisy Novelty to King of Cool*. New York: Farrar, Straus, and Giroux, 2005.

Selasi, Taiye. "Bye-Bye Babar," *The Lip*, March 3, 2005. http://thelip.robertsharp.co.uk/?p=76.

Shaftel, David. "The Black Eagle of Harlem: The Truth Behind the Tall Tales of Hubert Fauntleroy Julian." *Air and Space*. January 2009. www.airspacemag.com/history-of-flight/the-black-eagle-of-harlem-95208344/?no-ist.

Shakespeare, William. *The Second Part of King Henry the Fourth*. Edited by Samuel B. Hemingway. New Haven: Yale University Press, 1961.

Sharpley-Whiting, T. Denean. *Bricktop's Paris: African American Women in Paris between the Two World Wars*. Albany: State University of New York Press, 2015.

Shasimosa Tütü. *Lugano*. Plainisphare 815, 1986, LP.

Simon, Paul. *Graceland*. Warner Bros. 925 447-1, 1986, LP.

singleton, giovanni. *Ascension*. Denver: Counterpath, 2012.

Sir Ali. "La face B de Dibango Manu, le Maestro Afro-Saxo, sans tabou," *Le Jazzophone*, April 28, 2016. www.lejazzophone.com/interview-manu-dibango.

Skinner, Ryan Thomas. *Bamako Sounds: The Afropolitan Ethics of Malian Music*. Minneapolis: University of Minnesota Press, 2015.

Sklar, Pamela. "Claude Bolling: A Living Legend Turns 80." *Flutist Quarterly* 35, no. 4 (2010): 34–37.

Smudo. "Als der Hip-Hop Deutsch lernte: Durchbruch im Schwimmbad-Club," *Der Spiegel*, October 10, 2007. www.spiegel.de/einestages/als-der-hiphop-deutsch-lernte-a-949653.html.

Sounding Out! (blog). Edited by Jennifer Stoever-Ackerman. https://soundstudiesblog.com.

Sparti, Davide. "On the Edge: A Frame of Analysis for Improvisation." In *The Oxford Handbook of Critical Improvisation Studies*, edited by George E. Lewis and Benjamin Piekut, 1:182–201. New York: Oxford University Press, 2016.

Spellman, A. B. Liner notes to *John Coltrane and Johnny Hartman*, by John Coltrane and Johnny Hartman. Impulse! GR-157, 1995. CD.

Stander, Bella. "A Conversation with Paule Marshall." *Bella Stander*. February–March 2001. www.bellastander.com/paule.htm.

Stapleton, AnnClair. "U.S. Treasury Inquires about ISIS Use of Toyota Vehicles," CNN.com, October 7, 2015. www.cnn.com/2015/10/06/politics/u-s-treasury-isis-toyota.

Star Wars: Episode IV—Eine neue Hoffnung. YouTube, www.youtube.com/watch?v=CR8U7grGmxs.

Stearns, Marshall W. *The Story of Jazz*. Rev. ed. New York: Oxford University Press, 1970.

Sterne, Jonathan. *The Audible Past: Cultural Origins of Sound Reproduction*. Durham: Duke University Press, 2003.

———. "Sonic Imaginations." In *The Sound Studies Reader*, edited by Jonathan Sterne, 1–17. New York: Routledge, 2012.

Stewart, Gary. *Rumba on the River: A History of the Popular Music of the Two Congos*. London: Verso, 2000.

Stoever, Jennifer Lynn. *The Sonic Color Line: Race and the Cultural Politics of Listening*. New York: New York University Press, 2016.

Szwed, John. *Space Is the Place: The Lives and Times of Sun Ra*. New York: Da Capo, 1998.

The Terminal. Directed by Steven Spielberg. Glendale: Dreamworks, 2004, DVD.

Thomas, Lorenzo. *Extraordinary Measures: Afrocentric Modernism and Twentieth-Century American Poetry*. Tuscaloosa: University of Alabama Press, 2000.

Thomas, Rolf. "Lucas Niggli: Tätigkeitsbericht." *Jazzthetik*, May–June 2014, 34–35.

Thompson, Robert Farris. "African Art and Motion." In *The Jazz Cadence of American Culture*, edited by Robert G. O'Meally, 311–371. New York: Columbia University Press, 1998.

Tirro, Frank. "Jazz Leaves Home: The Dissemination of 'Hot' Music to Central Europe." In *Jazz and the Germans: Essays on the Influence of "Hot" American Idioms on 20th-Century German Music*, edited by Michael J. Budds, 61–82. Hillsdale: Pendragon, 2002.

"The Total Film Interview—Steven Spielberg," *GamesRadar+*, September 1, 2004. www.gamesradar.com/the-total-film-interview-steven-spielberg.

Townsend, Irving. "Ellington in Private." *Atlantic Monthly*, May 1975, 78–83.

———. Liner notes to *A Drum Is a Woman*, by Duke Ellington. Recorded 1956. Jazz Wax JWR 4527, 2010, LP.

Tracy, Steven C. *Langston Hughes and the Blues*. Urbana: University of Illinois Press, 2001.

Travelogue. *The Light Is On*. PBR J300, 2015, CD.

Turner, Richard Brent. *Jazz Religion, the Second Line, and Black New Orleans*. Bloomington: Indiana University Press, 2009.

Ulanov, Barry. "The Ellington Programme." In *The Jazz Cadence of American Culture*, edited by Robert G. O'Meally, 166–171. New York: Columbia University Press, 1998.

Under African Skies: Paul Simon's Graceland. Directed by Joe Berlinger. A&E, May 25, 2012.

Van de Leur, Walter. *Something to Live For: The Music of Billy Strayhorn*. New York: Oxford University Press, 2002.

Van Nuis, Petra, and Andy Brown. "Far Away Places." On *Far Away Places*. String Damper Records SDR-2133, 2009, CD.

Vertovec, Steven. *Transnationalism*. London: Routledge, 2009.

Virilio, Paul. *Negative Horizon: An Essay in Dromoscopy*. Translated by Michael Degener. London: Continuum, 2005.

Vogel, Shane. "Madam Zajj and U.S. Steel: Blackness, Bioperformance, and Duke Ellington's Calypso Theater." *Social Text* 30, no. 4 (2012): 1–24.

Von Eschen, Penny M. *Satchmo Blows Up the World: Jazz Ambassadors Play the Cold War*. Cambridge: Harvard University Press, 2004.

Wald, Elijah. *How the Beatles Destroyed Rock 'n' Roll: An Alternative History of American Popular Music*. New York: Oxford University Press, 2009.

Walker, Margaret. Preface to *I Wonder as I Wander*, by Langston Hughes, xi. New York: Thunder's Mouth Press, 1986.

Ward, Andrew. *Dark Midnight When I Rise: The Story of the Fisk Jubilee Singers*. New York: Amistad, 2001.

Washington, Grover, Jr. "Mr. Magic." On *Live at the Bijou*. Kudu 2 KU 35, 1977, 2 LPs.

Weheliye, Alexander G. *Phonographies: Grooves in Sonic Afro-Modernity*. Durham: Duke University Press, 2005.

Weiner, Marc A. "*Urwaldmusik* and the Borders of German Identity: Jazz and Literature of the Weimar Republic." *German Quarterly* 64, no. 4 (1991): 475–487.

Weinstein, Norman C. *A Night in Tunisia: Imaginings of Africa in Jazz*. Metuchen: Scarecrow, 1993.

Welburn, Ron. "Jazz Criticism." In *The Oxford Companion to Jazz*, edited by Bill Kirchner, 745–755. New York: Oxford University Press, 2000.

Werner, James V. "The Detective Gaze: Edgar A. Poe, the Flaneur, and the Physiognomy of Crime." *American Transcendental Quarterly* 15, no. 1 (2001): 5–21.

Wheatley, Phillis. "On Being Brought from Africa to America." In *Call and Response: The Riverside Anthology of the African American Literary Tradition*, edited by Patricia Liggins Hill et al., 98. Boston: Houghton Mifflin, 1998.

Wickihalder, Jürg. *Brandruf, Jürg Wickihalder*. n.d. www.juerg-wickihalder.ch/cms/index.php/arbeiten/kompositions/46-brandruf.

———. *Jump!* Intakt 194, 2011, CD.

———. *Jürg Wickihalder Directing the Interplay Collective*. Dreamscape DSM 4756, 1997, CD.

Wickihalder, Jürg, and BEYOND. *Beyond*. Intakt 277, 2017, CD.

Wickihalder, Jürg, Pierre Favre, Kurt Müller Klusman, and Glarner Kammerchor. Performance, Stadtkirche Glarus, June 19, 2004. Digital copy in author's possession.

Wickihalder, Jürg, Tim Krohn, Manuel Perovic, Isabelle Krieg, Ulrich Bruppacher, Harmoniemusik Glarus, and Harmoniemusik Netstal. *Brandruf*. Performance, Glarus, May 13, 2011.

Wickihalder, Jürg, and Irène Schweizer. "Monk and More . . ." Performance, Neumarkt Theater, Zurich, May 31, 2013.

Wickihalder, Jürg, and Jürg Wickihalder Orchestra. *Narziss und Echo*. Intakt 209, 2011, CD.

Wiegman, Robyn. *Object Lessons*. Durham: Duke University Press, 2012.

Wild, David A. Liner notes to *The Complete Africa/Brass Sessions*, by John Coltrane, 2–17. Recorded 1961. Impulse! IMPD-2-168, 1995, 2 CDs.

Willard, Patricia. "Dance: The Unsung Element of Ellingtonia." *Antioch Review* 57, no. 3 (1999): 402–414.

Williams, John. *The Terminal*. Decca 9862875, 2004, CD.

Williams, Richard. *The Blue Moment: Miles Davis's* Kind of Blue *and the Remaking of Modern Music*. New York: Norton, 2010.

Wipplinger, Jonathan O. *The Jazz Republic: Music, Race, and American Culture in Weimar Germany*. Ann Arbor: University of Michigan Press, 2017.

Witte, Bernd. *Walter Benjamin: An Intellectual Biography*. Translated by James Rolleston. Detroit: Wayne State University Press, 1997.

Woideck, Carl. "John Coltrane: Development of a Tenor Saxophonist, 1950–1954." *Jazz Perspectives* 2, no. 2 (2008): 165–213.

Wyss, Thomas. "Das archaische Herz der Finsternis." *Tages-Anzeiger*, November 25, 2009, 30.

Zenni, Stefano. "The Aesthetics of Duke Ellington's Suites: The Case of *Togo Brava*." *Black Music Research Journal* 21, no. 1 (2001): 1–28.

Ziegele, Omri, and Where's Africa? *Can Walk on Sand*. Intakt 167, 2009, CD.

Index

AACM (Association for the Advancement of Creative Musicians), 5, 25, 91
Adorno, Theodor, 59, 141n34
Africa/Brass (J. Coltrane), 25, 78, 80–84
Afro-kinesis, 7, 14–15, 19, 23–24, 60, 128; and Afropolitanism, 16, 21; and Coltrane, John, 74, 76, 87, 94; and Dibango, Manu, 17–18, 32, 34, 56; in *A Drum Is a Woman* (Ellington), 22, 25, 42–47, 51; and Ellington, Duke, 34, 49–50, 52, 96; in *The Fisher King* (Marshall), 104–108; and Gordon, Dexter, 12–13; in *High Fidelity* (Hornby), 92; and Hughes, Langston, 78, 83; and improvisation, 25–27, 95; in *Jazz* (Janowitz), 75; on "Last Jump" (Wickihalder), 132–135; in *The Terminal* (Spielberg), 119–124; and transnationalism, 96, 99; and Wickihalder, Jürg, 130, 136
Afropolitanism, 7, 16, 21, 95, 101; and Coltrane, John, 25, 75, 82, 94; and Dibango, Manu, 16–20, 31–33, 56; on "Die da!?!" (Fantastischen Vier), 97–98; in *A Drum Is a Woman* (Ellington), 42, 47, 56; and Ellington, Duke, 21–22, 50, 54; in *The Fisher King* (Marshall), 26, 107–108, 113; and Hughes, Langston 24, 78, 82–87 passim, 94; in *Jazz* (Janowitz), 72, 75; on "Last Jump" (Wickihalder), 132–134;

in *The Terminal* (Spielberg), 117, 120, 123–124, 127, 130
Akiyoshi, Toshiko, 8
Albrectsen, Klaus, 13–14
Alexander, Eric, 95, 97, 99
Allen, Carl, 120
Allman Brothers Band, 95
Ansermet, Ernst-Alexandre, 127–128
Appel, Alfred, 7
Armstrong, Louis, 14, 66, 150n30; and Dibango, Manu, 16; and Ellington, Duke, 21–22; and Hughes, Langston 77, 83
Ashby, Harold, 53
Asheru, 96–97
Ashkenazy, Vladimir, 127
Association for the Advancement of Creative Musicians (AACM), 5, 25, 91
Ayler, Albert, 133

Bach, Johann Sebastian, 52, 59, 105
Bailey, Benny, 129
Bailey, Ozzie, 37, 41, 43
Baker, Josephine, 48, 60, 64, 67, 69
Baldwin, James, 6, 9, 18, 110–111, 136
Baraka, Amiri, 21, 76
Barnet, Charlie, 93, 99
Basie, Count, 13, 31, 34, 115
Baudelaire, Charles, 20, 45, 141–142n34
Beatty, Talley, 37, 40
bebop, 10, 33, 37. *See also* Parker, Charlie

Bechet, Sidney, 2, 6, 66, 69, 127; and Dibango, Manu, 17, 31, 143n6; and Ellington, Duke, 21
Beckford, Wayne, 55–56
Beethoven, Ludwig van, 52, 93, 100
Beiderbecke, Bix, 21
Belafonte, Harry, 40
Bell, Aaron, 96
Benjamin, Sathima Bea, 132–133
Benjamin, Walter, 19–20, 23, 51, 114, 134, 136; and Adorno, Theodor, 141–142n34; and angel of history, 78–80, 83, 100; and collecting, 85–87; and flânerie, 20–22, 25, 45–47, 55, 57, 63, 83, 123–124, 146n45; and jazz, 146n44, 147n69; and photography, 122–123; mentioned, 72, 73
Benton, Robert, 121
Berendt, Joachim Ernst, 13–14
Berlin, Irving, 73
Bernard, Emily, 48–49
Berry, Chuck, 93
Big Sea, The (Hughes), 76–77
Black, Brown, and Beige (Ellington), 6, 34–35
Bley, Paul, 132
Blue Note (label), 9–10, 12, 16
Blue Notes (group), 132, 133
blues, 9, 13, 61, 85, 102, 132; in Chicago, 25, 91–93, 94; and Coltrane, John, 81–82; and Dibango, Manu, 31, 143n6; and Ellington, Duke, 33, 47, 119; and Ellison, Ralph, 15; and Hughes, Langston, 94; mentioned, 45, 110
Bolden, Buddy, 21, 36, 37, 42
Bolling, Claude, 22, 32–33
Bonet, Lisa, 89–90
bop (bebop), 10, 33, 37. *See also* Parker, Charlie
Born, Georgina, 5, 98
bossa nova, 9, 52
Bowen, Justin, 17
Bowie, David, 55
Braggs, Rashida K., 6, 18–19, 99–100, 134, 139n9

Brahms, Johannes, 93
Brand, Dollar (Abdullah Ibrahim), 129, 132–133
Brandruf (Wickihalder), 135–136
Broonzy, Big Bill, 91–92
Brown, Clifford, 156n41
Brown, James, 30
Bryant, Ray, 120
Buckley, Jules, 98
Burgie, Irving, 44
Burke, Solomon, 94
Butler, Judith, 47

Cale, J. J., 97, 98
calypso, 22, 37, 40, 41, 44, 52
Camero, Candido, 37, 47
Candido, 37, 47
Carter, Benny, 23
Casucci, Leonello, 131
chanson, 10, 18, 70, 146n44
Cheney, Dick, 109, 210
Cherry, Don, 130
Clarke, Kenny, 6, 9
Clinton, George, 17, 55
Coleman, Denardo, 41, 145n28
Coleman, Ornette, 97, 130, 133, 145n28
Coleman, Steve, 6
Coltrane, Alice, 109, 152n62
Coltrane, John, 7, 76, 85, 87, 94–95, 130; *Africa/Brass*, 25, 78, 80–84; and Dibango, Manu, 31; *Duke Ellington and John Coltrane*, 96, 98; and sheets of sound, 24, 63, 73–75, 152n61; mentioned, 99, 150n32, 152n62
Cook, Will Marion, 127
Cortez, Jayne, 41, 44–45, 145n28
cosmodernism, 4, 22, 27, 82, 93
cosmopolitanism, 4, 24, 27, 63, 128
Cotton Club, 22, 33, 47–52, 54, 56, 132
Cusack, John, 88, 93

Dauner, Flo, 97
Davis, Francis, 102

INDEX

Davis, Miles, 7, 17, 56, 73, 152n61
Debussy, Claude, 52
de Lavallade, Carmen, 37, 46, 47, 64, 81
Dibango, Manu, 75, 107, 124, 129, 130–133 passim, 143n5; and *A Drum Is a Woman* (Ellington), 32–33; and Ellington, Duke, 20, 22–23, 143–144n7; "Négropolitaines," 16–19; "Soul Makossa," 17, 30, 55–56; "Toyota Makossa," 30–31, 54, 57, 143n2
Dimock, Wai Chee, 3, 6
disco, 98
Dixieland, 66, 83, 132, 150n30
Dixon, Willie, 93
Docteur Nico (Nicolas Kasanda), 17
Dolphy, Eric, 81
Douglas, Dave, 150n27
Douglass, Frederick, 111–112
Dresser, Mark, 150n27
Drum Is a Woman, A (Ellington and Strayhorn), 22, 35–48, 50–52, 55–57, 144n18, 145n28, 148n82
Duke Ellington and John Coltrane (Ellington and Coltrane), 96, 98
Dupree, Champion Jack, 132
Dyani, Johnny, 132, 133

Eldridge, Roy, 121
Ellington, Duke, 11, 58, 72, 127–136 passim, 142n43, 148n76; *Black, Brown, and Beige*, 6, 34–35; and Dibango, Manu, 16, 17, 20, 31–32, 144n7; *A Drum Is a Woman*, 22, 35–48, 50–52, 55–57, 144n18, 145n28, 148n82; *Duke Ellington and John Coltrane*, 96, 98; "Immigration Blues," 119, 156n39; jungle style of, 22, 47–54, 99, 122, 156n39; misogyny of, 41, 45, 145n30; and Strayhorn, Billy, 21, 33–35; *Togo Brava* suite, 52–55, 148n73; mentioned, 19, 25, 71, 76, 93, 99, 140n4
Ellison, Ralph, 15, 20, 21, 84; *Invisible Man*, 7–8, 12, 14, 43; mentioned, 4, 25, 119
Europe, James Reese, 58–59
Ewart, Douglas, 25–26

Fantastischen Vier, 97–98, 99
Farmer, Art, 120, 122
Favre, Pierre, 130
Feige, Daniel Martin, 126, 157n3
Fischer, Werner Tian, and Travelogue, 130
Fisher Fishkin, Shelley, 4–5
Fisk Jubilee Singers, 68–70
Fitzgerald, Ella, 103
folk music, 24, 31, 78–83, 88–89, 135, 140n4
Frampton, Peter, 91
Frears, Stephen, 88–90, 92, 154n39
free jazz, 2, 128, 145n28
Fueter, Daniel, 28, 136

Gabler, Milt, 102, 155n5
Garfunkel, Art, 91, 93, 94
Garland, Red, 152n61
Garzone, George, 129
Gaye, Marvin, 91, 93, 94, 100
Gershwin, George, 50, 133, 142n43, 152n52
Gertze, Johnny, 132
Gettin' Around (Gordon), 9–11
Giddins, Gary, 136–137
Gillespie, Dizzy, 22, 115, 121
Gitler, Ira, 73–75
Goll, Ivan, 23
Golson, Benny, 27, 127, 156n41; "Killer Joe," 120, 122; "Something in B flat," 120; in *The Terminal*, 27, 115, 117–118, 126
Gonsalves, Paul, 33–34, 53
Goodman, Benny, 93, 99
Gordon, Dexter, 9–12, 16, 27, 117, 133, 140n8; and Afro-kinesis, 13–14, 17, 63, 149n17; and Afropolitanism, 19; *Gettin' Around*, 9–11; and Wickihalder, Jürg, 129, 130; mentioned, 122
gospel, 9. *See also* spirituals
Gov't Mule, 94–95, 97
Goyal, Yogita, 6
Greer, Sonny, 47, 49, 50, 122
Guillory, John, 87
Guy, Barry, 130
Guy, Joe, 102

Haentzschel, Georg, 150n30, 150n32
Häfner, Lutz, 97
Hammond, John 56, 102
Hancock, Herbie, 129
Hanks, Tom, 114, 156–157n41
Hawkins, Coleman, 21, 22, 52, 115
Heath, Jimmy, 83
Henderson, Fletcher, 21
Hesse, Herman, 59, 60, 61, 73
Hessel, Franz, 45, 146n45
Higginbotham, Irene, 155n3
hip-hop, 96–98
Hjejle, Iben, 90, 135n39
Ho, Fred, 3
Hodges, Johnny, 33–34, 37, 76, 144n18
Holiday, Billie, 13, 102–103, 109–110, 120, 155n3, 155n10
Hollaender, Friedrich, 60, 71, 150n32
Hooker, John Lee, 93
Hornby, Nick, 25, 85–94 passim, 154n33
Howlin' Wolf, 93
Hubbard, Freddie, 81
Hughes, Langston, 3, 47, 81, 87, 134; *The Big Sea*, 76–77; and Ellington, Duke, 34, 39, 48; *I Wonder as I Wander*, 24–25, 77–80, 82–85, 93–94, 99–102; mentioned, 86, 96, 121
Hummel, Johann Nepomuk, 139n10

Ibrahim, Abdullah, 129, 132–133
"Immigration Blues" (Ellington), 119, 156n39
improvisation, 14, 19–20, 25, 98, 120–123, 126–127; and Afro-kinesis, 21, 27, 95, 122, 136; and Coltrane, John, 84; and Douglass, Frederick, 111–112; in *A Drum Is a Woman*, 32, 47; in *The Fisher King*, 26, 103–104, 108–110, 112–113; and Gordon, Dexter, 10–11; and Hughes, Langston, 101–102; in *Jazz* (Janowitz), 63, 68; in *The Terminal* (Spielberg), 26–27, 113–118, 123–127; and Wickihalder, Jürg, 2–3, 27, 112–113, 130–131, 134, 136–137; mentioned, 139n10, 156n26, 157n59, 158n17
Invisible Man (Ellison), 7–8, 12, 14, 43
I Wonder as I Wander (Hughes), 24–25, 77–80, 82–85, 93–94, 99–102
Iyer, Vijay, 109–110, 116, 124, 126–127, 157n59

Jacquet, Illinois, 91
James, Etta, 93
Janowitz, Hans, 76, 101, 127, 149n10, 150n32, 151n37; *Jazz*, 24, 60–67, 70–75, 97, 149n9, 149n27, 152n61; mentioned, 25, 151n33
Jazz (Janowitz), 24, 60–67, 70–75, 97, 149n9, 149n27, 152n61
Jones, Elvin, 81–82, 96
Jones, Jo, 13, 34, 115
Jones, Omi Osun Joni L., 6
Jones, Rufus, 53
Joyce, James, 1, 7
Julian, Hubert Fauntleroy, 50

Kabasele, Joseph, 17, 31
Kafka, Franz, 60, 115
Kane, Art, 26, 115, 121–123, 127, 156n37
Käppeli, Marco, 130
Kasanda, Nicolas, 17
"Killer Joe" (Golson), 120, 122
Krenek, Ernst, 59, 68
Krohn, Tim, 128–129, 135–136
Kubik, Gerhard, 16, 52
Kuti, Fela, 16, 133
kwela, 133
Kweli, Talib, 96–97

Lacy, Steve, 66, 112, 130, 156n31
"Last Jump" (Wickihalder), 130–134
Laswell, Bill, 55
Levitas, Willard, 36, 40
Lewis, Eric, 5
Lewis, George, 56

Lind, Jenny, 5
Little Richard, 96
Living Colour, 96
Lunceford, Jimmy, 93, 99, 100

MacAllan, Willi, 69
Mackey, Nathaniel, 19
Makeba, Miriam, 17, 18, 30
makossa, 16, 30–32, 55. *See also* Dibango, Manu
Malekani, Jerry, 17, 30–31
Mance, Junior, 132
Maroney, Denman, 150n27
Marsalis, Wynton, 21, 130
Marshall, Paule, 26, 108–113 passim, 124, 155n10
Massey, Cal, 81
Mbembe, Achille, 16
McGregor, Chris, 132, 133
McPartland, Marian, 122
Meyer, Tommy, and Root Down, 133
Michelot, Pierre, 9
Miley, James "Bubber," 47, 49–50, 53, 156n39
Miller, Glenn, 16, 129
Miller, R. Baxter, 80, 82, 134, 156n26
Mills, Irving, 48, 50
Mitchell, Roscoe, 109
modernism, 7, 15, 20, 49
Moholo, Louis, 132
Monk, Thelonious, 1–3, 73, 95, 115, 131
"Monk and More . . ." (Wickihalder), 2–3, 14
Montoliu, Tete, 10, 12, 19, 140n4, 149n17
Moraru, Christian, 4, 22, 27, 82, 134–135
Morrison, Toni, 42, 61, 72, 147n61, 149n9
Moten, Fred, 27
Mozart, Wolfgang Amadeus, 59

Nanton, Joe "Tricky Sam," 47–50, 53
"Négropolitaines" (Dibango), 16–19
Nichols, Nichelle, 148n76

Niggli, Lucas, 125, 130
Niles, John Jacob, 78–80, 83
Ntshoko, Makaya, 132–133

Oliver, King, 21
opera, 5, 37, 39, 50, 59, 98
Osgood Mason, Charlotte, 48, 77
Ostendorf, Berndt, 120

Parker, Charlie, 103, 107, 119, 155n10; and Coltrane, John, 83; and Dibango, Manu, 31; and improvisation, 109; and Wickihalder, Jürg, 130
Parker, Maceo, 96
Partsch, Cornelius, 59, 72
Pedersen, Niels-Henning Ørsted, 12
Perovic, Manuel, 135
postmodernism, 7, 95, 114
Powell, Bud, 9, 16, 140n8, 155n10
Pukwana, Dudu, 132
punk, 91, 99
Puthli, Asha, 97

Ra, Sun, 55, 91, 137
Rachmaninoff, Sergei, 18, 127
ragtime, 6, 69
Rainey, Ma, 60
rap, 55, 96–98
Rasula, Jed, 25, 59
Rathert, Wolfgang, 120
rhythm and blues, 33, 73
Richard, Little, 96
Riel, Alex, 12, 14, 19, 133
Roach, Max, 14–15, 50
rock, 25, 53, 85–87, 91, 93, 94–96, 98–99
Rollins, Sonny, 157n59
Roth, Joseph, 70–71

samba, 31
Schiltknecht, Roland, 129
Schmidt, Michael Bernd, 97; Fantastischen Vier, 97–98, 99

Schuller, Gunther, 67
Schweizer, Irène, 2–4, 27, 131–134, 158n17
Scott, Tony, 102–103
Sears, Al, 33
Segona, Peter Tholo, 17
Selasi, Taiye, 16
Shakespeare, William, 34, 64
Shasimosa Tütü, 128, 129
Sherrill, Joya, 37, 38
Simon, Paul, 95–96
singleton, giovanni, 152n62
Smith, Ada Beatrice Queen Victoria Louise Virginia "Bricktop," 60
Smith, Bessie, 15, 77
Smudo (Michael Bernd Schmidt), 97; Fantastischen Vier, 97–98, 99
Snyder, Terry, 47
"Something in B flat" (Golson), 120
soukous, 16, 18, 30
soul, 92, 130
"Soul Makossa" (Dibango), 17, 30, 55–56
Spellman, A. B., 24
Spielberg, Steven, 26, 113–114, 117–120, 123–126, 156–157n41. See also *Terminal, The*
spirituals, 18, 78, 81
Springer, Joe, 102
Stearns, Marshall, 49–50
Sterne, Jonathan, 5
Stoever, Jennifer Lynn, 5
Strayhorn, Billy, 40, 153n5; *A Drum Is a Woman*, 33, 37, 39–40, 47; and Ellington, Duke, 21, 35, 39, 54
Stuckenschmidt, Hans Heinz, 68
Sullivan, Maxine, 122
swing (genre), 13, 22, 32, 33, 37, 93
swing (rhythm), 10, 13–15, 46, 140n4; and African swing belt, 16, 52; and democratization, 67; and Ellington, Duke, 21–22, and Schweizer, Irène, 132

Taylor, Cecil, 133
Taylor Greenfield, Elizabeth, 5

Tchakouté, Pierre Didi, 17
Terminal, The (Spielberg), 26–27, 113–127 passim, 156n35, 156n37
Terry, Clark, 54
Thomas, Lorenzo, 124
Togo Brava suite (Ellington), 52–55, 148n73
township jazz, 132–134
"Toyota Makossa" (Dibango), 30–31, 54, 57, 143n2
transnationalism, 3–7, 27–28, 86, 97–98, 127, 139n10, 139–140n20; and Afro-kinesis, 96, 99, 56, 96, 119–120; and Afropolitanism, 16, 117, 123; and Benjamin, Walter, 20–21; and Coltrane, John, 24; and Dibango, Manu, 18–19, 31, 56, 75; in *A Drum Is a Woman* (Ellington), 22, 25, 36, 45, 51; and Ellington, Duke, 21, 52, 54, 144n8, 146n45; in *The Fisher King* (Marshall), 26, 103, 107–110; and Gordon, Dexter, 9–12; and Hughes, Langston, 77–84, 94, 99; in *Jazz* (Janowitz), 62, 65, 67, 71, 73; in *The Terminal* (Spielberg), 113–120, 124–125; and Wickihalder, Jürg, 130, 133–137, 158n16
Tyner, McCoy, 24, 81
Tynes, Margaret, 37–39, 43

Ulanov, Barry, 39, 50

Van Gelder, Rudy, 10, 12, 81, 96
Viola, Joe, 129

Wagner, Richard, 25, 68, 93
Walker, Margaret, 78, 80, 83
Washington, Grover, 97
Waters, Ethel, 77
Waters, Muddy, 93
Webb, Chick, 21
Webster, Ben, 11, 13
Welles, Orson, 35, 153n5
Wheatley, Phillis, 51
Whiteman, Paul, 21, 50, 72, 142n43, 150n32, 152n52

Wickihalder, Jürg, 27, 129–130, 137, 158n17; *Brandruf*, 135–136; and improvisation, 112–113, 120; "Last Jump," 130–134; "Monk and More . . . ," 2–3, 14
Wiegman, Robyn, 3–4
Williams, John, 120, 127
Williams, Mary Lou, 109, 122
Wilson, Teddy, 102, 155n3

Wonder, Stevie, 91
Wooding, Sam, 67, 70
Woodyard, Sam, 44, 47
Workman, Reggie, 81

Xenakis, Yannis, 133

Ziegele, Omri, and Where's Africa?, 133

www.ingramcontent.com/pod-product-compliance
Lightning Source LLC
Chambersburg PA
CBHW030654230426
43665CB00011B/1091